To my lovely wife Mary

Contents

Part 2
CD-ROMs

Part 3
Finding databases

Appendices

Permissions

The following information contained in the book is reprinted with permission:

Excerpts from ABI/Inform, © 1992, University Microfilms Inc., Ann Arbor, MI.

Excerpts from America Online, © 1993 America Online, Vienna VA.

Excerpt from American Health Magazine, © 1992 Readers Digest Publications, New York, NY.

Excerpt from Business Database Plus, Computer Database Plus, Health Database Plus, and Magazine Database Plus, © 1993 Information Access Company, Foster City, CA.

Excerpts from Business Dateline, © 1992 University Microfilms Inc., Ann Arbor, MI.

Excerpt from CAIN, © 1993 Computerized AIDS Information Network, CA.

Excerpts from CompuServe, © 1993 CompuServe Inc., Columbus, OH.

Excerpt from Computergram International, frequency: daily, © 1993 APT Data Services, London, UK.

Acknowledgments

My thanks to everyone who helped with this book. I'm particularly grateful to Reva Basch, Peter Jacso, Alfred Glossbrenner, and Tracy LaQuey for their valuable comments and suggestions. Thanks also to University of Montana journalism professor Dennis Swibold. He lent his finely honed editing skills to expertly cut this book's fat—yet caused minimal pain to the author. I'd also like to thank all the press-relations people at the various online services who were so helpful: in particular, Debra Young at CompuServe went above and beyond the call of duty. Finally, thanks to Mary and Cecelia for putting up with the seemingly never-ending stacks of papers throughout our house.

Introduction

Did you ever need to find the answer to a question? Have you ever needed to look up a fact? Have you ever been in a situation where you needed an expert opinion?

Of course you have. Everyone needs and wants information—usually every single day and on a potentially infinite number of topics: What's the latest news on the new tax plan? Where can I learn about the Civil War? What does the latest research say about caffeine? Has anything been published recently on travel to Vietnam? Which home computer should I buy? Should I invest in the cellular phone industry? What's the latest sales figures and financial performance of General Motors? How's the outlook for home-based catering services? Which college offers what I'm looking for? And so on and so forth.

This type of a list is limitless. But although we all naturally have different problems and questions, there is a single type of information resource that virtually anyone can use to find his or her answers: the electronic database.

An electronic database is simply a collection of related information in electronic form—it might be a series of reports on apple growing or a compilation of economic statistics on Zimbabwe. Through a computer, you can search a database to find precisely what you need. Today there are thousands of such databases, and that number is increasing by about 20% every year.

The potential benefits you can reap from tapping into electronic databases are almost limitless. Now that might sound like a lot of hype, but just think about how you could benefit by instantly being able to locate facts, advice, and expertise on thousands and thousands of topics culled from literally millions of sources. Here are just a few ways that I and persons I know have personally benefited from by going online:

> A woman who lives in Virginia but once worked as a political organizer in El Salvador uses an electronic news-clipping service on CompuServe to monitor news stories on that country coming over the newswire, thereby staying informed—literally up to the minute—on new developments in that country.

> Another online user living in New York City who works as a financial writer regularly checks a couple of different online services to search financial newswires in order to keep up with the day's financial developments. Recently, for example, this writer, while working on a story on a three-person acquisition of a Seattle shipyard, was able to uncover, by searching on those person's names in other regional papers, that those individuals had been acquiring similar properties in other regions—something they had denied doing.

> A freelance advertising copywriter in Rochester, New York, who must stay on top of developments in graphics design and page-layout software, regularly searches for the latest product introductions and reviews—and for tips on how to best use the product once he has bought it.

I personally had the opportunity to use electronic databases to help a colleague of mine quickly find out as much as possible about her spouse's life-threatening heart condition. By searching thousands of popular and medical related journals, I was able to find the latest

developments in treatment and uncover the names of the most highly regarded surgeons in the country.

Other uses and benefits of online databases and online services are nearly limitless. You can:

- ➤ Find the address and phone number of a business or person you're trying to track down.
- ➤ Learn what the latest research says about diet and health.
- ➤ Research the biography of a famous artist, scientist, or politician.
- ➤ Get an income statement from a U.S. or non-U.S. public corporation.
- ➤ Compare features and characteristics of colleges and universities.
- ➤ Get up-to-the-minute news on the electronics and computer industry.
- ➤ Find out which consumer products are worth buying and which aren't.
- ➤ Pinpoint demographic and statistical trends for regions in the U.S.
- ➤ Discover side effects and problems of prescription drugs.
- ➤ Locate the latest national economic statistics—before reading about it in tomorrow's newspaper.
- ➤ Research the fastest-growing industries and career opportunities.
- ➤ Read the latest movie and video reviews.
- ➤ Obtain facts and insights on other countries' cultures and lifestyles.
- ➤ Access the latest publications issued by the federal government.
- ➤ Perform historical research.
- ➤ Look up the results and read about Supreme Court decisions.
- ➤ Read classic literature and search for specific phrases.
- ➤ Scan the latest popular journals and magazines to find an article you've been trying to track down.

> Search for patent applications and study the actual documents.

> Read the Bible.

> Locate in-depth engineering and technical reports.

> Obtain sociological research reports and findings.

> Get the latest sports scores and standings.

> Get travel tips for cities around the world.

> Meet others online, share information and ideas—and have fun!

 # Types of electronic databases

There are two major types of electronic information databases: *online databases* and *CD-ROMs*. The former refer to databases that are stored in mainframe computers that your computer can link up with and search remotely over your existing telephone lines. CD-ROMs, in contrast, are hard, shiny discs that look like audio CDs (and use the same laser technology to encode information), and are databases that you insert right into your computer—like a floppy disk. This book covers both of these powerful electronic technologies.

While online databases have been around since the 1970s, it really wasn't until the mid-1980s that they began affecting the broader, nonscientific, and technical population. CD-ROMs have also been around for some years (though not as long), but it wasn't until the early 1990s that they really became available in the broad consumer market.

Today the electronic database industry—particularly the CD-ROM segment—continues to grow at a phenomenal rate. What this has meant is an enormous selection of electronic databases for consumers to choose among. While this profusion of information resources is certainly a nice state of affairs, there's a distinct down side. There are so many different databases that it has become difficult and confusing to choose the best one. Many products cover the same subject material, though some are more comprehensive, timelier, and of higher quality than others. Often, two databases that appear to be

alike actually differ quite significantly in important areas like ease of use and power. And, of course, there is always the matter of cost; some very good databases are downright cheap, while others that might not be so useful are extremely expensive.

What this book will do for you

This book's mission is to cut a clear path through the thicket of data sources by clearly describing and comparing competing electronic data services and sources. With this book, you'll be able to choose which sources and services fit your information needs best and most cost-effectively.

I've tried to accomplish this task by breaking the book down into logical sections, each one covering a different aspect of electronic information searching. The first part of *Find It Online!* describes and compares key information databases found on the major consumer online database services America Online, Delphi, GEnie, Prodigy, and CompuServe. This first section of the book also contains a chapter on one of the hottest online areas: the Internet, which is a global "network of networks" linking about 20 million people in over 50 countries.

The second section of the book examines CD-ROMs. This section is actually broken down into two separate chapters. The first covers CD-ROMs you can buy yourself and use in your own computer; the second examines CD-ROMs that you can find at your local library and search for free.

The final section of this book (chapter 11) is actually a directory that's designed to help you locate specific online and CD-ROM databases, and is grouped by subject. Finally, at the end of the book are three appendices: the first is a price-comparison chart of different online services; the second explains Boolean logic and searching; and the third lists and describes selected books, journals, associations, and other resources that provide further information on electronic database searching.

Who is this book *not* for? Well, it's not really written for the expert or professional business searcher, though if you fall into this category you might still find it to be a useful reference and look-up tool. It's also not written for people who want to join an online service simply to exchange electronic mail, play games, shop, or do other nonresearch activities. While many people enjoy these aspects of going online, this particular book focuses on the *information* you can locate. (Check appendix C for books that cover other kinds of consumer online activities.)

There's a lot of media and advertising hype today about the "information highway" and how electronic information technologies are going to change the way we live our lives. These promises, while intriguing, still remain only claims—and contain a fair amount of self-serving marketing hype. But electronic information databases are *already* here—proven and waiting to be exploited. With this book at your side, virtually no question should remain unanswered.

One caution: the electronic information field is about the fastest changing arena anywhere. This book will get you started in understanding, finding, and searching databases. But if you want to stay on top of new electronic products and features as they're introduced, you'll need to read newspapers, journals, and trade magazines that monitor ongoing developments. You can find a list of some of the best of these in appendix C.

Good luck, and enjoy your searching!

1

Introduction to online database searching

If you're an information addict like me, signing up with an online service can be a bit overwhelming. It's like providing a food junkie with a 24-hour on-call butler service to an endless row of bottomless brunch buffets. You can gorge on whatever you want, as much as you want, and whenever you want—but your excitement over what's available is tempered with the fear of overdosing.

Well, who are the "chefs" behind these smorgasbords of information? What exactly are they serving up? And how do you find all the goodies? Let's take a closer look.

⇨ A basic explanation of online database terminology

Before defining and explaining all the terms and buzzwords in the database industry, I might as well first tell you up front that

terminology in the online field is a slippery area. Even the experts in the industry don't always agree on which words to use to describe the varying levels of information providers in the field. But we do need to sort through it all, so let's go and do it. But keep in mind that you might sometimes hear other terms or ones that are at variance with the following definitions.

For our purposes, an *online service* provides access to one or more online databases. These services (or, as the larger professional services are sometimes called, *hosts*) typically offer a wide variety of databases, which they "send" in digital form to you through ordinary telephone lines to your personal computer. That's not the only thing an online service provides, though. Most consumer online services also offer games, electronic mail and messaging, bulletin boards, free software, special interest groups, and much more. This book, however, focuses specifically on information that's available online.

What type of information can you find? It would probably be easier to answer the question "What type of information *can't* you find?" (Okay, maybe not—don't take me up on this one.) But the point here is that there is an incredible, amazing, vast, mind-boggling, enormous, gargantuan (tell me when you've had enough superlatives), monumental, breathtaking amount of information available online. Yes, there's quite a bit.

This information itself is organized in a variety of ways, and it's organized into searchable databases, each one of interest to different kinds of people. Although you might have heard the word before, many people are not exactly sure what a *database* actually is. Well, it's really not all that complicated. A database is simply a collection of related information. You might not realize it, but you already work with and regularly use the most familiar types of databases. For example, your rolodex is a database of the names and phone numbers of your business contacts. And your yellow pages is a database of addresses, phone numbers, and descriptive information on businesses operating in your area of the country.

Almost always, though, when speaking of a database, people are normally referring to a database that has been entered into a computer, and is then configured and programmed so it can be

conveniently searched by use of a computer. So, for example, if you could turn your yellow pages into an online database, you could then, when you needed to find someone's name or phone number, electronically search it instead of manually thumbing through the book. You could, for instance, instruct your computer to locate the names of all businesses providing locksmith services. Or, more narrowly, all locksmiths located on Route 11.

Okay, you might say, "big deal. Why is that so much better than just picking up the phone book?" And you'd be right—searching your own phone book on a computer might be convenient in some circumstances, but most of the time it wouldn't really be much more useful or efficient than picking up the book and finding what you needed the old fashioned way. But think about this: What if your question was more obscure, or you needed to search a much larger database than your local phone book? What if you needed to compile a list of all 24-hour emergency locksmiths located in your state? Would you want to read through 30 or more phone directories? Or what if you were searching, not for a locksmith, but a business that sold, say, lion feed? In that case you might have to look through the entire U.S. yellow pages in the hopes of finding a firm. Clearly, in instances like these, having your state's or the entire country's yellow pages on an online database would be of immeasurable help.

In fact, today there's a database of the entire United States yellow pages. And not only is there a database, there are a handful of competing ones!

Today there are over 7,000 online databases available for searching over a computer. And these vary enormously in what they cover and provide. Not only can you search for and locate, for example, the names and addresses of businesses across the country, but also:

> ➤ Articles published in thousands of popular magazines

> ➤ Reports and studies issued by the U.S. Government

> ➤ Financial information on corporations around the globe

> ➤ Management strategies from hundreds of business journals

> ➤ Demographic and statistical data from the Bureau of the Census

➤ Analyses from leading brokerage firms on companies and industries

➤ The latest results from leading educational researchers

➤ Today's news headlines, updated by the minute

. . . as well as results of political polls, high technology news reports, import/export figures, doctoral dissertations, findings from medical researchers, investment decision recommendations, and thousands of other subjects that we don't have room to list here!

Not only are these mountains of information available at your immediate disposal, but much of the time you can search for precisely what you want by using powerful and efficient *keyword* searches. In other words, if you're searching a database of one million journal articles from health related magazines, you can instruct your online service to search and retrieve only those articles that cover the topic of, say, heart disease and children . . . and were published in the last six months. This ability to search databases with keywords is enormously important, and your skill in constructing appropriate keyword searches is so crucial that I've devoted an entire section of the book (appendix B) to this topic.

Where do databases come from?

But let's start at the beginning. Where in the world does all this vast information come from? Does your great and powerful online service have omniscient knowledge of every fact ever created? No. In fact, in the vast majority of cases, an online service doesn't actually create or compile the information itself. Instead, it contracts with other organizations that supply the data. These "behind the curtain" organizations are what we call *database producers*.

The background of these database producers varies quite a bit. Sometimes they're true subject experts who turn information they already collect for their primary non-online business into computer-readable databases. Examples here include publications like *The Washington Post*, *Consumer Reports*, and *Grolier's Encyclopedia*,

which produce online versions of their information, but are better known for their longtime print products. (Sometimes these types of database producers are also called *information providers*.) More frequently, though, database producers are organizations that contract with multiple subject-expert entities to create a larger database consisting of these related information sources. An example of this type of database producer is Predicasts, which contracts with and obtains thousands of business and management trade magazines and journals to create a single searchable database of millions of published articles, called PROMT.

To further complicate things, there's yet another, broader, umbrella type of organization that you should be familiar with. These firms contract with many (often hundreds) of both types of database producers previously described—the subject expert and multiple database compiler—and make all of those databases available from a single "one-stop shopping" type of service. These organizations are called *online hosts* or *online vendors*. Examples of these companies include Dialog, Dow-Jones News Retrieval, and Nexis. Consumer online services can obtain their data from any or all of these types of providers.

⇨ Whew!

As you can see, the relationships between online database producer, vendor, and online service can be a bit confusing. Strike that. These relationships can be *very* confusing. The following analogy suggested by best-selling author Alfred Glossbrenner might help:

> The best analogy I know of is that online systems are like department stores and database producers are like the manufacturers whose products the stores sell. To extend this just a bit further, just as some products can be found in almost every store (*The Washington Post* is a good example of a frequently found "information product" available on many online systems), some stores have exclusive deals, like the fulltext of *The New York Times* being available only on the professional Mead Lexis/Nexis system.

Types of databases

What kind of information do databases actually provide you? Again, what you receive depends on the specific database you choose to search. Say, for example, you're looking for business articles published during the last year on the topic of implementing total quality management (TQM) techniques in the retail industry. There are a number of databases you could search to find those articles. However, what you'd actually get from those databases after you completed your search and located some published articles would typically be one of these three types of results:

Bibliographic citations of the article This would provide the name of the publication, date published, page number, and usually some accompanying information such as the author, page count, and so forth. If you wanted to then actually obtain a copy of that article, it would be up to you to either go to a library, order it directly from the publisher, or arrange some other method, such as using a "document delivery service." These databases are called *bibliographic* and provide just minimal identifying information so you can track down the source yourself.

A short summary of the original article You would receive this along with accompanying bibliographic information, as described previously. This summary is typically about a paragraph long, and is called an *abstract*. It's written by a professional abstractor whose job is to identify and describe the main points of the full article. (In a few cases, the summary is an *excerpt*, which lifts, word-for-word, a short section of the original article, normally the very beginning, to give you an idea of what the article is about.) These *abstract databases* provide a short, but very useful summary of the original article. You can then, if you think you want to read the whole piece, track down the original item yourself; or you might decide that the abstract had enough information for your purposes, and you don't need to go any further.

The complete text of the original article This is called, more properly, the *fulltext*. Fulltext databases capture all of the words that were contained in the article, as originally published. When you retrieve the fulltext, you then normally need to go no further on your own to track down the original.

You might think, after reading these comparisons, that the best databases are fulltext ones. Well, it's certainly true, that most of the time it's extremely useful and convenient to know that you can instantaneously have hundreds of thousands of complete articles at your fingertips on command. There's nothing like the satisfaction of watching your printer churn out article after article. No need to drive to the library, no need to get up and track down publishers by phone—you just sit back and watch the copy roll in.

But alas, fulltext databases are not perfect—at least not yet. For one thing, online databases today are still mainly incapable of reproducing graphs, pictures, and other nontextual elements from an original document. So you might find that even a fulltext database omits a crucial bar or pie chart that illustrates points made in the text. Similarly, the layout and graphic elements from the original article would be lost too, which means not just a loss of aesthetics, but readability and, in some cases, the proper context of important elements like sidebars and boxed text.

The other caution to keep in mind is that fulltext databases aren't always fulltext! Fulltext database producers have various policies defining exactly what kind of information in an original "qualifies" to be included in a fulltext database. So, for example, fulltext newspaper databases often omit elements such as letters to the editor, advertisements, very short articles, classifieds, and other items. What this means, of course, is that sometimes, if you want to really see the "full fulltext," you still need to track down the original. (Or you might find out whether an image-based CD-ROM database exists, which covers the same originals. By using certain CD-ROMs, which are examined in chapters 9 and 10, you might be able to obtain an exact duplicate of the original document—headlines, graphics, layout, and all.)

The final drawback to fulltext databases is that they're often tricky to search efficiently. If you aren't careful in how you construct your search, it's very easy to end up with a large number of irrelevant articles.

But let's not be too hard on fulltext databases. Most of the time they are, indeed, a true blessing to the online searcher. They're here to stay and, in fact, during the last 3 to 5 years or so, there has been an increasing number of databases that provide fulltext.

Other than traditional databases, what other types of information can you find online? Although the focus of this book is on databases, you should also know that there's another type of information resource available on consumer online services: *special-interest groups*, or SIGs. These are exactly as they sound, groups of people who have similar interests and have joined together to share ideas and information. The nature of these special interests can run the gamut, from airplanes to mountain climbing to yellow-bellied sapsuckers.

Not all online services call their affinity groups SIGs. In fact, on CompuServe they're called *forums*, and on GEnie they're called *roundtables* (or RTs). But although each service might use a different name, they all operate pretty similarly and offer the same type of information, usually including browsable "libraries" of data that members can upload for perusal, downloadable software, and bulletin boards where people can post questions and discuss common problems.

⇨ The key players

While there are hundreds of online services, there are only a handful of major services offering a great number of databases and services and who currently reach 50,000 or more consumers. The biggest and most well known of the general-consumer online services are Prodigy, CompuServe, GEnie, America Online, and Delphi. The rest of part 1 of this book examines each of their offerings and pricings in great detail. Here first, though, is a quick snapshot of each:

Prodigy Possibly the largest of the online services, with a claimed 2 million members in 950,000 homes, Prodigy is best known for its ease of use and family orientation—and the inability of joint owners IBM and Sears to make the service turn a profit.

CompuServe Equally well known in the consumer online world, CompuServe is another giant, with about 1½ million users. The company has built a name for itself by offering a vast array of broad and specialized information resources. CompuServe is owned by H&R Block.

GEnie Smaller than the previous two services with about 350,000 subscribers, GEnie still has a dedicated following and offers a wide range of databases and special interest groups. General Electric owns GEnie.

America Online With a current roster of about 500,000 users, America Online is the fastest growing of the consumer online services. In addition to its growing popularity, America Online is also renowned for its live discussion forums and its particularly friendly, easy to use, and attractive-looking user interface.

Delphi Although Delphi has under 100,000 customers—the smallest user base of the services covered in this book—it recently pulled a bit of a coup by being the first (and as of this writing still the only) consumer online service to offer full access to the Internet service. The Internet is a gigantic web of computer networks around the world, whose usage has skyrocketed during the last couple of years.

It's worth noting that use of consumer online services has been growing quite rapidly over the last several years. Keep in mind, though, that recent figures also show that, although the rate of growth has been impressive, only about 5 percent of U.S. households actually subscribe to an online service.

Although these consumer online services are the most popular, they aren't, of course, the only online services available. In fact, business librarians, information professionals, and other serious researchers rarely choose a consumer online service to do their heavy-duty database searching. Instead, they normally select one or more of the following professionally oriented online hosts:

Dialog Dialog provides access to more databases than any other online service. Currently, it offers over 400 databases covering everything from agriculture to finance to zoology. Dialog is owned by Knight-Ridder.

Mead Data Central Along with Dialog, Mead's powerful Lexis and Nexis services have been longtime favorites of the serious information professional. Mead made its mark by being one of the first online services to offer the complete versions (fulltext) of original data sources rather than shorter abstracts.

Dow-Jones News/Retrieval As you might expect, Dow Jones is the premier business and financial online vendor. Not only is it the only service to offer the fulltext of the *Wall Street Journal*, but it also has a wealth of company, industry, and financial market data.

NewsNet Smaller than the previous three services, NewsNet has made its mark in the information world by specializing in the fulltext of hundreds of specialized trade and professional newsletters. These publications, typically written by top analysts and covering inside industry news, are usually very expensive to obtain via normal print subscription. On NewsNet, however, users can perform selective searching at a much lower cost.

Data-Star This Swiss-based online host has been an up and comer in the online world for the past several years. It's known for its top-notch coverage of European information, as well as its innovations in search techniques. In March of 1993, Data-Star was acquired by Dialog.

Although this book focuses on consumer online services, there's no reason why, if you're serious about finding information, you couldn't or shouldn't sign up with one of these more heavyweight information services. While they might take longer to learn proficiently and can be expensive, you'll be rewarded with some of the finest electronic information available anywhere. A closer examination of these professional online services can be found in chapter 8.

Note, though, that you can also tap into some of these professional databases less expensively via *gateways* on Delphi, GEnie, and CompuServe. Very basically, a gateway is an electronic connection that allows a computer on one online system to connect to a computer on another.

Getting going

Are you ready to go online? Here's how to get started. All you need is a personal computer (it can be either an IBM/compatible or Macintosh), a modem, and communications software.

If you don't already own a modem, here are a few basics. A *modem* is a piece of equipment that allows your computer and the online service's computer to "speak" over the existing telephone lines. It does this by taking the digital data that comes out of your computer, and "translating" it to the analog wave of a phone line. When the signal reaches the computer on the other end of the line, it then translates that signal again back to digital form. This process is known as *mo*dulating and *dem*odulating—hence the name *modem*.

Today, virtually all modems you can buy work with any computer— the standard that they conform to is called Hayes (after the company that was a pioneer in modem technology). Modems differ in a number of ways, but the biggest difference is in their speed of data transfer, which is measured in bits per second, or bps. While older modems transfered data at the relatively slow rate of 300 or 1200 bps, today's modems are usually rated at 2,400 or 9,600 bits per second.

Even faster modems are now available—those are rated at 14,400 (or 14.4) bps. The advantage of using a faster modem is that you can capture and download information quicker, which could mean lower online costs if a service is pricing their service by the minute (as many do). However, not all online services can support 14.4-bps (or even 9,600-bps) modems and those that do often add a surcharge. However, it's true that most times it's still cheaper to download information with a faster modem, even if you're paying a surcharge.

Communications software is the software you install on your computer that instructs your modem to dial and connect up with the online service. It also manages the information and communications coming across the phone line to your computer, and is needed when using any online service. There are many good communication software packages available for both PCs and Macintoshes. Your dealer can probably help you pick out one that's appropriate. Note, though, that some online services provide their own communications software. America Online and Prodigy send disks that contain special software optimized to work with their own service. CompuServe offers a special front-end called CompuServe Information Manager, which automates search tasks and makes it easier and friendlier (it displays windows and icons like a Macintosh or Microsoft's windows).

I could say a lot more about modems and communications software, but it isn't really what this book is all about. For a much more detailed discussion, I'd recommend Alfred Glossbrenner's *The Complete Handbook of Personal Computer Communications* (St. Martin's Press) or David Hakala's *Modems Made Easy* (Osborne/McGraw-Hill).

Finally, if you're serious about online searching, you should know at least the basics about a sophisticated and powerful search method called Boolean searching. To find out what this is and how to apply it to your database searches, make sure you read appendix B.

Now you should be ready to take a look at the major consumer online services and see what information databases they have to offer. For each service reviewed, we'll examine the same kind of information:

➤ Overview of service

➤ How to sign up and get around the service

➤ Research databases, organized into seven key reference areas:
  • encyclopedias
  • magazines and journals
  • health and medical information
  • business information
    • business news
    • company directories
    • company financials
    • company and industry analyses
  • newspapers and newswires
  • college information
  • other useful reference databases

➤ Pricing and fees

I chose these seven reference categories because they typically contain the most broadly useful research databases for information-gathering projects. Note, however, that I'm not including pure investment-type databases, such as stock tracking, portfolio creation services, and related nonresearch services.

2
CompuServe

This chapter on CompuServe is the longest in this section on consumer online services—because CompuServe offers, by far, the most. So we're starting with the best!

This behemoth of a service, owned by H&R Block Inc., is currently used by almost 1.5 million people. Its 1,700+ databases, services, and forums make it the number-one consumer online service in terms of the amount of information products available. For the serious nonprofessional researcher, CompuServe has the most powerful, in-depth, comprehensive—and cost-effective—databases in the consumer online industry. Only the professional systems offer more.

Not that there aren't *any* drawbacks to CompuServe. Novice users can find it difficult to navigate, the graphics aren't quite the level of America Online's (though not too significantly less if you use CompuServe's excellent graphical interface, CompuServe Information Manager), and some of the premium services carry *very* hefty surcharges. But these trade-offs are fairly minor when compared to what you do get on CompuServe.

⇨ Signing up and getting started

Signing up with CompuServe is pretty straightforward. One approach is to set up a billing account and simply log on using your own

13

communications software (and a modem, of course). Unlike Prodigy and America Online, you don't absolutely need special CompuServe software. However, CompuServe does offer, with every membership kit, a software package called CompuServe Information Manager (CIM), which is the preferable way to use the service and is designed to make searching and navigating around CompuServe much easier and friendlier.

CIM is a graphical front-end package (for either IBM-compatible or Macintosh users) that makes getting around CompuServe a lot simpler and a lot more pleasant. Like the America Online and Prodigy software, CIM does its job by using windows, pull-down menus, icons, and other graphical elements that make navigating around CompuServe easier, as well as more fun. You can also program it to perform certain functions automatically, such as dialing the service, logging on, and immediately connecting up with a designated section or sections of CompuServe, thereby making the logon procedure more efficient. Other nice features of CIM include a graphical ticking clock that keeps track of the time you're spending online, and a fast and easy function for saving text to disk.

Not that it's all that hard to get around CompuServe without CIM. Like the other online services, you have a choice of either using hierarchic menus and entering option numbers, or keying in a command as a shortcut to get to a specified section of the service. Those quick reference words are called GO commands. (You enter the word GO followed by the section of CompuServe you want to access, e.g., GO Sports, GO Cars, etc.)

But because CompuServe's offerings are so vast, it's true that it can take quite some time before you feel proficient in knowing how to find and then efficiently get in and out of a particular section of the service. There are, of course, online Help commands that can be of assistance (you can key in GO Help for details). A couple other particularly useful commands are Index, to see a complete list of CompuServe's offerings, organized by subject, and Quick, for a list of all of CompuServe's GO command words.

It is important, then, to do as much reading as you can about the structure of CompuServe and learn as many navigational tips as you

can. The best way to do this is to read CompuServe's *New Member Guide* as well as its *CompuServe Magazine*. You might also consider buying a book devoted specifically to CompuServe users. These are listed in appendix C.

Tip: Another piece of front-end software that's received rave reviews for automating access to CompuServe and making searching more productive is a shareware product called OzCIS. You can get the latest version by sending $20 to Steve Sneed, Ozarks West Software, P.O. Box 50285, Colorado Springs, CO 80949-0285.

When you use CompuServe's Information Manager to enter the system's basic services, your screen will display an opening screen, as shown in Fig. 2-1.

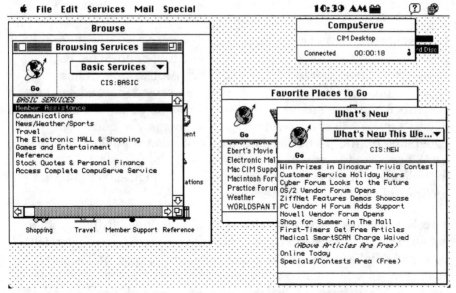

Figure 2-1

The opening screen of CompuServe's Information Manager, listing the system's basic services.

Let's now take a close look at the various information databases you can access on CompuServe. CompuServe categorizes all of its information files as either basic, which incurs no extra transaction fees; extended, where you pay an extra hourly fee; and premium,

where you not only pay the extra hourly fees but also pay a surcharge on top of those fees. Those surcharges vary widely depending on the particular database.

Because the CompuServe service is so large, this chapter will categorize them differently than those for the other online services. In this chapter, each covered database will be grouped into one of the following four categories:

Databases available through CompuServe's basic service
These are available to all CompuServe members, and carry no additional charges other than regular connect-time charges.

The Plus series of databases These are a series of general-interest but powerful and comprehensive databases that carry a relatively modest surcharge and are provided through an electronic gateway by Ziff-Davis.

IQuest databases These databases, like the Plus series in the previous category, are also made available to CompuServe users via an electronic gateway to Dialog and other professional online services, provided by a third-party gateway provider called Telebase Systems Inc. There are over 800 very powerful databases on the IQuest service. All carry a surcharge, which can run quite high, depending on the particular database. Note that the IQuest databases can be searched in one of two ways: all together as a full set, or individually as "seeded" databases, placed strategically in different sections of the CompuServe service.

The Knowledge Index service Knowledge Index (KI) is another gateway service. This one links CompuServe members to over 100 powerful databases found on the professional Dialog online system. KI databases, which can be searched only evenings and weekends, also carry a surcharge: $24 for each hour of search time.

Basic service offerings

Let's start with what's available on CompuServe's regular basic service, and don't carry any surcharge. As with the other online services, I'll concentrate on these key subject areas:

- ➤ Encyclopedias
- ➤ Magazines and journals
- ➤ Health and medical information
- ➤ Business information: news, company directories, company financials, and company and industry analyses
- ➤ Newspapers and newswires
- ➤ College information

⇨ Encyclopedias

✳ Grolier's Academic American Encyclopedia

CompuServe's online encyclopedia is located within its "reference" section of the service, as illustrated in Fig. 2-2.

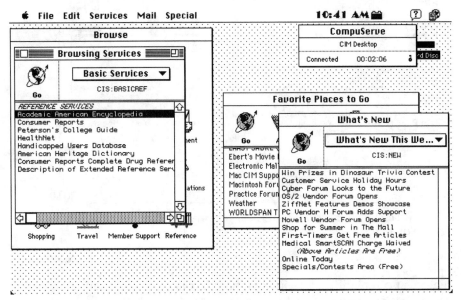

Figure 2-2

A list of the reference services available through CompuServe, including Grolier's Academic American Encyclopedia.

Like GEnie, Delphi, and Prodigy, CompuServe offers Grolier's Electronic Academic American Encyclopedia. It's a fulltext database, updated quarterly, consisting of 21 volumes, 33,000 articles, and 10 million words. You can search the encyclopedia by entering key words, as illustrated in the following sample search. First, you're prompted for your keyword or phrase, as shown in Fig. 2-3.

Figure 2-3

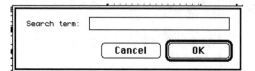

Being prompted for a keyword or phrase when conducting a search of Grolier's encyclopedia.

Say you decided to enter `Costa Rica`. The system would then search the encyclopedia and present you with a series of menu choices on the types of information you could find on that entry. If you choose the overview selection, you're then shown the excerpt shown in Fig. 2-4.

Figure 2-4

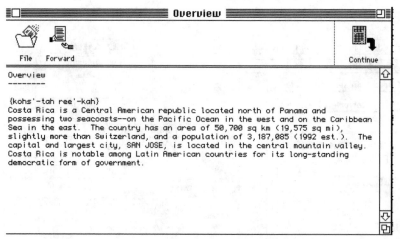

An overview of the term Costa Rica, *provided by the online encyclopedia.*

There's no real difference in searching Grolier's on CompuServe than on the other consumer online services. And as with the other online services, while search capabilities are somewhat limited, it's a handy resource to have nearby. Grolier's is updated quarterly on CompuServe.

⇨ Magazines and journals

✳ Consumer Reports

This database contains the fulltext of stories published from recent issues of *Consumer Reports* magazine, as well as automotive reports published since 1988. However, it isn't a very powerful system because you can search only by making menu selections from a predefined subject list, and not by your own keywords. A search for reviews of CD players, for example, is shown in Figs. 2-5 through 2-7.

Figure 2-5

The first part of a search in the Consumer Reports database for reviews of CD players.

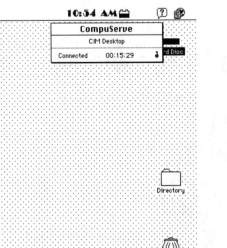

Figure 2-6

The second part of a Consumer Reports search for CD-player reviews: specifying Recommendations.

Figure 2-7

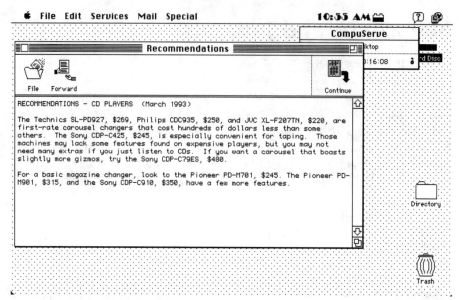

The third part of your search: a recent review in Consumer Reports magazine recommending several CD players.

As you can see, you can use the menus to narrow down broad subject categories into more specific ones, but you can't do any type of Boolean or even simple keyword phrase searches. So this database, while useful and convenient, is not one for real research purposes.

Health and medical information

✳ HealthNet

HealthNet is basically an online encyclopedia of health-related information. Although it offers fulltext articles on a variety of topics, you can't perform any keyword searches; instead you must use its menu system to choose subject categories and subcategories to narrow down the articles you need. Another online service that offers HealthNet is Delphi. Figures 2-8 through 2-10 show how the database worked to find information on the subject *Anxiety and Panic Disorders*.

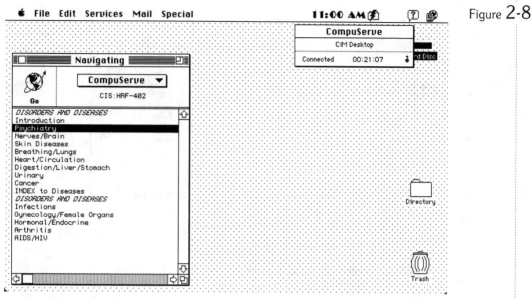

Figure 2-8

A search through CompuServe's HealthNet database for information on anxiety and panic disorders.

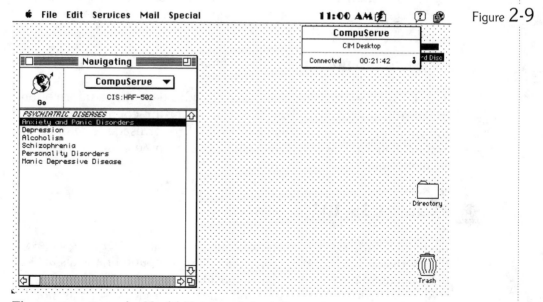

Figure 2-9

The continuation of a HealthNet search for information on anxiety and panic disorders.

Figure 2-10

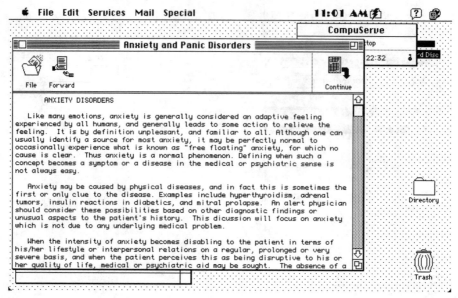

The culmination of your search: a lengthy discussion of the subject.

Again, as with the Consumer Reports database, HealthNet falls under the category of "nice, but not noteworthy," and is just marginally useful for any in-depth research.

✳ Consumer Reports Drug Reference

This is an interesting database that provides descriptive information on approximately 700 prescription and over-the-counter drugs. Information provided includes advice on proper usage, side effects, general cautions, and so forth. You can search by either the drug's common name or its generic name.

⇨ Business information

All of CompuServe's major searchable databases covering business directories, news, company analyses, and company financials are gateway databases and covered later in this chapter. (There are, though, a variety of nonsearchable business services, such as stock quote look-ups, investor services and forums, and so forth available under CompuServe's basic service.)

Newspapers and newswires

✳ NewsGrid

While not actually a CompuServe Basic service, NewsGrid is a very modestly priced extended service that gathers data from various newswires covering U.S. and world news, and is keyword searchable. There's only seven day's worth of a backfile, though, and the file is designed mainly as a headline news alert service, as opposed to a true comprehensive news database. NewsGrid is actually a service of a third-party news gathering organization called Comtex which gathers its news from a variety of newswire and news organizations, such as The Associated Press, UPI, the Securities and Exchange Commission, and various international newswires such as Agence France Press, Kyodo (Japan), and Deutche Press (Germany).

✳ Associated Press Online

Associated Press Online provides the latest headlines and news from the Associated Press newswire. However, it is not a searchable database; you can view only the latest news stories coming over the wire. Figures 2-11 through 2-13 are an example of what was found on a search to locate the latest national news stories, conducted on June 24, 1993 at 11:08 AM.

Note that the story's dateline displays a time of 10:10 AM—less than an hour previous to the time the search was run. That's one of the best features of online news services: they offer breaking stories that are just minutes, or even a few seconds old! The downside, though, is that the AP database is *not searchable*—you have no choice in determining which stories to locate. In the same vein, all of the following news databases fall under the same nonsearchable category.

✳ UK News Clips

This file is produced by the London-based wire service Reuters (which specializes in providing up-to-the-minute news reports from around the globe). It provides the latest political, economic, and financial news items from the U.K. Stories are held in this file for 24 hours, and are not keyword searchable.

Figure 2-11

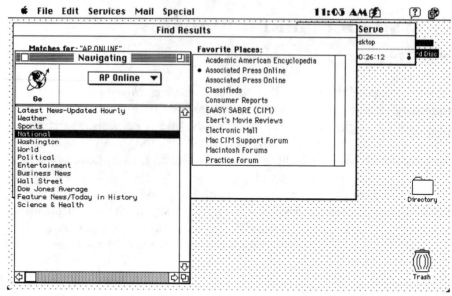

A search of the latest news stories in the Associated Press Online database.

Figure 2-12

Selecting a subject for your search.

Figure 2-13

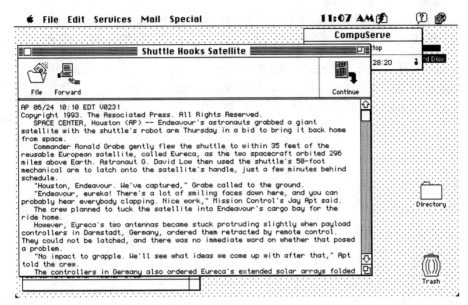

Recent news articles on the subject selected in Fig. 2-12.

✳ UK Sports Clips

Also produced by Reuters, UK Sports Clips contains only the latest headlines and fulltext stories covering a variety of sports and competitions held around the world.

✳ Online Today

Online Today provides daily updated computer and information industry news. You can view the current day's stories, the previous day's, or a week's review. Again, though, there's no online searching capability.

⇨ College information

✳ Peterson's College Database

This database is an online equivalent to the popular Peterson's print guides, which contain descriptive data on 3,400 U.S. and Canadian

four-year and two-year colleges. It's designed to help prospective students and parents pinpoint schools that have certain desirable characteristics and features. The following, for example, is an (edited) sample of a search I performed to uncover a list of small coed colleges that offer a communications major, located in a small to medium sized city in the New England region:

```
PETERSON'S COLLEGE DATABASE

Copyright (c) 1992

All (3404) Colleges Available

How would you like to search?
 1 College Name
 2 Location
 3 Coed/Single Sex
 4 Size
 5 Level of Study
 6 Public/Private
 7 Campus Setting
 8 Entrance Difficulty
 9 Majors
10 Sports
11 Housing

Enter choice or <CR> for more! 2

 1 City
 2 State
 3 Regions Inside United States
 4 Regions Outside United States

Enter choice! 3

REGIONS INSIDE THE
UNITED STATES
1 New England  CT,ME,MA,NH,RI,VT
2 Mid Atlantic  DE,DC,MD,NJ,NY,PA
3 South Atlantic  FL,GA,NC,SC
  VA,PR
4 South Central  AL,KY,MS,TN,
  WV,AR,LA,NM,OK,TX
5 Great Lakes  IL,IN,MI,OH,WI
6 Plains  IA,KS,MN,MS,NE,ND,SD
7 Mountain  AZ,CO,ID,MT,NV,UT,WY
8 Pacific  AK,CA,HI,OR,WA

Enter choice! 1

239 colleges selected
```

```
In what type of setting should
your college be located?

 1 Major metropolitan area (pop.
   over 500,000)
 2 Close to but not in a major
   metropolitan area
 3 Small to medium-sized city
   (pop. 50,000-500,000)
 4 Small town (pop. under
   50,000)
 5 Rural area

Enter choice! 3

27 colleges selected

What size range should your
college be in?  Note that the
total enrollment size (including
graduate students, if any) is
used here.

 1 Very small (under 1000)
 2 Small (1000-4999)
 3 Medium (5000-9999)
 4 Large (10,000-20,000)
 5 Very large (over 20,000)

Enter choice! 2

17 colleges selected
```

Now that I've entered all my criteria and have a manageable number of colleges to view, I can now instruct the database to show me the names of schools it has come up with.

Although this is a menu-only database, it actually serves its purposes quite well and is nicely designed.

⇨ The Ziff-Davis Plus databases

One of the best deals on CompuServe—and on any online service as a matter of fact—are the series of Plus databases, made available to CompuServe members via a gateway to the Ziff-Davis computer

network (a *gateway* is an electronic link from one computer database host to another.

The following is a list of the Plus databases and the corresponding research categories they fall under:

Database	Research category
Business Database Plus	Business news
Computer Database Plus	Magazines and journals
Health Database Plus	Health and medical
Magazine Database Plus	Magazines and journals

Let's take a closer look at each of these databases. Each section contains the search costs, including a sample price for a typical 15-minute search.

⇨ Business Database Plus (BUSDB)

➢ $15 hourly surcharge

➢ $1.50 per article retrieved

➢ 15-minute search plus three fulltext articles = $3.75 time + $4.50 = $8.25

This file provides the fulltext from five years' worth of about 500 regional, national, and international business and trade publications, as well as a selection of 550 industry newsletters. Business Database Plus is usually updated on a weekly basis.

Here's a good case study of a search on the industry newsletter segment of this file, and how I needed to modify it to better pinpoint what I needed to locate. In this case, my mission was to find any articles that discussed or analyzed the success of Eastman Kodak in selling its Photo CD product. Note that I started the search by instructing the system to locate keywords in the title of the article, to ensure that the subject was a major focus of items retrieved:

START A SEARCH for Articles

1 Words in Article Titles
2 Words in Article Text
3 Publication Names
4 Publication Dates
5 RETRIEVE an Article by Reference Number

Enter choice (? for help) ! *1*

Enter word or phrase
(? for help): *kodak and photo cd*

Searching..
Industry Newsletters   Search Summary

Search Method   Search Expression   Articles

Words in Titles   kodak and photo cd   28

Full-text articles that match ALL the search terms above: 28

NEXT ACTION

 1 Display Article Selection Menu
 2 Narrow the Search
 3 Replace or Erase a Search Expression
 4 Start a New Search
 5 Display Charge Summary

Enter choice (? for help) ! *1*

Industry Newsletters   Article Selection Menu

1   KODAK BUILDS ON SUCCESS OF PHOTO CD TO SEEK A MAJOR ROLE IN OPTICAL
STORAGE AND RETRIEVAL OF IMAGES, Computergram International, February 9,
1993 i2103.
    Reference # N1757827   Text: Yes (3031 chars)

2   ACORN PREPARES TO EQUIP ARCHIMEDES MACHINES FOR MULTIMEDIA, CD ROM,
AND KODAK's PHOTO CD, Computergram International, February 5, 1993 i2101.
    Reference # N1754668   Text: Yes (1518 chars)

3   MULTIMEDIA: NEW WINSTORM MULTIMEDIA UPGRADE KIT TRANSFORMS ORDINARY PC
INTO MULTIMEDIA PC; CD-ROM KIT COMES BUNDLED WITH OVER $1,000 OF FREE
FULL APPLICATION SOFTWARE INCLUDING KODAK'S NEW PHOTO CD ACCESS SOFTWARE,
Edge
    Work-Group Computing Report, January 18, 1993 v4 i139.   Reference #
N1760727   Text: Yes (3375 chars)

(the text continues)

Let's take a look at a portion of the fulltext from item #1:

```
Enter as many as 20 choices (<CR> for more, ? for help) ! 1

Citation:  Computergram International, February 9, 1993 i2103

Coverage:  Computers and Electronics (CE)

Publisher: Apt Data Services Ltd.

Subscription: 695 British pounds Sterling as of 1/92. Contact Apt Data
Services Ltd., 12 Sutton Row, London WIV 5FH, UK. Phone 1 528-7083. FAX 1
439-1105.


================================================================

Title: KODAK BUILDS ON SUCCESS OF PHOTO CD TO SEEK A MAJOR ROLE IN
OPTICAL STORAGE AND RETRIEVAL OF IMAGES

Eastman-Kodak Co reckons compact disks could be as ubiquitous a storage
medium as floppy disks are today thanks to its new low-cost rewritable CD
player. The company is also continuing to push Photo CD for personal
computers with the official UK launch of its PhotoEdge and Renaissance
imaging software, the announcement of its Shoebox Photo CD archiving
system, and the promise of additional authoring software later this year.
The aim is simple: Kodak wants to triple the number of users with Photo
CDs installed on their personal computers. The new PCD Writer 200 player,
Kodak says, owes much to the development of Photo CD. It is being
manufactured by business partner Philips Electronics NV to Kodak
specifications - that is to say it has a special security system that
reads the individual bar-codes on Kodak Writable CD disks. It can also
write to non-Kodak disks for all standard CD-ROM, CD-ROM-XA, CD-I
players.

(the text continues)
```

Although this is an interesting piece, it doesn't actually mention any specific sales figures, which was the data I was hoping to find. Let's start again and try a title search; this time I'll broaden my search by just entering `Photo CD` and leaving off the word *Kodak* since, upon some reflection, I don't want to eliminate any articles that discuss Photo CD sales but just don't happen to use the word *Kodak* in the title:

```
START A SEARCH for Articles

1 Words in Article Titles
2 Words in Article Text
3 Publication Names
4 Publication Dates
5 RETRIEVE an Article by Reference Number
```

```
Enter choice (? for help) ! 1

Enter word or phrase
(? for help): photo cd

Searching..

Industry Newsletters                                    Search Summary

Search Method     Search Expression                        Articles

Words in Titles   photo cd                                    48

Full-text articles that match ALL the search terms above:   48
```

Aha! By eliminating the requirement that the word *Kodak* be found in the headline, I've broadened my search so that it now finds a total of 48 items. But now, after broadening my search, I want to appropriately *narrow* it:

```
NEXT ACTION

 1 Display Article Selection Menu
 2 Narrow the Search
 3 Replace or Erase a Search Expression
 4 Start a New Search
 5 Display Charge Summary

Enter choice (? for help) ! 2

Industry Newsletters                           Search Methods Menu

NARROW the Search for Articles

1 Words in Article Titles
2 Words in Article Text
3 Publication Names
4 Publication Dates
5 Publication Areas of Coverage
6 Return to Search Summary menu
```

I've decided I want to specify words in the article text now, since I'm really hoping to locate just those news items that—somewhere in the body of the article—mention how the product's sales are doing or are expected to do:

```
Enter choice (? for help) ! 2

Narrowing the Search.

Enter word or phrase (<CR> no change, ? for help):
sales or forecast or forecasts
```

31

```
Searching..

Industry Newsletters                                    Search Summary

Search Method      Search Expression                    Articles

Words in Titles    photo cd                              48
Words in Text      (sales or forecast or forecasts)      35317

Full-text articles that match ALL the search terms above:  8
```

Hmmm . . . it looks like I might have hit pay-dirt. Let's take a look:

```
NEXT ACTION

  1 Display Article Selection Menu
  2 Narrow the Search
  3 Replace or Erase a Search Expression
  4 Start a New Search
  5 Display Charge Summary

Enter choice (? for help) ! 1

Industry Newsletters                    Article Selection Menu

1   KODAK CUTS PHOTO CD PRICES; SALES EXCEED FORECAST, Computergram
    International, January 11, 1993 i2082.
    Reference # N1730186    Text: Yes (855 chars)

2   MULTIMEDIA: AST INTROS 486-BASED MULTIMEDIA PC WITH PHOTO CD
CAPABILITIES,
    Edge Work-Group Computing Report, January 11, 1993 v4 i138.
    Reference # N1739388    Text: Yes (2973 chars)

3   AST's 486-Based Multimedia PC With Photo CD 01/11/93, Newsbytes News
    Network, January 11, 1993.
    Reference # N1732800    Text: Yes (2365 chars)

4   CD-ROM Expo: 1st Multisession Photo CD Drive 10/06/92, Newsbytes News
    Network, October 6, 1992.
    Reference # N1635194    Text: Yes (1405 chars)
```

Number one sure looks like a winner. Let's see it:

```
Enter as many as  8 choices (<CR> for more, ? for help) ! 1

Citation:  Computergram International, January 11, 1993 i2082

Coverage:  Computers and Electronics (CE)

Publisher: Apt Data Services Ltd.

Subscription: 695 British pounds Sterling as of 1/92. Contact Apt Data
```

Services Ltd., 12 Sutton Row, London WIV 5FH, UK. Phone 1 528-7083. FAX 1 439-1105.

```
=================================================================
```

Title: KODAK CUTS PHOTO CD PRICES; SALES EXCEED FORECAST

Eastman Kodak Co announced it was cutting prices on its Photo CD players to between $380 and $550, and claimed that sales of machines and related services were exceeding expectations, with the prospect of 100,000 sold in the first year if the present rate continues. Kodak declined comment on a report it had allied with Canon Inc. on microfilm cameras and Photo CD technology.

COPYRIGHT 1993 by Apt Data Services Ltd.

There it is: a projected 100,000 sold in the first year. Success! A little postmortem, however, is in order. First of all, note that although the word *sales* was found in the headline, it didn't really matter since I also searched for it in the text. You might also wonder why the first search didn't turn up the article. After all, it did meet the original search criteria: a title containing the words *Kodak* and *Photo CD*. Well, as it turns out, it *was* located in the first search. I just didn't get around to viewing it since it was a little older than the ones displayed and I hadn't yet called it up. So, in fact, the first search, while not really as targeted or well thought-out, also located the same piece.

This really speaks to the somewhat slippery nature of online searching. Although there's no question that there's both an art and science to the process, every search is different, there's rarely any single "perfect" search statement, and you never know exactly what you're going to locate until you view it. The only way to get around this is to keep searching and experimenting until you either find what you need or decide to try another database or information source.

Computer Database Plus (COMPDB)

➢ $15 hourly surcharge

➢ $2.50 per article retrieved

➢ 1.00 per abstract

➢ 15-minute search plus three fulltext articles = $3.75 time + $7.50 = $11.25

This is another winner from Ziff-Davis. Computer Database Plus provides abstracts and fulltext from over 230 computer or computer-related magazines, newspapers, and journals, and contains over 250,000 articles back through 1987. As with other Ziff databases, you can search not only by keyword, but by specific sections, or "fields," of each article. On this file, the fields include company name, product name, featured people, publication name, and publication date. (This database is available on CD-ROM, titled *Computer Select*, and is also available at many libraries).

If you want to move from one CompuServe service to another, you can just enter a GO command, like this one shown in Fig. 2-14, which is followed by a screen describing the file (Fig. 2-15.)

Figure 2-14

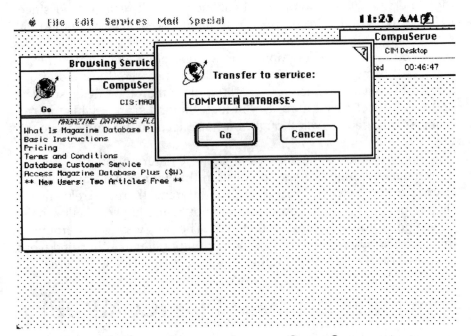

Entering the GO command to move from one CompuServe service to another.

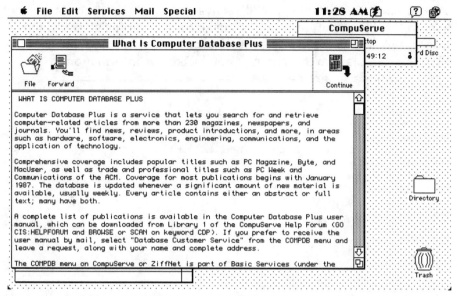

Figure 2-15

A screen describing the file selected by the the GO command shown in Fig. 2-14.

⇨ Health Database Plus (HLTDB)

➤ $0 hourly surcharge

➤ $1.50 per fulltext article retrieved

➤ $1.00 per abstract article retrieved

➤ 15-minute search plus 3 fulltext articles = $0 time + $4.50 = $4.50

This Ziff file includes over 100,000 articles, derived from both technical health journals and consumer magazines. The database provides abstracts from the health journals (back through 1989) and the fulltext for articles culled from the consumer magazines (from 1983). Health Database Plus is usually updated on a weekly basis.

You can search by keyword, article title, subject descriptor, company name, or product name. Searches can be narrowed by keyword or year of publication.

Again, Ziff has created a very attractive database. Not only do you get search flexibility, but, as a way to make for more precise searching, you can view a list of the database's own subject-heading index terms. Here's a sample search I recently conducted for information on chronic fatigue syndrome:

```
Health Database Plus
Copyright 1989, 1993 Ziff Communications Company

  1 Search
    For articles on health, nutrition, and fitness
    (132,679 articles; last updated Mar. 4, 1993)
  2 Quick Reference
  3 Exit


Enter choice (? for help) ! 1


Health Database Plus                      Search Methods Menu

START A SEARCH for Articles

  1 Key Words (words in article titles, subject headings
    or the names of featured companies or products)
  2 Subject Headings
  3 Publication Names
  4 Publication Dates
  5 Words in Article Text
  6 RETRIEVE an Article by Reference Number


Enter choice (? for help) ! 1


Enter key word or phrase

(? for help): chronic fatigue syndrome

Searching..

Health Database Plus                         Search Summary

Search Methods   Search Expression             Articles

Key Words        chronic fatigue syndrome         99

Articles that match ALL the search terms above:    99
```

Ninety-nine articles are more than I want to read. Now I'd like to focus the search and narrow down the count:

```
NARROW the Search for Articles
```

```
1 Key Words
2 Subject Headings
3 Publication Names
4 Publication Dates
5 Words in Article Text
7 Return to Search Summary menu
```

Let's narrow the search to only the most recent journal articles. I can do this by inputting option 4:

```
Enter choice (? for help) ! 4
Narrowing the Search
```

According to the database's help screen, I can narrow by month and year by using the word *since*, as follows:

```
Enter publication date or range (<CR> no change, ? for help):
since jan 1992

Searching..

Health Database Plus                    Search Summary

Search Methods   Search Expression           Articles

Key Words        chronic fatigue syndrome    99
Dates            since jan 1992              32681

Articles that match ALL the search terms above:    24
```

Now that's a more manageable number. And, even more importantly, it's a better, more focused search of the latest research. To see what was retrieved:

```
Health Database Plus               Article Selection Menu

1  Clinical ecology. (report of the American Medical Association's
Council on Scientific Affairs), JAMA, The Journal of the American Medical
Association Dec 23, 1992 v268 n24 p3465(3).
   Reference # A13088299   Text: Yes (12267 chars)   Abstract: Yes

2  Skeletal muscle metabolism in the chronic fatigue syndrome: in vivo
assessment by 31P nuclear magnetic resonance spectroscopy. (phosphorous),
Chest, Dec 1992 v102 n6 p1716(7).
   Reference # A13373732   Text: Yes (10794 chars)   Abstract: No

3  Doesn't anyone consider the effects of caffeine upon fatigue?
(ordinary fatigue, and possibly chronic fatigue syndrome, is responsive
to the therapeutic benefits of imbibing tea or coffee) (Column), Tea &
Coffee Trade Journal, Oct 1992 v164 n10 p5(2).
   Reference # A12728116   Text: Yes (3544 chars)   Abstract: No
```

Those are the first three entries. Note how complete and well-labeled the titles are. Ah, an online researcher's dream . . . if only other databases could be like these. Well, back to reality! Now it's time to take a look at the full record. Why don't we take a look at #3, about the impact of caffeine on chronic fatigue:

```
Enter as many as 20 choices (<CR> for more, ? for help) ! 3

Citation:    Tea & Coffee Trade Journal, Oct 1992 v164 n10 p5(2)

-----------------------------------------------------------------------

Doesn't anyone consider the effects of caffeine upon fatigue? (ordinary
fatigue, and possibly chronic fatigue syndrome, is responsive to the
therapeutic benefits of imbibing tea or coffee) (Column)

Authors: Lee, Samuel

-----------------------------------------------------------------------


Subjects: Caffeine-Health aspects
          Coffee-Health aspects
          Tea-Health aspects
          Fatigue-Prevention
          Chronic fatigue syndrome-Care and treatment
Reference #: A12728116


=================================================================
Full Text COPYRIGHT Lockwood Book Publishing Company Inc. 1992

Coffee and tea have long been recognized as the best all around remedy
for both mental and physical fatigue by practically everybody except the
medical profession. Nearly all cerebral workers, sooner or later, reach a
mental block where their mind refuses to function and they can no longer
proceed. A cup of brew does wonders for their mental processes,
clarifying their thoughts, and permitting progress in their tasks. Even
routine workers reach points where they can no longer continue in their
dull clerical work and must break its monotony by a shot of caffeine.

Physical fatigue, too, is quickly overcome by a cup of stimulant.
Muscular worker's weariness is rapidly alleviated by a cup of either of
these beverages. Not only is a return to work hastened but with
appreciably less physical effort and greater accuracy after one of these
drinks, and with less protest; yet physicians rarely recommend them for
this common symptom of many diverse ailments. They have been brain-washed
to believe that their recommendations might lead to excess ingestion of
these palliative, which in their estimation is more objectionable than
the relief obtained. Rare and horrible cases of excessive usage and
addiction to coffee have been published in medical journals periodically
for over a century. Instances of benefits of these beverages are seldom
reported.

(the text continues)
```

That was a pretty interesting article. But whether or not there truly exists a relationship between caffeine and chronic fatigue syndrome is another question. Remember, you can't automatically believe what you read just because it's coming off of a computer.

 Magazine Database Plus (MAGDB)

➤ $0 hourly surcharge

➤ $1.50 per article retrieved

➤ 15-minute search plus 3 fulltext articles = $0 time + $4.50 = $4.50

Magazine Database Plus, like the other Ziff files, is an outstanding database. It provides the fulltext to magazine articles for over 130 popular periodicals. You can search by keyword or field (e.g., title or subject heading), use proximity operators, and view a complete title list before choosing which articles to view in full. An extra nice feature of this database is its display of a "last updated" notice, so you have a good sense of just how timely the information is going to be. Here's a sample of a search conducted on the topic of food irradiation:

```
                    Magazine Database Plus
          Copyright 1990, 1993 Ziff Communications Company

1 Search Magazine Database Plus
  For full-text articles from general-interest publications
  (162,123 articles; last updated May 12, 1993)
2 Quick Reference
3 Exit

Enter choice (? for help) ! 1


Magazine Database Plus                 Search Methods Menu

Start A SEARCH for Articles

1 Key Words (words in article titles, subject headings, or
  the names of featured persons, companies or products)
2 Subject Headings
3 Publication Names
4 Publication Dates
5 Words in Article Text
6 RETRIEVE an Article by Reference Number
```

```
Enter choice (? for help) ! 1

Enter key word or phrase
```

Before conducting the search, let's see what kinds of keyword searching Magazine Database Plus allows, and get some hints by entering a question mark and receiving help:

```
(? for help): ?

KEY WORD SEARCH METHOD

A keyword search finds articles in which the search term occurs in the
title (including annotations), subject headings, or the names of featured
companies or products.

To search for articles using keywords, you can enter one or more words at
the prompt. You can use the following operators: NEAR or N, WITHIN or W,
AND, OR, NOT, (, ), *, and ?.

Examples:

PRESIDENT* NOT REAGAN finds articles in which words like 'president' and
'presidential' occur but in which the word 'reagan' does not.

JAPAN N10 ECONOM* finds articles in which the word 'japan' and words like
'economics' and 'economy' occur 10 or fewer words apart in either
direction.
```

Now you have a better idea of what you can and can't do in these searches. The following instructs the computer to find all instances where the word *food* is located either three words before or after the word stem *irradiat* (so you can pick up words like *irradiate*, *irradiation*, and so on):

```
Enter key word or phrase
(? for help): food n3 irradiat*
```

Here's what you'd see:

```
Searching..

Magazine Database Plus                       Search Summary

Search Methods     Search Expression            Articles

Key Words          food n3 irradiat*               18
```

Articles that match ALL the search terms above: 18

NEXT ACTION

  1 Display Article Selection Menu
  2 Narrow the Search
  3 Undo Last Search Step
  4 Start a New Search
  5 Display Charge Summary

Enter choice (? for help) ! *1*

Magazine Database Plus   Article Selection Menu

1 Nuking food. (irradiation-treated food products), Buzzworm, Jan-Feb
1993 v5 n1 p24(1).
    Reference # A13687506   Text: Yes (3111 chars)   Abstract: Yes

2 Food irradiation: the story behind the scare., American Health:
Fitness of Body and Mind, Dec 1992 v11 n10 p60(8).
    Reference # A12946125   Text: Yes (25124 chars) Abstract: Yes

3 What drives the critics? (food irradiation), American Health: Fitness
of Body and Mind, Dec 1992 v11 n10 p64(2).
    Reference # A12946905   Text: Yes (7402 chars)   Abstract: Yes

4 Food irradiation: a hot issue., Harvard Health Letter, August 1992 v17
n10 p1(3).
    Reference # A12532699   Text: Yes (13222 chars)   Abstract: Yes

Enter as many as 18 choices (<CR> for more, ? for help) ! *2*

Citation: American Health: Fitness of Body and Mind, Dec 1992 v11 n10
          p60(8)

Title: Food irradiation: the story behind the scare.
Authors: Katzenstein, Larry

Subjects: Radiation preservation of food-Health aspects
          Irradiated foods-Health aspects

Reference #: A12946125

==

Abstract: Food irradiation is a process in which food is exposed to
radiation to kill bacteria and insects and to prolong shelf life.
Opponents

```
Press <CR> for more (? for help) !

claim that irradiation destroys the nutritional value of foods.
Proponents say irradiation makes foods safer.
=================================================================

Full Text COPYRIGHT RD Publications Inc. 1992

In the summer of 1991, millions of Floridians heard this radio
advertisement, aired repeatedly on 57 stations: "What if you found out
that those fresh fruits and vegetables everyone keeps telling you to
eat more of might kill you? No joke.... Supermarkets have started
selling radiation-exposed foods: spices, processed foods, and soon,
meats and fruits and vegetables.... Many scientists are saying
irradiation makes foods unsafe, changes the molecular structure of
food, destroys nutrients. And new studies show that ingesting
radiation-exposed foods causes genetic damage, which can lead to cancer
and birth defects...."

The ad was paid for by Food & Water, a Marshfield, Vt.-based consumer
group that's leading a nationwide campaign to keep food irradiation—a
process that exposes food to radiation to rid it of harmful bacteria and
insects and prolong shelf life—from winning public acceptance. The
campaign plays on two of our deepest concerns: anxiety over food safety
and, more than ever after Chernobyl and Three Mile Island, mistrust of
anything involving radiation.

(the text continues)
```

The IQUEST databases

Full IQuest service

➤ $9 each search (provides up to 10/15 headings, plus one fulltext article, where applicable. Each additional 10/15 headings cost $9; each additional fulltext costs $9)

➤ $3 each abstract retrieved

➤ $2 to $70 surcharge, depending on database (a surcharge is added everywhere the $9 fee applies)

⇨ Seeded IQuest databases

➤ $2 to $20 each search (provides up to 5/10 headings, depending on the database)

➤ $2 to $75 per full record; some databases include full records as part of the initial search

If you're a CompuServe member, you have the opportunity to access a huge number of powerful professional databases. There are actually two completely separate—and even competing—services vying for your attention here: IQuest from Telebase Systems, Inc., and Dialog's Knowledge Index. Let's look at IQuest first.

IQuest is the name that CompuServe gives to the special online gateway service that links its members to over 850 of some of the most in-depth professional online databases in existence.

IQuest is run by Telebase Systems, Inc., a firm that's a well-known and respected player in the information industry. Today, Telebase markets this gateway to a variety of users under different names and distribution channels. But its easy-to-use menu search approach and flat-rate pricing have remained the same (though now it normally charges a $1 fee even if a search doesn't turn anything up). Its major consumer distribution method is via CompuServe.

The first thing you should know are the names of the online host services that IQuest links up with. If you'll remember from chapter 1, online host services are themselves resellers of databases, usually making hundreds available under one "umbrella." Here is a list of the online vendors available through IQuest:

➤ Dialog Information Services, Inc.

➤ NewsNet, Inc.

➤ BRS Information Technologies

➤ Data-Star

➤ FT Information Online, Ltd. (FT Profile)

➤ G.Cam-L'Europeenne De Donnees

➤ The HW Wilson Company

➤ Orbit Search Service

➤ Questel, Inc.

➤ Waterlow Ltd. (formerly Pergamon Financial Data Services)

These online hosts represent some of the best-known and most widely used systems in the online industry. And they include a few non-U.S. hosts as well: Data-Star (Swiss-based), FT Profile (U.K.), G.Cam-L'Europeenne De Donnees and Questel (France). No other online service anywhere provides access to so many databases. I should point out, though, that as wide-ranging as IQuest's range is, it is not, of course, completely comprehensive. Two major players not available through IQuest, for example, are Mead Data Central (Lexis/Nexis) and Dow Jones News/Retrieval. It's also important to point out that just because an online service is in the previous list, it doesn't mean that *all* of that service's databases are available through IQuest. Telebase Systems, the gateway developer of the IQuest offering, says that it's selective in what it chooses to make available, providing access to only those databases that it feels its customers desire.

How do you access the IQuest service? There are actually two ways: through seeded databases or through the full IQuest system. *Seeded files* are a subset of the full system, a selection of databases that CompuServe extracts and places in relevant sections of its own subject categories. Once you've logged onto CompuServe, you can download the names of all 850 available databases. Here are just a few to give you the flavor of this service's scope: Dissertation Abstracts, European Company Library, Criminal Justice Periodicals, Mergers & Acquisitions International, McGraw-Hill, Legal Resources Index, Publications, Patent Research Center, and TRW Business Profiles.

There is another subtle but significant difference between searching the regular IQuest and seeded databases. When you search a database on the full IQuest system, you have additional search and display options and flexibility. For example, you can perform field searching, view more items, and display the items you retrieved from your search in a wider variety of formats. However, you also pay a bit more on IQuest. See the beginning of this section for more details on pricing.

Both systems, however, generally conduct a search in a similar fashion, that is, by presenting you with a menu of choices and allowing you to enter basic Boolean search phrases. You're restricted, though, in the level and sophistication of your searches. For example, you can't use "proximity operators" and specify precisely how far apart you want your keywords or phrases to be located. You're also restricted in modifying your search mid-stream. So, for instance, if a search isn't providing the results you had hoped, you'll often have to start a new search completely instead of combining or altering preexisting search statements. (In contrast, Knowledge Index's command search system allows all of these advanced features—see later in this chapter.)

One especially useful and innovative feature that's unique to IQuest, though, is its online S.O.S. feature. This is a "live" expert that users can communicate with online, right in the middle of a search, to receive immediate expert assistance. This can be a real lifesaver if you're having difficulties and aren't sure what to do.

Now let's examine the IQuest databases that cover the special research focus areas. I'll identify and describe the seeded databases only, since the full range of the 800+ IQuest full system is too large to cover here. The special research focus areas are as follows:

➤ Encyclopedias

➤ Magazines and journals

➤ Health and medical information

➤ Business information: news, company directories, company financials, company and industry analyses

➤ Newspapers and newswires

➤ College information

⇨ Encyclopedias

There are no IQuest seeded encyclopedia databases. CompuServe offers its online encyclopedia on its basic service.

 # Magazines and journals

✳ Books in Print

While Books in Print is not really a magazine or journal reference database, it's worth including here because it's such an important general reference tool. This database is the online equivalent to the print version of the well-known, popular *Books in Print* volumes, used in libraries and bookstores to identify all books currently in print. This is one of IQuest's more flexible databases, as it allows users to search by subject heading, title, and author. Each entry provides the name of the book, author, publisher, date of publication, edition, hardcover or paperback, and list price. The database also contains information on books that publishers have scheduled to release during the next six months, and those books that went out of print or out of stock in the last two years.

 # Health and medical information

✳ PDQ Cancer-Patient Information File (GO PDQ)

Information on 80 cancer types, treatment alternatives, and related data.

Business information: directories

✳ Dun's Electronic Business Directory/IQ via Dialog (GO DUNSEBD)

➤ $8 per hour CompuServe extended rate (2400 bps)

➤ $7.50 search to display up to 5 full records

➤ $7.50 for each additional full record

➤ 15-minute search plus 10 displayed full records = $2 time + $15 for 10 full displays = $17

By searching Dun's Electronic Business Directory, you can find information on over 8.5 million public and private U.S. companies.

Each record contains the company name, address, phone number,
type of business, and SIC code. Many also provide the number of
employees, information on parent company, and other data.

You have a good deal of flexibility in how you can search this file.
Here, for instance, is the opening menu of the file and the search
choices you're given:

```
* D & B -- DUN'S ELECTRONIC BUSINESS DIRECTORY *

PRESS  TO SELECT                        PRESS  TO SELECT

1  by company name                      6   by county
2  by SIC description of product/service 7  by MSA code
3  by primary SIC code                   8  by state
4  by primary or secondary SIC code      9  by telephone number
5  by city                              10  by zip code
                                        11  by number of employees
```

Let's try to find a listing of modem manufacturers by entering an SIC
description of the product. After selecting item 2, the system will ask
you to enter the proper SIC description, which identifies the industry.
Had I known the exact numerical code (and could have found it by
using the IQuest's live online support system), I would have chosen
option numbers 3 and 4, and been more precise.

The U.S. government assigns every industry a specific SIC, or
Standard Industrial Classification, code, which is a unique
identification number. The first two digits of an SIC code correspond
to a major industry group, and the following digits further specify that
industry's subcategory.

Many databases, especially company directory databases, utilize these
SIC codes as a way to categorize businesses in their files. For this
reason, you should be familiar with the codes. Although some
databases will help you narrow down your industry to its appropriate
SIC code, you'll be much better off just looking it up in an SIC
manual. You can either find one in your library or order it from the
government at the following address:

SIC Manual, Superintendent of Documents
United States Government Printing Office
Washington, DC 20402

```
ENTER THE SIC DESCRIPTION OF A PRODUCT OR SERVICE
-> modem/

Is:
MODEM/
Correct ? (Yes/No) -> yes

PRESS    TO SELECT

  1  Narrow your search  (add more fields)
  2  Begin your search now
  H  for Help,    C  for Commands

Total charges thus far:    $0.00
-> 1
```

Now we can narrow the search by state. By the way, note how IQuest informs you, step by step, of how much in search fees you've incurred— a very nice feature. Since I haven't yet sent the search to the host computer for record retrieval, I haven't incurred any costs so far.

```
-> 8
                    * ENTER STATE CODE *

SEARCH TIPS:  Enter a 2-letter state code.  Enter the code for Oregon
              immediately followed by the WILD LETTER slash (/).

SEARCH EXAMPLES:   MA
                   OR/
                   NC OR SC

Type H for a list of state codes and more help.

ENTER A STATE CODE
-> MA

Is MA Correct ? (Yes/No) -> yes

PRESS    TO SELECT

  1  Narrow your search  (add more fields)
  2  Begin your search now
  H  for Help,    C  for Commands

Total charges thus far:    $0.00
-> 2

There are 41 item(s) which
satisfy your search phrase.

We will show you the most recent 5

You may wish to PRINT or CAPTURE this data if possible.

Total charges thus far:    $7.00
```

✳ Dun's Market Identifiers (DUNS)

➤ $8 per hour CompuServe extended rate (2400 bps)

➤ $7.50 search to display up to 5 names

➤ $7.50 for each additional 5 names

➤ $7.50 for each record displayed in full

➤ 15-minute search plus 10 displayed names and 3 full records = $2 time + $15 for name display + $22.50 for 3 full displays = $39.50

Dun's Market Identifiers contains information on over 6.7 million U.S. public and private establishments having more than five employees or with over $1 million in sales. Information on a listed company includes its name, address, phone number, and sometimes number of employees, sales figures, corporate family relationships, and executive names and titles. This database differs from the previously described Dun's directory, Dun's Electronic Business Directory, in that this one covers fewer companies but might have additional information on those it does cover.

You can search this database by company name or by a special identification number. Here's a sample search:

```
* D&B — DUN'S MARKET IDENTIFIERS *
Company Menu

PRESS   TO SELECT
  1  by company name
  2  by DUN'S number
  3  previous menu

  H  for Help,  C  for Commands

Total charges thus far:    $0.00
-> 1

* ENTER COMPANY NAME *

SEARCH TIPS:  Omit punctuation (examples: & + = - ! $ * , .) and words
such as Co., Company, Inc., Corp.

SEARCH EXAMPLES:  Narricot
                  Boykins Fabric
                  Black Decker
                  IBM OR International Business Machines
```

```
Type H for more help and examples.

ENTER A COMPANY NAME

There are 4 item(s) which
satisfy your search phrase.

You may wish to PRINT or CAPTURE this data if possible.
```

After viewing these four items, it looked like the fourth was the one
that I wanted to see in detail, so I instructed the system to retrieve
and display that one.

✳ Corporate Affiliations (AFFILIATIONS)

➤ $8 per hour CompuServe extended rate (2400 bps)

➤ $7.50 search to display up to 10 companies

➤ $7.50 for each additional 10 companies

➤ $7.50 for each record displayed in full

➤ 15-minute search plus 10 displayed names and 3 full records =
$2 time + $7.50 for name display + $22.50 for 3 full displays
= $32

Another company directory, Corporate Affiliations, specializes in
providing information on the relationships between parent and
subsidiary firms for most large U.S. public companies (including all
firms on the New York, American, and Over The Counter exchanges),
top privately-held firms, and most large public and private firms in
the world. A typical record includes the business name, address,
phone number, business description, names of executives, and where
it fits in the corporate family hierarchy. Here's a sample search I
conducted to uncover subsidiaries of the media giant Paramount:

```
ENTER YOUR PARENT COMPANY NAME
-> Paramount/

Is:
PARAMOUNT/
Correct ? (Yes/No) -> yes

PRESS    TO SELECT
  1  Narrow your search  (add more fields)
  2  Begin your search now
```

```
   H  for Help,    C  for Commands
Total charges thus far:      $0.00
-> 2
```

There are 90 item(s) which
satisfy your search phrase.

We will show you the most recent 10

You may wish to PRINT or CAPTURE this data if possible.

Heading # 1   Searched: 05-21-1
993 09:01
G+W Entertainment
One Gulf+Western Plaza
New York, NY 10023
USA

Heading # 2

Madison Square Garden Corporation
Two Pennsylvania Plaza
New York, NY 10121
USA

Heading # 3

Madison Square Garden Center Inc
Two Pennsylvania Plaza
New York, NY 10121
USA

Heading # 4

Madison Square Garden Network
Two Pennsylvania Plaza
New York, NY 10121
USA

Heading # 5

Miss Universe Inc
6420 Wilshire Blvd.
Los Angeles, CA 90048
USA

Heading # 6

New York Knickerbockers Basketball
Two Pennsylvania Plaza
New York, NY 10121
USA

```
Heading # 7
New York Rangers Hockey Club
Two Pennsylvania Plaza
New York, NY 10121
USA


Heading # 8

Festival Inc.
9200 Sunset Blvd.
Los Angeles, CA 90060
USA


Heading # 9

Paramount Pictures Corporation
5555 Melrose Ave.
Los Angeles, CA 90038
USA


Heading # 10

Famous Music Corporation
One Gulf+Western Plaza
New York, NY 10023
USA
```

These are some pretty interesting results. I didn't know, for example, that the Miss Universe contest was owned by Paramount!

✳ Thomas Register Online (THOMAS)

- ➤ $8 per hour CompuServe extended rate (2400 bps)
- ➤ $5.00 search to display up to 10 names
- ➤ $5.00 for each additional 10 names
- ➤ $5.00 for each record displayed in full
- ➤ 15-minute search plus 10 displayed names and 3 full records = $2 time + $5.00 for name display + $15.00 for 3 full displays = $22

A third type of business company directory is offered by Thomas, whose specialty is listing information on who makes what product. For each of the nearly 150,000 public and private U.S. and Canadian companies listed in this database, you can find names and addresses, as well as a listing of products or services provided. Here's a sample of a search conducted on Thomas to find manufacturers of tuning forks:

```
ENTER A PRODUCT NAME
-> tuning fork/

Is:
TUNING FORK/
Correct ? (Yes/No) -> yes

PRESS    TO SELECT
  1  Narrow your search  (add more fields)
  2  Begin your search now
  H  for Help,    C  for Commands

Total charges thus far:     $0.00
-> 2

There are 3 item(s) which
satisfy your search phrase.

You may wish to PRINT or CAPTURE this data if possible.

Heading # 1           Searched: 05-21-1993  08:54
01039128    DIALOG File 535: Thomas Register Online
Saronix

Heading # 2
01029795    DIALOG File 535: Thomas Register Online
Riverbank Laboratories Physics Research Facility

Heading # 3
01004047    DIALOG File 535: Thomas Register Online
Jonard Industries Corp.

PRESS        TO SELECT
  1      Review results again
  2      See full record
  5      Start a new search
  6      Leave System

Total charges thus far:     $5.00
-> 2

The available Heading numbers currently range between 1 and 3.

Please enter the heading number(s) of the full record(s) you wish to see.
Separate each with a comma. (e.g. 1,5,6)
-> 1-3

Retrieving 3 full records will cost:  $15.00

Do you wish to continue (Yes/No) -> yes

Heading # 1           Searched: 05-21-1993  08:55
```

```
01039128    DIALOG File 535: Thomas Register Online
Saronix
151-T Laura Lane
Palo Alto, CA  94303    USA

TELEPHONE: 415-856-6900
FAX:       415-856-4732  FAX
OTHER:     348465 SARONIX PLA  TELEX
           800-227-8974  In CA: 800-422-3355

LOCATION: U.S.-SOUTHWEST
COUNTY: San Mateo
CMSA: 7362 SAN FRANCISCO-OAKLAND-SAN JOSE, CA
ADI: 688 SAN FRANCISCO-OAKLAND-SAN JOSE (SANTA ROSA & VALLEJO)

TRADE STATUS:
    EXPORTER

DESCRIPTION OF BUSINESS:
    Piezoelectric Quartz Crystals & Clock Oscillators.

ASSETS:            5M+ ($5,000,000 - $9,999,999)
NUMBER OF EMPLOYEES: 32

MANAGEMENT:
    Bulechek, D.W.   P.   GENERAL MGMT.
    Baldwin, W.   Tech. Mgr.   ENGINEERING
    Kim, G.T.   G.M.   PRODUCTION
    Talens, R.   Purch. Mgr.   PURCHASING
    Blewett, M.   N.S.M.   SALES MGMT.
    Sponholz, R.E.   V.P.   INTL. SLS.
    Aldaffer, M.   Comm. Mgr.   ADVERTISING
    Finlay, J.   Nat. Mktg. Mgr.   MARKETING
    Dosch, W.G.   Chf. Fin. Exec.   FINANCIAL

PRODUCTS AND SIC CODES:
    CAPACITORS—CERAMIC  3675
    CRYSTALS—QUARTZ  3679
    *FORKS*—*TUNING*  3931
    OSCILLATORS—CLOCK  3679
    OSCILLATORS—CRYSTAL  3679, 3825

TRADENAMES:
    Nymph   (All)

SOURCE: Thomas Register of American Manufacturers  1992
        ( 57354896 ) (TR)
```

And so on. This search, including printing out three full records, ended up costing $20. That's a fair bit of cash, so keep in mind that Thomas Register, like certain other information resources that are available online, also have print equivalents—which can be searched for free at your local library!

⇨ International business directories

IQuest seeded databases also include a selection of very impressive international directory databases. These contain a mixture of basic identifying information as well as selected financial data on firms located around the world. The databases include:

✳ Australia New Zealand Company Library

> ➤ $8 per hour CompuServe extended rate (2400 bps)

> ➤ $5.00 to $7.50 search to display 5–10 items, depending on database

> ➤ $5.00 to $7.50 for each additional 5–10 items, depending on database

> ➤ $5.00 to $30 for each record displayed in full

> ➤ 15-minute search plus 10 displayed names and 3 full records = ($17+ depending on database)

This group file is composed of a variety of relevant databases, including D&B Dun's Asia-Pacific Market Identifiers, which contains information on a total of 95,000 Australian and New Zealand businesses, Extel Cards financial data, the Asia-Pacific news database, and Reuter's international textline file.

✳ D&B Dun's Canadian Dun's Market Identifiers (DUNS)

> ➤ $8 per hour CompuServe extended rate (2400 bps)

> ➤ $7.50 search to display 5 names

> ➤ $7.50 for each additional 5 names

> ➤ $7.50 for each record displayed in full

> ➤ 15 minute search plus 10 displayed names and 3 full records = $2 time + $15.00 for name display + $22.50 for 3 full displays = $39.50

Contains data on over 350,000 Canadian companies.

✳ D&B Dun's International Dun's Market Identifiers (DUNS)

➢ $8 per hour CompuServe extended rate (2400 bps)

➢ $7.50 search to display 5 names

➢ $7.50 for each additional 5 names

➢ $7.50 for each record displayed in full

➢ 15-minute search plus 10 displayed names and 3 full records = $2 time + $15.00 for name display + $22.50 for 3 full displays = $39.50

Contains information on over 2.1 million public and private companies, as well as government-controlled firms in 120 countries, including Asia, Africa, Europe, Middle East, South America, Australia, and the Pacific Rim.

✳ European Company Library (EUROLIB)

A multiple database file providing directory and financial data on over two million European firms. Databases covered include ABC Europe, D&B Dun's European Market Identifiers, Kompass, databases from Financial Times (FT), European Community databases, and other leading files. (Pricing varies widely depending on the specific database selected.)

✳ German Company Library (GERLIB)

Contains directory, financial, and product information for over 48,000 public and private German companies. (Pricing varies widely depending on the specific database selected.)

✳ Patent Research Center (GO PAT)

➢ $8 per hour CompuServe extended rate (2400 bps)

➢ $1 scan for hits and obtain search results menu

➢ $4.00 search to display 10 titles

➢ $4.00 for each additional 10 titles

➢ $7.50 for each record displayed in full

➢ 15-minute search plus scan plus 10 displayed names and 3 full records = $2 time + $1 scan + $4.00 search + $22.50 for 3 full displays = $29.50

While not really a company directory, it's worth mentioning CompuServe's Patent Research Center (GO PAT), which contains summaries of U.S. patents granted in chemical, mechanical, electrical, and design areas, as well as international patent summaries from the middle of the 1970s. The data is derived from two well-known Dialog databases: Claims/U.S. Patents and Derwent's World Patents Index.

⇨ Business information: news

✳ Marketing/Management Research Center (MGMTRC)

- ➢ $8 per hour CompuServe extended rate (2400 bps)
- ➢ $1 scan for hits and obtain search results menu
- ➢ $5.00 search to display 10 titles
- ➢ $5.00 for each additional 10 titles
- ➢ $5.00 for each record displayed in full
- ➢ 15-minute search plus 10 displayed names and 3 full records = $2 time + $1 scan + $5.00 for title display + $15.00 for 3 full displays = $23

This file is actually composed of nine different databases on Dialog: ABI/Inform, Findex, FINIS, Infomat International Business, McGraw-Hill Publications Online, PTS MARS, PTS New Product Announcements, and PTS PROMT. Some contain fulltext, others abstracts, and some are bibliographic. Coverage and update frequency varies by database.

All of these databases are leaders in the business information field, making this mega-database a very powerful choice. A search in this "research center" works like this: first, you conduct a scan of the nine databases to find out how many records each contains that match your search statement. Second, you're provided with the counts and asked to select a database to search. You can, of course, search more than one, though not at the same time. You must complete one search first before going on to another.

You can also order reprints of articles retrieved for $18 each. In my opinion, however it's *way* too expensive. Check the appendix for the names of guides listing document delivery firms who can quote you better prices. Better yet, call your local library and ask for a free interlibrary loan!

⇨ Business information: company reports and analyses

In this category, I'll identify databases that provide knowledgeable insights into crucial operational and management areas of companies, such as sales and earnings forecasts, new product development, strategic planning, competition, and other data not easily located.

Some of the best company analysis reports are those derived from Wall Street brokerage analysts and market research firms. Both employ staffs whose job is to study a company and/or industry in-depth, and comment knowledgeably about how the firm is really doing and how it's expected to do. The first source listed, called Investext, is the industry leader in supplying these reports.

❋ Investext (GO INV)

> $8 per hour CompuServe extended rate (2400 bps)

> $7.50 search to display 10 titles

> $7.50 for each additional 10 titles

> $15.00 for each single page displayed in full

> 15-minute search plus 10 displayed names and 3 pages = $2 time + $7.50 for title display + $45.00 for 3 full page displays = $54.50

Investext contains the fulltext of company and industry research reports compiled during the most recent two years by analysts in more than 50 Wall Street, regional, and international brokerage houses and research firms such as Merrill Lynch and Bear Stearns. As of the summer of 1993, the file included 8,200 reports on publicly held companies, 2,300 on privately held ones, and industry reports covering 50

different segments. Company reports typically include historical information such as a company profile, revenues, earnings, and other financial operating results such as stock performances. Many also contain the research brokerage's recommendations and forecasts.

Investext is a powerful and extremely valuable company research tool, often providing insider-type insights unavailable from other sources. However, it's a difficult database to master and in fact can be difficult to search even passably well. For this reason, I highly recommend that before you search Investext that you contact the IQuest user services staff (SOS) and obtain some search assistance.

You can search Investext by company, industry, or report number. Here is a sample of an Investext *company* report:

```
1239720
H&R Block - Company Report
CYRUS J. LAWRENCE INCORPORATED
Raiman, G.M.


DATE: 890629
INVESTEXT(tm) REPORT NUMBER: 921781,  PAGE 1 OF 2
This is a(n) COMPANY report.

SECTION HEADINGS:
    Highlights & Rating
    Investment Conclusion
    Earnings Update

TABLE HEADINGS:
    Stock Price & Financial Data 1988-90

TEXT:
RECOMMENDATION: Hold

H&R BLOCK (NYSE - HRB - $31 3/8)

    * Lowering opinion to HOLD from BUY, based on valuation.
    * Year-end results in line with expectations.
    * Expect moderate, yet consistent growth over next few years.
    * Company's earnings are highly recession-resistant.
    * Shares appear fully valued on growth rate expectation yet sell
      at a 30% discount to estimated asset values.
    * Clean balance sheet; excess cash totals $300 million.

                    (*) Earnings/Cash     P/E-P/CF                 Return on
                        Flow Per Share       Ratio       Ind. Current  Avg. Equity
    52-Week Range   1988 1989A 1990E    1989A 1990E    Div.  Yield   1989E 1990E
    $34-$20         $1.72 $1.90 $2.15   16.5x 14.6x    $1.28  4.1%    24.8% 25.3%
```

(*) Fiscal year ends April 30.

Capitalization
(1/31/89)   Millions   %

Long-Term Debt $4.8   1.3%
Deferred Taxes   10.1   2.8
Other   7.5   2.0
Equity   343.7   93.9
Total $366.1   100.0%

Common Shares: 52.4 million
Book Value Per Share: $6.56
Institutional Ownership: 67%

[Graphical Material Omitted: Stock Chart]

Quarterly Earnings

	1988(a)	1989A	1990E
July	$(0.07)	$(0.10)	$(0.12)
October	(0.03)	(0.02)	(0.03)
January	(0.21)	(0.18)	(0.21)
April	2.03	2.20	2.51
Year	$1.72	$1.90	$2.15

(a) Numbers have been restated to reflect Access Technologies
acquisition.

INVESTMENT CONCLUSION

  We are lowering our investment opinion to a HOLD from a BUY. In our
opinion, the shares appear reasonably valued based on a future 12% to 14%
growth rate, helped by roughly 2% to 4% in fiscal 1990 and 1991 by
increased penetration of Rapid Refund (electronic filing to the IRS). The
company's overall growth rate would be only 10% to 12% without Rapid
Refund, which is less than spectacular, down from 14% over the past four
years. At the same time, the shares are selling at the high end of their
relative multiple range of 0.9x to 1.3x the S&P Industrials. We do not
want to minimize the highly consistent, recession-resistant nature of
this company's earnings. Rather, we feel that absent any near-term tax
changes and a full valuation, there are better growth stock opportunities
elsewhere.
  We continue to be impressed with the values within the company. The tax
preparation franchise is very valuable, in our opinion, being the only
large-scale tax preparer in the industry to the middle market. Margins
are high, and it is virtually a cash cow, requiring little capital
investment. The company is so firmly entrenched that American Express
(NYSE - AXP - $35 1/4) which is interested in getting into this business,
has determined that it would be too costly to go after the mass market
that Block services. In addition, Block owns two other valuable

companies, Personnel Pool of America, the third-largest temporary-help company in the industry, and CompuServe, a commercial and consumer database company with the largest videotex network in the country. The total value of these properties, including excess cash on the books is roughly $43 per share, according to our calculations (see Table I). However, we do not believe the company is particularly interested in selling or in realizing these values at the current time.

EARNINGS UPDATE

   H&R Block recently reported fiscal 1989 earnings per share of $1.90, which includes a $0.03 capital gain from the sale of National Data (OTC (#) - NDTA - $30 3/4) stock. The earnings were in line with our expectations, reflecting only a 9% growth rate, down from a 20% rate in the prior years. This year, the growth rate in the tax preparation business was slow by comparison, as it usually is in the second year of a major tax law change. All other divisions came in as expected, except Path Management, which was slightly below expectations. Rapid Refund added roughly $25 to $30 million in revenues, which should double next year, as it is expanded to close to 100% of the offices from 50% this year.

(the text continues)

You can see from the example the great level of financial detail and analysis. It's a very expensive database, though. You're charged $7.50 for every report title search you run (for retrieval up to 10 report titles), and on top of that you pay an additional $15 for every *page* from a report that you choose to display. Obviously, if you choose to search this file, you had better know what you're doing! Unless you're a very accomplished searcher, you might be better off hiring a professional information broker to search this file for you.

✳ TRW Business Profiles (TRW)

➤ $8 per hour CompuServe extended rate (2400 bps)

➤ $9.00 search to display 24 titles

➤ $34 for first full record displayed

➤ $9 for each of the next four full records displayed

➤ 15-minute search plus 10 displayed titles and 3 full records = $2 time + $9 for title display + $52.00 for 3 full displays = $63.00

A different kind of company financial database is available from TRW. TRW is a credit rating firm and, as such, keeps close track of how a company pays its bills and its credit history. This database provides this and related data on over 13 million organizations. Information in a credit report typically contains credit histories, financial information and ratios, UCC filings, tax liens, judgments, bankruptcies, and an executive summary.

While this can be a very valuable database, it's extremely expensive. A single credit report will cost you $34 on top of the normal search rates. There's also not much in the way of search flexibility, as you can search only by company name and state locator.

❊ Business Dateline (BUSDATE)

> $8 per hour CompuServe extended rate (2400 bps)

> $7.50 search to display 5 titles

> $7.50 for each additional 5 titles

> $7.50 for each full record displayed

> 15-minute search plus 10 displayed titles and 3 full records = $2 time + $15.00 for title display + $22.50 for 3 full displays = $39.50

Another intriguing source for insights into companies is Business Dateline. Business Dateline contains the fulltext of articles from more than 115 regional business publications in the U.S. and Canada. Regional business journals are some of the best sources around for learning about private and smaller companies—the types of firms for which there's much less public information available. For example, say you needed to do research on a small, privately held real estate developer located in Dayton, Ohio. Chances are that firm would have been profiled at some point in Dayton's regional business journal. Typically, these profiles identify key management personnel, provide some company background, and talk about strategic plans and competition.

Business Dateline's coverage extends back to 1985, and is updated weekly. You can search the database by subject, author, company names, geographic location, or publication date. Here's a sample of

some research that I did to locate any news items or analyses on a
small, privately held, computer training firm called Logical Operations.

```
* BUSINESS DATELINE *

PRESS   TO SELECT
  1  by subject words
  2  by author name
  3  by company name
  4  by geographic location
  5  by publication date

  H  for Help, C for Commands

3

ENTER A COMPANY NAME
-> logical operations

There are 8 item(s) which
satisfy your search phrase.

We will show you the most recent 5

You may wish to PRINT or CAPTURE this data if possible.

Heading # 1                     Searched: 06-24-1993  14:58

0350672   93-00632
Personal Training Systems Now Available at Logical Operations
Conway, Ronald
Business Wire (San Francisco, CA, US) s1  p1
PUBL DATE: 921207
JOURNAL CODE: BWRE
DOC TYPE:  Report
DATELINE:  San Jose, CA, US       WORD COUNT: 416

COMPANY NAMES: Personal Training Systems, San Jose, CA, US, SIC:7372,
*Logical* *Operations* Inc, Rochester, NY, US, SIC:7372;8299

CLASSIFICATION CODES: 8302 (Software and computer services); 7500
(Product planning & development)

DESCRIPTORS: Software industry; Product introduction; Pacific

Heading # 2

0327538   92-76706
The Slow Road
Cosgrove, Michael
Rochester Business Journal (Rochester, NY, US), v8 n22 s1  p17
PUBL DATE: 920918
JOURNAL CODE: ROCH
```

```
DOC TYPE:  Newspaper article
DATELINE:  Rochester, NY, US        WORD COUNT: 1,524

SPECIAL FEATURE: Drawing

COMPANY NAMES: Buck & Pulleyn, Rochester, NY, US, SIC:7311, Paychex,
Rochester, NY, US, DUNS:09-439-9359, SIC:7374, Ticker:PAYX Moscom Corp.,
Rochester, NY, US, DUNS:01-916-3161, SIC:3661;3577, Ticker:MSCM *Logical*
*Operations* Inc, Rochester, NY, US, SIC:7372;8299

CLASSIFICATION CODES: 2310 (Planning); 2500
  (Organizational behavior)

DESCRIPTORS:  Expansion; Business conditions; Management styles; Trends;
Middle Atlantic

Heading # 3

0315359   92-63200
Logical Operations Halts Expansion Into Europe
Hovis, Kathy
Rochester Business Journal (Rochester, NY, US), v8 n16 s1  p4
PUBL DATE: 920807
JOURNAL CODE: ROCH
DOC TYPE:  Newspaper article
DATELINE:  Rochester, NY, US        WORD COUNT: 588

COMPANY NAMES: *Logical* *Operations* Inc, Rochester, NY, US,
SIC:7372;8299

CLASSIFICATION CODES: 8690 (Publishing industry); 1300 (International
trade & foreign investment)

DESCRIPTORS: Publishing industry; Educational services; Personal
computers; Training; Foreign investment; Europe; Middle Atlantic

(the text continues)
```

Well, we've turned up a number of very interesting articles. Say we want to look at the full record for item #3, about Logical Operations halting its expansion into Europe:

```
Heading # 3

0315359   92-63200
Logical Operations Halts Expansion Into Europe
Hovis, Kathy
Rochester Business Journal (Rochester, NY, US), v8 n16 s1  p4
PUBL DATE: 920807
JOURNAL CODE: ROCH
DOC TYPE:  Newspaper article
DATELINE:  Rochester, NY, US        WORD COUNT: 588
```

TEXT:
   Logical Operations Inc. has decided to log off its overseas ventures
and concentrate on operations back home, its president said this week.
   At the same time, a hiring surge at the 180-employee firm is leveling
off. Logical Operations six weeks ago halted its plan to open an office
in Munich, Germany, President Barry Keesan said. We thought we were
getting ahead of ourselves," he said. "It's an example of being
overzealous, overambitious."
   The company decided the European venture, slated also to involve
translating company computer training materials into other languages,
would have been a drain on its core business. Gains would not have been
seen in the European market for several years, and translating materials
was more complicated than first thought, Keesan said.
   Logical Operations already has six titles in French and two in German,
he said, but all translating plans are on hold. With the introduction of
new products, including a software line, since the business was bought by
Ziff Communications Co. in 1991, Keesan said it made sense to train its
focus closer to home.

(the text continues)

   COPYRIGHT: Copyright Rochester Business Journal 1992

COMPANY NAMES: *Logical* *Operations* Inc, Rochester, NY, US,
SIC:7372;8299

CLASSIFICATION CODES: 8690 (Publishing industry); 1300 (International
trade & foreign investment)

DESCRIPTORS: Publishing industry; Educational services; Personal
computers; Training; Foreign investment; Europe; Middle Atlantic

Wow. That's a lot of good information—especially on a smaller
company. Included are the names of officers, employment figures,
strategic plans, problem areas, and a number of insights that can be
quite valuable if you're studying a particular company.

Business: financial analyses

Databases in this category are similar to the business directories
described previously, but contain more than just basic identifying
information like address, number of employees, and total sales.
Depending on the database, this might include sales trends by year,
earnings, profit and loss statements, balance sheets, credit ratings,
and so forth.

✳ S&P Online (S&P)

> ➤ 15-minute search plus 10 displayed titles and 3 full records =
> $2 time + $15.00 for title display + $22.50 for 3 full displays
> = $39.50

S&P Online is produced by the well-known credit rating firm of Standard & Poor's. This database contains information on approximately 5,600 companies and includes data such as earning outlooks, historical earnings, dividends, and business summaries. The database is updated weekly.

Unfortunately, this S&P file is less useful than other S&P databases found elsewhere. Here it can be confusing to use, and doesn't present the data itself in a particularly friendly manner. In fact, an excellent alternative would be to search the S&P file on the Knowledge Index system, described later in this chapter.

✳ Disclosure II (Disclosure)

> ➤ $8 per hour CompuServe extended rate (2400 bps)

> ➤ $5 to $25 per report

The Disclosure database contains financial information on all publicly owned companies that file a 10K and other reports with the U.S. Securities and Exchange Commission (SEC). Among the data offered in this database are a business description, detailed financial statements, management discussions, five-year financial summaries, a list of SEC filings, lists of subsidiaries and insider owners, and names of directors. Disclosure II is updated on a daily, weekly, and quarterly basis, depending on the type of data being revised.

Again, while Disclosure itself is a top notch source for in-depth financial information on public companies, it's difficult to search and might not be at its best through the CompuServe system. As with the Investext file, I would strongly recommend either obtaining a good deal of preliminary customer assistance before attempting to search this file, or hiring an expert to do the search for you.

⇨ News and newspapers

✳ Newspaper Library

- ➤ $8 per hour CompuServe extended rate (2400 bps)
- ➤ $4.00 search to display 5 titles
- ➤ $3.00 for each full record displayed
- ➤ 15-minute search plus 10 displayed titles and 3 full records = $2 time + $8 for title display + $9 for 3 full displays = $19.00

The Newspaper Library consists of the fulltext (except for classifieds) for 48 daily newspapers around the country. This is an exceptionally powerful database, valuable for virtually any project. The file, derived from Dialog, is updated daily, but there's a two-day time lag between the time a newspaper is updated until the time it's available online. These are the newspapers available:

- ➤ Akron (OH) Beacon Journal
- ➤ Albany (NY) Times-Union
- ➤ Allentown (PA) Morning Call
- ➤ Anchorage (AK) Daily News
- ➤ Arizona Republic/Phoenix Gazette
- ➤ Atlanta (GA) Constitution/Atlanta Journal
- ➤ Baltimore (MD) Sun
- ➤ Boston (MA) Globe
- ➤ Buffalo (NY) News
- ➤ Charlotte (NC) Observer
- ➤ Chicago (IL) Tribune
- ➤ Christian Science Monitor
- ➤ Cincinnati (OH) / Kentucky Post
- ➤ Cleveland (OH) Plain Dealer
- ➤ Columbia (SC) State

➤ Columbus (OH) Dispatch

➤ Dayton (OH) Daily News

➤ Denver (CO) Rocky Mountain News

➤ Detroit (MI) Free Press

➤ Ft. Lauderdale (FL) Sun-Sentinel

➤ Fresno (CA) Bee

➤ Houston (TX) Post

➤ Lexington (KY) Herald-Leader

➤ Los Angeles (CA) Daily News

➤ Los Angeles (CA) Times

➤ Memphis (TN) Commercial Appeal

➤ Miami (FL) Herald

➤ Minneapolis (MN) Star Tribune

➤ New Jersey Record

➤ New Orleans (LA) Times-Picayune

➤ Newsday (NY)

➤ Norfolk (VA) Ledger-Star & Virginian-Pilot

➤ Orlando (FL) Sentinel

➤ Palm Beach (FL) Post

➤ Philadelphia (PA) Daily News

➤ Philadelphia (PA) Inquirer

➤ Pittsburgh (PA) Press

➤ Portland (OR) Oregonian

➤ Richmond (VA) News Leader / Richmond Times-Dispatch

➤ Sacramento (CA) Bee

➤ San Francisco (CA) Chronicle

➤ San Francisco (CA) Examiner

➢ San Jose (CA) Mercury News

➢ Seattle (WA) Post-Intelligencer

➢ Seattle (WA) Times

➢ St. Louis (MO) Post-Dispatch

➢ St. Paul (MN) Pioneer Press

➢ St. Petersburg (FL) Times

➢ USA Today

➢ Washington (DC) Post

➢ Washington (DC) Times

➢ Wichita (KS) Eagle-Beacon

➢ Wisconsin State Journal & Madison Capital Times

✳ Executive News Service

CompuServe has some interesting offerings in the news and newspaper department. Although the wires previously discussed in the "basic" section aren't searchable, CompuServe does offer its Executive News Service, a nicely designed electronic news-clip service that monitors AP news wires, the Washington Post, UPI, and Reuters news wires for stories that contain words or phrases that you specify. Stories are "clipped" for you as they come across the wires and held in electronic folders for you to review at your convenience (see Fig. 2-16).

In online lingo, this process is called an SDI, for *selective dissemination of information*, and can be a very convenient and powerful method for tracking and collecting news items that pertain to just your subject or subjects of interest. However, Executive News Service is a premium-based service, which charges an additional $15 per hour fee and is available only for those members who have signed up for the Executive Service Option, which is a $10 per month minimum commitment.

My only caution in using this very useful research tool is that the Executive News Service contains no business journals, so you shouldn't rely on it as your sole source of information.

Figure 2-16

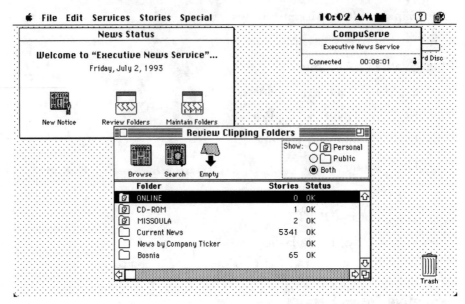

A screen from the Executive News Service, showing how you can retrieve
"clipped" stories from several electronic folders.

College information databases

CompuServe's college information database can be found in its
"basic" offering, and is described earlier in this chapter.

Other databases of interest

CompuServe has many other databases available. As I said earlier,
IQuest alone provides access to over 850! Here, however, I'd like to
present a selective list of databases that I think have the broadest
appeal to the serious researcher.

❋ **Demographic information**

> Supersite (SUPERSITE)

> Demographics (DEMOGRAPHICS)

> Census Data (CENDATA)

These are demographic reports containing information on population, income, housing, education, employment, and forecasts for the entire U.S., each state, county, and metropolitan area. Also available are sales potential reports and target marketing profiles on U.S. households, based on demographic, socioeconomic, and housing characteristics of the neighborhood. Data from SuperSite is derived from the well-known CACI data analysis firm. This is a powerful and extraordinarily useful database.

✳ Commerce Business Daily (COMBUS)

Includes the fulltext of U.S. Commerce Department publications, listing all significant federal contracts, requests for proposals, and related data.

✳ Government Publications (GPO)

Includes both a catalog of government publications and books, with online ordering. It also includes online consumer information articles from government publications, covering topics such as personal finance, health, automotive, food, parenting, and so on.

✳ NTIS—Government Sponsored Research (NTIS)

The U.S. National Technical Information Service is the source of government-sponsored research, development, and engineering reports. This database doesn't provide the actual reports, but references key information so users can place an order for what they need.

✳ PhoneFile (PHONEFILE)

This very useful database contains the names, addresses, phone numbers, and length of residency for more than 80 million households. You can search by name and address, last name and state, city and zip code, or phone number. The information is obtained from public record or published information, including phone-book directories, published birth announcements, real estate transactions, and information from public agencies.

* Marquis Who's Who (BIOGRAPHY)

This database offers biographical information describing key North American professionals. A typical biography includes the person's name, occupation, and date and location of birth; parents', spouse's, and children's names; education; positions held during career; civic, military, and political activities; memberships; awards; and other organizational affiliations.

⇨ The Knowledge Index databases

CompuServe's Knowledge Index probably provides the best information "bang for the buck" available on *any* consumer online service. The reason? You get access to some of the most powerful professional online databases in the world—at the bargain rate of $24 per hour—and that *includes* CompuServe's standard search rates, up to and including 9,600 bps. That's about 50% to 80% off of those databases' normal hourly search rates, and 100% off the normal per-document print rates.

There's only one catch, and it's not a very burdensome one either. You can search Knowledge Index only on the weekends (Fridays from 6 PM to Monday 5:00 AM local time) or weekday evening hours (Mondays through Thursdays 6 PM to 5 AM local time). Not a bad deal at all.

What exactly is Knowledge Index? The service is actually composed of a series of databases made available from Dialog Information Services, one of the leaders of the online database industry. Out of the 400+ online databases available through Dialog's regular service, Knowledge Index contains over 100 of them and is geared specifically for nonprofessionals such as students, teachers, consumers, and other "amateur" researchers. In fact, users of the Knowledge Index must agree that the information retrieved on the service is for their personal use only and that they will not resell it or use it for commercial purposes.

Until April of 1993, if you wanted to sign up with Knowledge Index you would have had to go through Dialog itself, which made the

service available to its own membership. However, for strategic planning purposes, Dialog decided that it wanted to make Knowledge Index available at an intersection that was already frequented by many nonprofessional database searchers. And so (with the exception of a few databases that couldn't be offered due to contractual limitations), Dialog said adieu to the Knowledge Index and sent it over to CompuServe, its new home.

The following, then, is a complete listing and short description of all of the databases currently on the Knowledge Index system:

✳ AGRICULTURE section

AGRI1 - AGRICOLA Worldwide information on agriculture. 1970 to present. Bibliographic database.

AGRI3 - CAB ABSTRACTS 1984–present. Detailed summaries of worldwide agricultural and biological research. Bibliographic database.

AGRI4 - CAB ABSTRACTS 1972–1983. Detailed summaries of worldwide agricultural and biological research. Bibliographic database.

✳ ARTS section

ARTS1 - ART BIBLIOGRAPHIES MODERN Comprehensive coverage of all modern art. 1974 to present. Bibliographic database.

ARTS2 - ART LITERATURE INTERNATIONAL (RILA) Worldwide historic coverage of Western art. 1973 to present. Bibliographic database.

✳ BIOLOGY, BIOSCIENCES, and BIOTECHNOLOGY section

BIOL1 - LIFE SCIENCES COLLECTION Worldwide coverage of research in biology, medicine, biochemistry, ecology, and microbiology. 1978 to present. Bibliographic database.

BIOL2 - CURRENT BIOTECHNOLGY ABSTRACTS Covers all aspects of biotechnology, including genetic manipulation, monoclonal antibodies, and fermentation technology. 1983 to present. Bibliographic database.

✳ **BOOKS section**

BOOK1 - BOOKS IN PRINT Currently published, forthcoming, and recently out-of-print books. Current. Directory database.

✳ **BUSINESS INFORMATION and CORPORATE NEWS section**

BUSI1 - ABI/INFORM Business practices, corporate strategies, and trends. August 1971 to present. Bibliographic, fulltext database.

BUSI2 - TRADE AND INDUSTRY INDEX Indexes of popular general business publications and industry trade journals. 1981 to present. Bibliographic database.

BUSI3 - HARVARD BUSINESS REVIEW Complete text of the *Harvard Business Review*. Covers full range of strategic management subjects. 1976 to present. Fulltext database.

BUSI4 - CHEMICAL BUSINESS NEWSBASE International trade and business coverage of the chemical industry. October 1984 to present. Bibliographic database.

BUSI5 - BUSINESSWIRE Unedited text of news released from over 10,000 U.S. organizations and corporations; emphasis on U.S. companies.

BUSI6 - PR NEWSWIRE Complete text of news releases covering entire spectrum. May 1, 1987 to present. Fulltext database.

CORP1 - STANDARD & POOR'S NEWS Financial news on U.S. public companies. June 1985 to present. Fulltext, numeric database.

CORP2 - ICC BRITISH COMPANY DIRECTORY Listing of every limited-liability company in England, Scotland, and Wales. Current. Directory database.

CORP3 - STANDARD & POOR'S CORPORATE DESCRIPTIONS Information and news on over 12,000 publicly held U.S. companies. Current. Directory database.

CORP4 - STANDARD & POOR'S NEWS Financial news on U.S. public companies. 1979 to June 1985. Fulltext, numeric database.

CORP5 - STANDARD & POOR'S REGISTER - BIOGRAPHICAL Information on approximately 72,000 key business executives. Current. Directory database.

✳ CHEMISTRY section

CHEM1 - CHAPMAN AND HALL CHEMICAL DATABASE Physical property data of over 175,000 substances. Current. Directory database.

CHEM2 - ANALYTICAL ABSTRACTS Comprehensive coverage of analytical chemistry. 1980 to present. Bibliographic database.

CHEM3 - THE AGROCHEMICALS HANDBOOK Detailed scientific data on agrochemicals. Current. Directory database.

CHEM5 - KIRK-OTHMER ONLINE Online encyclopedia of applied chemical science and industrial technology. Third edition of the Kirk Othmer Encyclopedia of Chemical Technology. Fulltext database.

✳ COMPUTERS AND ELECTRONICS section

COMP3 - MICROCOMPUTER INDEX Microcomputer products and developments. 1981 to present. Bibliographic database.

COMP4 - COMPUTER DATABASE Summaries of computer-related articles and publications. 1983 to present. Bibliographic database.

COMP5 - MICROCOMPUTERSOFTWARE GUIDE Complete information on available U.S. software programs. Current. Directory database.

COMP6 - BUSINESS SOFTWARE DATABASE Descriptions of software packages that have business applications for use with micro- and minicomputers. Current. Directory database.

COMP7 - MICRO SOFTWARE DIRECTORY (SOFT) Provides critical reviews of leading software packages. Current. Directory database.

COMP8 - COMPUTER NEWS FULLTEXT Complete articles from *ComputerWorld* and *Network World*. *ComputerWorld* August 1989 to present, *Network World* October 1989 to present. Fulltext database.

✻ **DRUG section**

DRUG1 - INTERNATIONAL PHARMACEUTICAL ABSTRACTS Research and current health-related drug literature. 1970 to present. Bibliographic database.

DRUG2 - DRUG INFORMATION FULLTEXT Complete text of the *American Hospital Formulary Service* and the *Handbook on Injectable Drugs*. Current. Fulltext, directory database.

DRUG3 - CONSUMER DRUG INFORMATION FULLTEXT Complete text of *Consumer Drug Digest*. Current. Fulltext, directory database.

DRUG4 - THE MERCK INDEX ONLINE(sm) Updated and expanded version of the *Merck Index*, an internationally recognized encyclopedia of chemicals, drugs, and biologicals. Late 19th century to present. Fulltext database.

✻ **ECONOMICS section**

ECON1 - ECONOMIC LITERATURE INDEX Comprehensive coverage of economic research. 1969 to present. Bibliographic database.

✻ **EDUCATION section**

EDUC1 - ERIC Research reports, articles, and projects significant to education. 1966 to present. Bibliographic database.

EDUC2 - PETERSON'S COLLEGE DATABASE Provides descriptions of over 4,700 colleges and universities with two- and four-year degree programs. Current. Directory database.

EDUC3 - PETERSON'S GRADLINE Provides descriptions of over 2,600 accredited institutions in the U.S. and Canada that offer post-baccalaureate degrees. Current. Directory database.

EDUC4 - A-V ONLINE Information on all nonprint media (films, transparencies, videos, slides, etc.) covering all levels of education. 1964 to present. Bibliographic, directory database.

EDUC5 - ACADEMIC INDEX Provides one-stop access to general-interest, social sciences, and humanities literature with an emphasis on academic journals. 1976 to present. Bibliographic database.

✳ ENGINEERING section

ENGI1 - COMPENDEX*PLUS(tm) Comprehensive coverage of 3,000 engineering journals. 1970 to present. Bibliographic database.

ENGI2 - CHEMICAL ENGINEERING AND BIOTECHNOLOGY ABSTRACTS Information on industrial practice and theoretical chemical engineering. 1971 to present. Bibliographic database.

✳ ENVIRONMENT section

ENVI1 - POLLUTION ABSTRACTS Information on pollution, its sources, and its control. 1970 to present. Bibliographic database.

✳ FOOD section

FOOD1 - FOOD SCIENCE AND TECHNOLOGY ABSTRACTS 1969 to present. Provides access to research and new development literature in the areas related to food science and technology. Basic allied disciplines such as chemistry, physics, biochemistry, and agriculture are covered as well. Coverage of a wide range of topics,

including food microbiology, food hygiene and packaging, beverages, food additives, food laws, and information on fruits, vegetables, nuts, sugars, fish, meat, poultry, dairy products, and more.

✻ GOVERNMENT PUBLICATIONS section

GOVE1 - GPO PUBLICATIONS REFERENCE FILE Publications for sale by U.S. Superintendent of Documents. 1971 to present. Bibliographic database.

GOVE2 - NTIS Indexes U.S. government produced technical reports. 1964 to present. Bibliographic database.

✻ HISTORY section

HIST1 - AMERICA: HISTORY AND LIFE Wide range of information on U.S. and Canadian history. 1964 to present. Bibliographic database.

HIST2 - HISTORICAL ABSTRACTS Article summaries of the history of the world from 1450 to present. 1973 to present. Bibliographic database.

✻ LEGAL section

LEGA1 - LEGAL RESOURCE INDEX Indexing of over 750 law journals and reviews. 1980 to present. Bibliographic database.

LEGA2 - BNA DAILY NEWS Daily, comprehensive news coverage of national and international government and private-sector activities. 1990 to present. Fulltext database.

✻ LITERATURE and LANGUAGE section

LITS2 - LINGUISTICS & LANGUAGE BEHAVIOR ABSTRACTS Abstracts of the world's literature on linguistics and language behavior. 1973 to present. Bibliographic database.

✻ MAGAZINES section

MAGA1 - MAGAZINE INDEX Index to articles in over 400 general-interest U.S. magazines. 1959 to March 1970 and 1973 to present. Bibliographic database.

MAGA2 - CANADIAN BUSINESS AND CURRENT AFFAIRS Index to articles appearing in 180 Canadian business publications, nearly 300 popular magazines, and 10 newspapers. July 1980 to present. Bibliographic database.

✳ **MATHEMATICS section**

MATH1 - MATHSCI Research on pure and applied mathematics. 1973 to present. Bibliographic database.

✳ **MEDICINE section**

MEDI1 - MEDLINE 1983-present. Biomedical literature and research. Bibliographic database.

MEDI2 - MEDLINE 1966-present. Biomedical literature and research. Bibliographic database.

MEDI10 - CANCERLIT Wide coverage of cancer research. 1963 to present. Bibliographic database.

MEDI11 - HEALTH PLANNING AND ADMINISTRATION Nonclinical research on all aspects of health care. 1975 to present. Bibliographic database.

MEDI3 - EMBASE One of the leading sources for searching biomedical literature. June 1974 to present. Bibliographic database.

MEDI13 - SPORT Coverage of sports medicine research and fitness. 1949 to present for theses and monographs; 1975 to present for journals. Bibliographic database.

MEDI14 - NURSING AND ALLIED HEALTH Covers all aspects of nursing and related health fields. 1983 to present. Bibliographic database.

MEDI16 - SMOKING AND HEALTH Information from journal articles, reports, and other literature concerning the effects of smoking on health. 1960 to present. Bibliographic database.

MEDI17 - AIDSLINE(tm) Provides complete access to the medical literature related to AIDS. 1980 to present. Bibliographic database.

✳ NEWS section

The following files contain the complete text of stories found in the daily editions of the print newspapers of the same names.

NEWS6 - USA TODAY 1988 to present. Fulltext database.

NEWS8 - WASHINGTON POST ONLINE 1983 to present. Fulltext database.

NEWS9 - PHILADELPHIA INQUIRER 1983 to present. Fulltext database.

NEWS10 - LOS ANGELES TIMES 1985 to present. Fulltext database.

NEWS11 - SAN JOSE MERCURY NEWS 1985 to present. Fulltext database.

NEWS12 - CHICAGO TRIBUNE 1988 to present. Fulltext database.

NEWS13 - BOSTON GLOBE 1980 to present. Fulltext database.

NEWS14 - SAN FRANCISCO CHRONICLE 1988 to present. Fulltext database.

NEWS15 - NEWSDAY AND NEW YORK NEWSDAY 1987 to present. Fulltext database.

NEWS16 - AKRON BEACON JOURNAL 1989 to present. Fulltext database.

NEWS17 - ARIZONA REPUBLIC/PHOENIX GAZETTE 1988 to present. Fulltext database.

NEWS18 - ATLANTA JOURNAL/ATLANTA CONSTITUTION 1989 to present. Fulltext database.

NEWS19 - BALTIMORE SUN 1989 to present. Fulltext database.

NEWS20 - CHARLOTTE OBSERVER 1989 to present. Fulltext database.

NEWS21 - CHRISTIAN SCIENCE MONITOR 1989 to present. Fulltext database.

NEWS22 - COLUMBUS DISPATCH 1988 to present. Fulltext database.

NEWS23 - DAILY NEWS OF LOS ANGELES 1989 to present. Fulltext database.

NEWS24 - DETROIT FREE PRESS 1987 to present. Fulltext database.

NEWS25 - HOUSTON POST 1988 to present. Fulltext database.

NEWS26 - MIAMI HERALD 1983 to present. Fulltext database.

NEWS27 - OREGONIAN (Portland) 1989 to present. Fulltext database.

NEWS28 - ORLANDO SENTINEL 1988 to present. Fulltext database.

NEWS29 - PALM BEACH POST 1989 to present. Fulltext database.

NEWS30 - RICHMOND NEWS LEADER/RICHMOND TIMES DISPATCH 1989 to present. Fulltext database.

NEWS31 - ROCKY MOUNTAIN NEWS 1989 to present. Fulltext database.

NEWS32 - SACRAMENTO BEE 1988 to present. Fulltext database.

NEWS33 - SEATTLE TIMES 1989 to present. Fulltext database.

NEWS34 - ST. LOUIS POST-DISPATCH 1988 to present. Fulltext database.

NEWS35 - ST. PAUL PIONEER PRESS 1988 to present. Fulltext database.

NEWS36 - SUN-SENTINEL (Fort Lauderdale) 1988 to present. Fulltext database.

NEWS37 - TIMES-PICAYUNE (New Orleans) 1989 to present. Fulltext database.

NEWS38 - WASHINGTON TIMES 1989 to present. Fulltext database.

NEWS39 - PITTSBURGH PRESS 1989 to present. Fulltext database.

✳ NEWS - ABSTRACTS section

NEWS1 - NEWSEARCH Daily index to over 2,000 news stories. Current month. Bibliographic database.

NEWS2 - NATIONAL NEWSPAPER INDEX Indexes the *Wall Street Journal*, the *New York Times*, the *Christian Science Monitor*, the *Los Angeles Times*, and *The Washington Post*. Other journals are also covered selectively. 1979 to present, 1982 to present for the *Los Angeles Times* and *The Washington Post*. Bibliographic database.

NEWS3, NEWS4 - UPI NEWS Complete text of news stories carried on the United Press International Newswire for the most current six months. Fulltext database.

NEWS7 - CURRENT DIGEST OF THE SOVIET PRESS
Translations and abstracts from major Soviet newspapers and magazines. 1982 to present. Fulltext, bibliographic database.

✳ **PSYCHOLOGY section**

PSYC1 - PsycINFO Leading source of published research in psychology and behavioral sciences. 1967 to present. Bibliographic database.

PSYC2 - MENTAL HEALTH ABSTRACTS Worldwide information on mental health from 1,200 journals. 1969 to present. Bibliographic database.

✳ **REFERENCE section**

REFR1 - QUOTATIONS DATABASE Omnibus file of literary, political, and other quotations of note. Ancient times through 1979. Bibliographic, fulltext database.

REFR2 - MARQUIS WHO'S WHO Detailed biographies on nearly 75,000 professionals. Current. Directory database.

REFR3 - EVENTLINE Multidisciplinary and multinational information on past and forthcoming events. October 1989 through 2000+. Directory database.

REFR4 - MAGILL'S SURVEY OF CINEMA Review articles on over 1,800 notable films. 1902 to present. Bibliographic database.

REFR5 - DISSERTATION ABSTRACTS ONLINE Abstracts of all U.S. dissertations since 1861 and citations for some Canadian dissertations. Also includes selected Masters theses since 1962. 1861 to present. Bibliographic database.

REFR6 - CONSUMER REPORTS The complete text of the monthly issues of *Consumer Reports*. 1982 to present. Fulltext database.

REFR7 - EVERYMAN'S ENCYCLOPAEDIA Comprehensive reference work providing detailed and informative articles that cover the full range of human knowledge. Sixth edition. Fulltext database.

REFR8 - PUBLIC OPINION ONLINE (POLL) Comprehensive, complete text collection of public-opinion surveys conducted in the United States. 1960 to present. Fulltext database.

✳ **RELIGION section**

RELI1 - BIBLE (KING JAMES VERSION) The complete text of the King James version of the Bible. Fulltext database.

RELI2 - RELIGION INDEX Index to articles covering church history, biblical literature, theology, history of religions, the sociology and psychology of religion, and related areas. 1975 to present. Bibliographic database.

✳ **SOCIAL SCIENCES section**

SOCS1 - SOCIOLOGICAL ABSTRACTS Worldwide coverage of sociological research. 1963 to present. Bibliographic database.

SOCS2 - PAIS INTERNATIONAL Broad-based source for all areas of public and current policy. 1972 to present for the PAIS Foreign Language Index; 1976 to present for the PAIS Bulletin. Bibliographic database.

SOCS3 - PHILOSOPHER'S INDEX Index to journal articles and books on the subject of philosophy and related fields. 1940 to present. Bibliographic database.

SOCS4 - AGELINE Index journals covering social gerontology (the study of aging in social, psychological, health related, and economic contexts). 1978 to present. Bibliographic database.

According to Knowledge Index, those databases represent coverage of a total of over 50,000 different journals and periodicals! As you can see from this list, every database is grouped into a subject category. This is important to note because each database is assigned a four-letter name that corresponds to a subject category. For example, all databases in the Business Information and Corporate News section begin with the letters BUSI. In addition, each database is given an identifying number that follows its four-letter name.

Another important point is the different types of databases available on Knowledge Index. They include bibliographic, directory (which provides names, addresses, phone numbers, etc., of individuals and organizations), abstract, and fulltext information. Remember, fulltext databases provide the complete (or nearly complete) version of the original item, abstracts provide a one- to two-paragraph summary, directories provide a numerical or address-like listing, and bibliographics provide only enough information so you can find the original source yourself.

Finally, another key difference is the databases' varying years of coverage. Make sure you take this information into account when selecting a database to search.

Searching the Knowledge Index

How do you go about searching the Knowledge Index? The first thing you need to do is join CompuServe. Then, after you've logged on, you can select CompuServe's Search Knowledge Index menu item, or just type GO KI. Then after waiting a couple of seconds as CompuServe logs onto the system, you're in!

Once you're connected to the Knowledge Index, you have two main decisions to make. The first one is to decide whether to search the database by menus or by command. Then you need to choose which database to search.

Menu searching

If you're a novice searcher, you'd probably be better off selecting the menu method, which guides you step by step through the search process. If you choose the menu option, the system will also help you choose the right database. Let's take a fairly typical information problem, and walk it through Knowledge Index's menu-assisted search.

Say your mission was to learn the latest news and analysis of Sony Corporation's venture into creating hardware to read "electronic books." These are those little hand-held CD-ROM readers you might encounter in a consumer electronics store, which are geared not to professionals or businesspeople, but for the mass market.

You should be prepared, then, to have some kind of search statement ready to key in when prompted by the system. Although the exact form of that statement can vary depending on the particular database you select, you still need to come up with a basic Boolean statement, which can always be modified later if need be. Unlike most other consumer online databases, the Knowledge Index allows you to use advanced Boolean search functions, including full truncation and proximity operators. On the Knowledge Index, the truncation command is signified with a question mark, and proximity operators with the letter *n*.

You should already know the basics of Boolean searching before reading much further in this chapter. A full discussion and explanation of Boolean searching can be found in appendix B of this book.

In this particular case, the basic Boolean statement might simply be "Sony AND electronic book?" This statement would be designed to retrieve any articles that contained *both* the word Sony *and* the two-word phrase electronic book or electronic books.

When you enter the Knowledge Index's search menu program, you're first shown a list of all of the major subject categories, and asked to choose one:

➤ Agriculture & nutrition

➤ Bibliography—books & monographs

➤ Business information

➤ Chemistry

➤ Computers & electronics

➤ Directories and reference

➤ Education

> ➤ Law & government

> ➤ Medicine, biosciences, & drugs

> ➤ News & current affairs

> ➤ Popular information

> ➤ Science & technology

> ➤ Social sciences & humanities

Actually, you're offered a few choices here: you can simply choose a category by entering the appropriate number, but if you're unsure which category would be best (and this will happen frequently), you can instead choose to see the names of the specific databases within a category or get additional information about that category. While it's possible that the Business Information category would be appropriate, let's choose a more specific grouping and try out the Computers & Electronics section:

```
Computers & Electronics

Each category consists of list databases containing information relevant
to that subject.

Category

1. Computer Science
2. Computer & Electronics Industry
3. Personal Computer Information

Enter D for the section description. Enter S<category number> to search
term(s) in all files for each section category. Enter the category number
(e.g., 1) to proceed to the list of the database.
```

So now you can either obtain a textual description of this section, search the databases in one of the categories, or obtain a listing of the specific databases in one of the categories. Let's see which databases are in the Computers & Electronics Industry category, which sounds promising. Do this by entering the term s2:

```
Computers & Electronics   Category 2 or 3
Computer & Electronics Industry
    1 ABI/Inform (R) 1971 - present
    2 Business Dateline 1985 - present
    3 Computer Database (TM) 1983 - present
    4 Computer News Fulltext 1989 - present
    5 Trade & Industry Index (TM) 1981 - present
```

```
Press ENTER to see additional databases.

Choose a file by entering the option NUMBER. Enter D<option number>
(e.g., D2) for a specific database description.

/H = Help   /L = Logoff   /M = Previous Menu   /MM = Main Menu
?
```

Now that you know which databases are included in that category,
you might as well run your search. Do this by first typing in /M to get
back to the previous menu, and then instruct the system to go ahead
and run the search against the databases in the subcategory number
2. Type in your choice: 2. Now the system will prompt you for the
search statement. There's no turning back now; you have your
Boolean operators lined up correctly and the truncation symbol set
into place. Key in:

```
Sony and Electronic Book?
```

and wait. After what seems like an eternity, but is actually just
several seconds, the system will respond with these nebulous,
noncommittal words:

```
Your Search is being processed.
```

and then, after a few more seconds:

```
The following database(s) contain information on SONY AND ELECTRONIC
BOOK?
```

Database Name	No. of Records
1. ABI/Inform (r) (Management/Business) 1971+	12
2. Business Dateline (r) 1985+	20
3. Computer Database (tm) 1983+	15
4. Trade & Industry Index (tm) 1981+	25

Success! What just occurred? Well, the system performed a
preliminary search; it took your search statement and ran it against
the list of databases in the subcategory Computer & Electronics
Industry. This preliminary search provides only a count of how many
records in the database match your search statement, and is designed
to help you pinpoint which one or ones would be worth a complete
search. From the looks of what was retrieved, all four databases
appear to be very good prospects! So let's take a look at a sampling
of records from each of those four files. The system prompts for a
response with the statement:

```
Enter option number, Halt, /M to Modify Search, or /H for Help
?
```

Starting from the bottom up, let's take a look at the Trade & Industry
Index item by keying in its identifying number, 4. The system will
then display the titles of only the first ten articles found in that
database:

```
                Trade & Industry Index (tm) 1981+
                    **25** records for DISPLAY
                    Enter HALT to exit Display


Option                    TITLE
No.-----------------------------------------------------------------

 1 Asian enigma (why Japanese companies have not completely dominated
 2 Audio EBs (Sony Electronic Publishing Co. introduces audio electro
 3 Sony's Data Discman authoring for the new platform (hand-held CD-R
 4 Electronic Book newsletter. (a United Kingdom electronic publishing
 5 Sony. (new and improved version of Data Discman Electronic Book int
 6 Sony announced new Data Discman with audio...three audio electronic
 7 Sony adds five new electronic book titles (Sony Electronic Publishin
 8 Multimedia for the masses (electronic books)
 9 Sony electronic books hit French market (Data Discman) (Brief Artic
10 Sony shows off new hand-held PC: CD-ROM discs allow tiny machine t

Enter option number(s), HALT,/H for help or press ENTER for next screen:
```

The Knowledge Index displays the first 10 citations located, with the
most recent citation displayed first and older ones following in order. It
appears that we've struck some electronic gold here. Note though, that
the last few words from each title are cut off—this is an unfortunate
result of the system's software. But it looks like we've retrieved some
very relevant and interesting citations. You could hit the Enter key to
view additional citations, but let's take a closer look at these first, at
least to find out their publication dates. Why don't we, then, view the
first three on the list. To do so, all you need to do is key in 1-3. The
Knowledge Index will then happily churn out the following:

```
selection 1 of 3
13349436  DIALOG File 148: TRADE & INDUSTRY INDEX
TITLE: Asian enigma. (why Japanese companies have not completely
dominated the portable computer market) (The Wall Street Journal Reports:
Technology) (supplement)
AUTHOR: Schlesinger, Jacob M.
JOURNAL: The Wall Street Journal
PG: pR26(W) pR26(E)    col 1; 40 col in  EDITION: Mon
PUB DATE: Nov 16, 1992
ISSN: 0193-2241
```

SUBFILE: BUS Business, General
SOURCE FILE: NNI File 111
ABSTRACT: Many analysts had predicted that the Japanese would dominate
the portable-computer market, but US companies have proven the leaders in
portable computing technology and the few Japanese forays into hand-held
multimedia devices have fizzled. Apple, IBM, HP and other US firms 'have
the vision of multimedia,' according to Apple Japan Pres Shigechika
Takeuchi. The distinction between microcomputers and home electronics, a
field the Japanese have long dominated, has not yet broken down; Sony,
the only major Japanese firm to experiment with portable multimedia, has
not been successful with its Data Discman electronic book. Most Japanese
firms view multimedia as a technology that is not yet clearly defined,
but US firms are rushing to develop it. The Kaleida joint venture between
IBM and Apple is working on a new operating system for hand-held
multimedia devices and is seeking alliances with Japanese firms. Both US
and Japanese executives say that the main reason the Japanese do not lead
portable-computing technology is that they do not feel confident setting
standards, dictating the direction of the industry or writing software.
GEOGRAPHIC LOCATION: Japan
GEOGRAPHIC CODE: AEJA
DESCRIPTORS: Portable computers—Market share; Japan—Business and industry
IDENTIFIERS: Japanese Competition; Portable computers; Market Analysis;
Miniaturization; Trends; Japan

Copyright 1993 Information Access Company

selection 2 of 3
12939155 DIALOG File 148: TRADE & INDUSTRY INDEX
TITLE: Audio EBs. (Sony Electronic Publishing Co. introduces audio
electronic book)
JOURNAL: The Electronic Library
VOL: v10   ISSUE: n4   PG: p245(1)
PUB DATE: August, 1992
ISSN: 0264-0473
SUBFILE: LIB Library and Information Science
SOURCE FILE: TI File 148
COMPANY: Sony Electronic Publishing—Product introduction
SIC CODE: 3652 Prerecorded records and tapes
        7372 Prepackaged software
DESCRIPTORS: Compact disc industry—Product introduction

Copyright 1993 Information Access Company

selection 3 of 3
12566154 DIALOG File 148: TRADE & INDUSTRY INDEX
TITLE: Sony's Data Discman authoring for the new platform. (hand-held
CD-ROM data machine)
AUTHOR: Bonime, Andrew
JOURNAL: CD-ROM Professional
VOL: v5   ISSUE: n5   PG: p118(4)
PUB DATE: Sept, 1992
ISSN: 1049-0833
SUBFILE: LIB Library and Information Science

```
SOURCE FILE: TI File 148
ILLUSTRATION: illustration; diagram
ABSTRACT: Writing CD-ROM software for Data Discman requires a PC with DOS
and Sony's SEBAS (Sony Electronic Book Authoring Software). It also
requires a 650+ megabyte hard drive and a replicating output device to
use when taking the software to be copied. The authoring procedure is
outlined in ten steps which include data capture, data refinement, format
conversion, editing and cleaning data, search method design, data
tagging, menu building, indexing, simulation and refinement, and
mastering and replication.
PRODUCT: Sony Data Discman (Hand-held data device)—Computer programs
DESCRIPTORS: CD-ROM—Product development; Software packages—Development

Copyright 1993 Information Access Company
```

What did we find? A couple of key points right off the bat. First, note that the most recent items are displayed first—the "pub date" for the first selection is November 16, 1992, the second is August, 1992, and so on. This is crucial. In a fast-moving high-tech field like electronic books, you might decide that you want to read items no older than six months.

The other thing that jumps out is the fact that two of the items include an abstract, while one provides only bibliographic data. You'll often come upon these variations, even within the same database, since database producers establish different contractual arrangements with the original sources.

Let's keep working our way up the list. Now that you've seen what Trade & Industry has to offer, go ahead and instruct the Knowledge Index to display titles from the next database in the list:

```
         Computer Database (tm) 1983-
         ** 15 ** records for DISPLAY
         Enter HALT to exit DISPLAY


Option            TITLE
No. -------------------------------------------------------------------
 1  Asian enigma. (why Japanese companies have not completely dominated
 2  Multimedia puts books on the brink of a new technological revolutio
 3  Japan: Matsushita marketing blitz for electronic book player. (Matsu
 4  Sony's recipe: one part hardware, one part software. (Sony Corp.'s
 5  Sanyo releases Electronic Book based on Sony design. (portable com
 6  Sony shows off new hand-held PC: CD-ROM discs allow tiny machine to
 7  Quanta to offer CIA World Factbook as electronic book. (the US Cent
 8  Is the electronic book closer than you think? (electronic publishin
 9  A new chapter for electronic books. (data bases on Sony Corp.'s Data
10  Walkman of words: Sony's Data Discman can squeeze into a portable e
```

```
Enter option number(s), HALT, /H for help, or press ENTER for next
screen:
```

That first item looks familiar, but the rest look new—and also right on
the money. Let's take a look again at items two and three from this list:

```
selection 2 of 3
12657609  DATABASE: CD FILE 275  *Use Format 9 for FULL TEXT*
TITLE: Multimedia puts books on the brink of a new technological
revolution. (Column)
AUTHOR: Saffo, Paul
JOURNAL: PC-Computing VOL.: v5 ISSUE: n10 PAGINATION: p72(1)
PUBLICATION DATE: Oct, 1992
ARTICLE TYPE: Column
AVAILABILITY: FULL TEXT Online  LINE COUNT: 00085
SOURCE FILE: CD File 275
ABSTRACT: The 'electronic book' is a promising new entrant into the
market for multimedia technologies. Software companies developing
products include Voyager Co, Broderbund Software Inc and Mathsoft Inc.
Companies from other industries, such as IBM and Sony Corp, are also
involved. Products being developed are called books, but they are
typically developed and marketed as compact disk-read only memory (CD-
ROM) data bases that function interactively. They are not very much like
books at all. Electronic books are a bridge between print and electronic
technologies. Today's electronic books are a sort of electronic
incunabula - infant examples of what electronic publishing will produce
in the future.
COMPANY NAME(S): Broderbund Software Inc. - Product development
SIC CODE: 7372; 3651; 2700
ISSN: 0899-1847
DESCRIPTORS: Product Development; Future Technologies; Books; Multimedia
Software; Multimedia Technology; Electronic Publishing; Publishing
Industry

Copyright 1993 Information Access Company

selection 3 of 3
12633306  DATABASE: CD FILE 275  *Use Format 9 for FULL TEXT*
TITLE: Japan: Matsushita marketing blitz for electronic book player.
(Matsushita Electronics)
AUTHOR: Miyazawa, Masayuki
JOURNAL: Newsbytes  PAGINATION: NEW09300003
PUBLICATION DATE: Sept 30, 1992
AVAILABILITY: FULL TEXT Online  LINE COUNT: 00027
SOURCE FILE: NW File 649
COMPANY NAME(S): Matsushita Electronics Corp. - Marketing; Sony Corp. -
Licenses
SIC CODE: 3571; 3670
DESCRIPTORS: Electronic Publishing; Marketing Strategy

Copyright 1993 Information Access Company
```

Let's move up another notch on the list, and take a look at the titles uncovered on the next database, called Business Dateline. Here's what's displayed:

```
               Business Dateline (r) 1985-
               ** 20 ** records for DISPLAY
               Enter HALT to exit DISPLAY

Option               TITLE
No. ----------------------------------------------------------------
 1  Firm channels hopes to two-way TV
 2  Future Fixtures, or Flops? Some Educated Guesses About Which of t
 3  CD-ROM Technology Matures: No. of Titles Now Doubling Every Year
 4  Sony Electronic Publishing Names Randall Their Vice President of In
 5  Through the Looking Glass: San Francisco's "Multimedia Gulch" Leads
 6  Cadre Turns 10: Esoteric Software Maker Grows in R.I., Grumbles Abo
 7  Read 'em and Beep: Electronic Books Coming to a Screen Near You
 8  Computer Books Turn Reading Into Audiovisual Event
 9  Creative Multimedia Corp. Introduces Beyond the Wall of Stars — a
10  Looking for the Next Wave in Electronics

Enter option number(s), HALT, /H for help, or press ENTER for next
screen:
```

This time, let's zip right to option number 4, and take a look at the piece titled Sony Electronic Publishing Names. Here's what you're shown:

```
selection 4 of 5
0350037    92-98229
Sony Electronic Publishing Names Randall Thier Vice President of
International Operations
Dille, Peter
Business Wire (San Francisco, CA, US) s1  p1
PUBL DATE: 920729
JOURNAL CODE: BWRE
DOC TYPE: Report
DATELINE: New York, NY, US          WORD COUNT: 365


TEXT:
     Sony Electronic Publishing Co. announced Tuesday that Randall Thier
has joined the company as vice president.
     Thier will direct Sony Electronic Publishing's international
operations, and also be responsible for the Multimedia Productions
division of the company's North American operations.
     Thier's international operations responsibilities include
distribution, marketing and sales. Responsibilities for Multimedia
Productions include the division's electronic book product line for the
Sony Data Discman electronic book player, and its Affiliated Label CD-ROM
product line for PC, Mac, and MPC personal computer platforms. Thier will
also be responsible for expanding the company's publishing activities in
the computer software business.
```

Thier will report to Olaf Olafsson, president of Sony Electronic Publishing.

"We're pleased to add someone with Randy's proven track record to Sony Electronic Publishing," said Olafsson. "He brings experience and knowledge of the computer software industry in many areas which mesh with our plans. We expect Randy will play a key role in our growth."

(the text continues)

NAMED PERSONS: Thier, Randall
COMPANY NAMES: Sony Electronic Publishing Co, New York, NY, US, SIC:Ticker:7372

CLASSIFICATION CODES: 8302 (Software and computer services); 2130 (Executives)
DESCRIPTORS: Software industry; Appointments & personnel changes; Executives; Personal profiles; Middle Atlantic

Copyright 1993 UMI/Data Courier

Note that this item is not a bibliographic citation or even an abstract, but a fulltext record. Also important to observe is that this database, Business Dateline, utilizes *classification codes* and *descriptors*, which are designed to help you make your searches much more precise. For more information on how to perform searches using these and other special fields, see appendix B.

Finally, let's take a look at the ABI/Inform database. Here's KI's listing of the most recent ten titles it found for that file:

```
             ABI/Inform (r) (Management/business) 1971-
                  ** 12 ** records for DISPLAY
                  Enter HALT to exit DISPLAY

Option              TITLE  No. -------------------------------------
   1  See, hear, look, learn
   2  The Information Age Has Arrived or "Much Ado About Everything"
   3  The UK Book Business: Literally Behind the Times
   4  Disc Directories: Nynex Sells Business, White Pages Listings on CD
   5  Sony's Data Discman - Authoring for the New Platform
   6  Sony's Data Discman: A Look at These New Portable Information
Machines an
   7  Scrolled Any Good Books Lately?
   8  Center for Missing Children Adopts Multimedia Tech
   9  Put an Office in the Palm of Your Hand
  10  The Writing Is on the Screen

Enter option number(s), HALT, /H for help, or press ENTER for next
screen:
```

Let's take a closer look at item 7:

```
1/M/7
00633974      DIALOG FILE 15     ABI/INFORM     92-48914
Scrolled Any Good Books Lately?
Schwartz, Evan I.
Business Week  n3282 (Industrial/Technology Edition)  PP: 61  Sep 7, 1992
CODEN: BWITEU  ISSN: 0739-8395  JRNL CODE: BWE
DOC TYPE: Journal article  LANGUAGE: English   LENGTH: 1 Pages
AVAILABILITY: Photocopy available from ABI/INFORM 36.00

ABSTRACT: A growing number of publishers believe that consumers will
succumb to electronic books when they see how the technology adds
interaction to the printed word. By combining software and text, readers
of electronic books will be able to call up footnotes, illustrations, and
music at any point in their reading. Leading  the  realm  of  electronic
publishing are electronic encyclopedias, which already outsell their
printed counterparts in school libraries. It is not clear who will
capitalize most on the new market - the publishers that own the content
or the software companies that know how to create interesting,
interactive programs. Sony Electronic Publishing Co. and Encyclopedia
Britannica Inc.'s Compton's NewMedia unit are among the most aggressive.
In addition to creating their own titles, they are signing up dozens of
small publishers as affiliates. By controlling hundreds of titles, they
should gain clout in distribution channels.

GEOGRAPHIC NAMES: US

DESCRIPTORS: Product development; Electronic; Publications; Product
acceptance; Systems design
CLASSIFICATION CODES: 7500 (CN=Product planning & development); 5240
(CN=Software & systems); 8690 (CN=Publishing industry)
**********************************************************************
```

By now you should have a basic feel for how a menu-based search works and the kinds of information you can find. By the way, this whole procedure took only about 15 minutes—and cost about $6. Is that a deal, or what?

Before leaving the Knowledge Index's menu service, let's try one more case-study search. This time, let's see what you might find if you want to locate some background information on a major company. Let's say you're trying to dig up data on the media conglomerate Time Warner, Inc. The first step is to choose the appropriate category from the Knowledge Index's 13 major sections. (See the list under *Searching the Knowledge Index*, earlier in this chapter.)

Although the third category, Business Information, might turn up some interesting information, we're really interested in locating basic statistical and descriptive data on the firm, and that's the kind of information you'd get in a directory, which corresponds to category 6 (Directories and Reference). So input the number 6. At this point, the system gives you a further choice by presenting the different types of reference and directory sources available:

```
Directories & Reference

Each category consists of a list of databases containing information
relevant to that subject.

Category
    1  Biographical Directories
    2  Books, Government Publications & Dissertations
    3  Company Directories
    4  Drug/Pharmaceutical Directories
    5  Encyclopedias & Quotations
    6  Films & Audio Visual Materials
    7  Public Affairs, Opinions & Events
    8  School/University Directories
    9  Software Directories

Enter D for the section description. Enter S<category number> to search
term(s) in all files for each section category. Enter the category number
(e.g., 1) to proceed to the list of databases.

?
```

Choose option #3, Company Directories, and you'll be given a further choice of three distinct databases that comprise that category:

➤ ICC British Company Directory (current)

➤ Standard & Poor's Corporate Descriptions (current)

➤ Standard & Poor's Register—Corporate (current)

Let's try searching Standard & Poor's Register - Corporate. The Knowledge Index will then display the following:

```
S&P Register - Corporate
Search Mode Options

Select one of the following options:

1. Company Name Search
2. Company Location Search
3. Line(s) Of Business Search
4. Company Size Search
```

```
Enter option NUMBER and press ENTER to continue.
/H = Help    /L = Logoff    /M- = Previous Menu    /MM = Main Menu
```

Since you already know the name of the company you want to locate, input 1. Displayed on the screen next is:

```
Enter Company Name: (e.g., BEECH AIRCRAFT)
?
```

Now you can enter the name of the company, Time-Warner. The system will respond with a small chart, identifying how many items it retrieved that correspond with that precise name, or with names spelled closely. The exact term is designated on the left with an asterisk.

```
S&P Register - Corporate
Company Name Index


COMPANY NAME                             NO. OF ITEMS
---------------------------------------------------
   1   TIME ZERO CORP.                        1
   2   TIME-O-MATIC, INC.                     1
   *   TIME-WARNER                            0
   4   TIMEC COMPANY INC.                     1
   5   TIMELY PRODUCTS DIVISION               1
   6   TIMEMED LABELING SYSTEMS, INC.         1
   7   TIMES                                  1
   8   TIMES & ALLEGANIAN CO.                 1
   9   TIMES & NEWS PUBLISHING COMPANY        1
  10   TIMES COMPANY                          1

Enter option number(s), HALT to exit, /H for help,
or press ENTER for next screen:
```

Uh oh. What happened? According to the system, there are no items in this file that are indexed as Time-Warner. Does this mean that this firm is not included in this database? That's *very* unlikely. Much more likely is that there was something wrong with the way you entered the company name. Let's see, what could have been the problem? The words Time and Warner are spelled correctly and you don't need to worry about upper- and lowercase since the online system doesn't care what case a letter is in. Hmmm . . . maybe there isn't a hyphen in Time-Warner. Type the word *halt* to exit the process and try a new search. This time enter Time Warner. Here's what the system will now display:

```
S&P Register - Corporate
          Company Name Index
```

```
COMPANY NAME                                 NO. OF ITEMS
--------------------------------------------------------
    1   TIME MARK CORP.                           1
    2   TIME PRODUCTS DIVISION                    1
    *   TIME WARNER                               0
    4   TIME WARNER INC.                          1
    5   TIME ZERO CORP.                           1
    6   TIME-O-MATIC, INC.                        1
    7   TIMEC COMPANY INC.                        1
    8   TIMELY PRODUCTS DIVISION                  1
    9   TIMEMED LABELING SYSTEMS, INC.            1
   10   TIMES                                     1
```

Enter option number(s), HALT to exit, /H for help,or press ENTER for next screen:

Hmmm . . . I still don't see any matching items. Wait, directly underneath that heading is an entry for Time Warner *Inc*. Aha! You know those computers—they're so literal-minded. It can tell me only that there's no entry for a Time Warner company, but there just happens to be one for a certain Time Warner Inc. Type in that option number (4) and see what happens:

```
0050473
TIME WARNER INC.
75 Rockefeller Plaza
New York, NY  10019
TELEPHONE: 212-484-8000

BUSINESS: Magazine & book publishing, music, filmed entertainment, cable
& programming
PRIMARY SIC:      2721
SECONDARY SIC(S): 2711; 2731; 4841; 4899; 7822

YEAR STARTED:     1922
REVENUE:          $12.02 Bil
EMPLOYEE TOTAL:   41,700

MARKET TERRITORY:
   NATIONAL
   INTERNATIONAL

THIS IS:
   A PUBLIC COMPANY
   An S&P 500 Company
   Included in Corporate Descriptions (File 133)

STOCK EXCHANGE:  NYS; BST; PAC; MID; PSE
CUSIP NUMBER:    887315
ACCOUNTING FIRM: Ernst & Young, New York, NY
LAW FIRM:        Cravath, Swaine & Moore
```

```
EXECUTIVES AND DIRECTORS:
* Chrm & Co-Chief Exec Officer  Ross, Steven J.
  Chairman, Chief Executive Officer, Inside Director
  Administration

* Pres & Co-Chief Exec Officer  Levin, Gerald M.
  Chief Executive Officer, President, Inside Director
  Administration

* Chrm Exec Comm               Munro, J. R.
  Chairman Executive Committee, Inside Director
  Administration

* Vice-Chrm                    Payson, Martin D.
  Chairman, Inside Director
  Administration

* Exec V-P & Chief Fin Officer  Wasserman, Bert W.
  Chief Financial Officer, Vice President-Executive, Inside Director
  Finance, Administration

* Editor-in-Chief              McManus, Jason
  Editor, Inside Director
  Administration, Operations, Manufacturing

* Secy                        Ecker, Allan B.
  Secretary, Inside Director
  Administration

(about 20 VPs are listed here)

* ALSO DIRECTORS

OTHER DIRECTORS:
  Adelson, Merv             Buttenwieser, Lawrence B.
  Culverhouse, Hugh F.      Dingman, Michael D.
  Finkelstein, Edward S.    Greenough, Beverly S.
  Holloway, Benjamin D.     Horner, Matina S.
  Johnson, Deane F.         Luce, Henry III
  Opel, John R.             Parsons, Richard D.
  Perkins, Donald S.        Troubh, Raymond S.
  van den Heuvel, William

Copyright 1993 Standard & Poor's Corp.
```

Hey, not bad! Note how much more information this S&P database provided compared to some of those very basic business company directory databases offered by other consumer online services. There's hardly even a comparison. And, if you wanted to, you could also search the other Standard & Poor's database, which actually provides a complete balance sheet.

Note that you can search this database not only by company, but by other variables too, such as company location, line of business, and size. This is a very useful feature if you want to create a list of companies that fit a certain criteria (e.g., a list of firms with fewer than 100 people, located in New York state, who sell computers, etc.).

⇨ Command searching

Now let's look in detail at the other way you can conduct searches on the Knowledge Index—by inputting commands. So you can best see the difference between the two, let's conduct the same two searches you conducted on the menu system. Let's start with the search for articles covering Sony Corporation and electronic books.

The first step, again, is to select the right database. This time, though, you aren't offered a listing of subject categories to choose from. Instead, you need to already have determined which database you want to search and enter the name of that database. Again, you can learn about the choices by either requesting a list of all databases or by obtaining a more extensive "database brief" by using the HELP command along with the database title (e.g., enter HELP REFR2, or HELP COMP1).

After you've read through the descriptions and selected a database, enter the BEGIN command to tell KI that you want to search that particular database. So if you decided to search The Computer Database, you'd enter the command Begin Comp4.

The key command you use to instruct KI to undertake a search is the word FIND. As with the previous search, you'll try to locate occurrences of articles that contained the word *Sony* along with *electronic book* or *electronic books* (again, you can merge *electronic book* and *electronic books* by using the question mark truncation symbol, for *electronic book?*).

Although you might be tempted to simply enter the phrase *Find Sony and electronic book?* when you're searching for occurrences of a company name in a command search system, it's very important that you first see precisely how that database has indexed the company.

(Remember my mistake with Time Warner?) Otherwise, if you don't enter the company name *just* right, the database might come up with zero citations—even if there are a lot of records indexed another way. To find out how a database has indexed a company, you need to perform an EXPAND command, which lets you peek in on the database's own index terms. Most databases have a special, separate index for company names that can be located by using the abbreviation *Co* for company. So the next command is:

```
Expand Co=Sony
```

KI then searches its company index and prints out:

```
Ref    Items  Index-term
E1         1  CO=SONOCO PRODUCTS CO.
E2         1  CO=SONUS CORP.
E3         1  CO=SONY
E4         1  CO=SONY (U.K.) LTD.
E5         1  CO=SONY AUDIO VISUAL PRODUCTS
E6         1  CO=SONY BROADCAST AND COMMUNICATIONS INC.
E7         1  CO=SONY BROADCAST PRODUCTS CO.
E8         3  CO=SONY COMMUNICATIONS PRODUCTS CO.
E9         1  CO=SONY COMPUTER SCIENCE LABORATORY INC.
E10        2  CO=SONY CORP
E11        1  CO=SONY CORP OPTICAL STORAGE SYSTEM DIV
E12      642  CO=SONY CORP.
```

Now, from the above listing, you can see that the preferred and broadest way that this database indexes Sony is specifically by the phrase Sony Corp. Note that the word Corp. must include a period at the end to retrieve all those hundreds of citations. If you keyed in just Sony Corp without the period, you'd get only the two citations listed two headings above. Most databases contain these kinds of inconsistencies in their indexing, which can prove to be a real danger to searchers who don't first check to see exactly how a person's or company's name has been entered.

So now you can type in `Find Sony Corp` (or take a bit of a shortcut and tell KI that you want to use its results displayed under E12 and use that abbreviation as the first part of the search). So the full command would be:

```
Find E12 and Electronic Book?
```

And the system would respond as follows:

```
642     CO=SONY CORP.
35088   ELECTRONIC
7910    BOOK?
94      ELECTRONIC BOOK?

S1      9  CO="SONY CORP." AND ELECTRONIC BOOK?
```

So you've located nine articles that meet the criteria of the search statement. The S1 simply stands for Set 1, where a *set* is the result of one of the search statements. Because this is your first search statement, that set is designated as S1. The advantage to having all your search statements designated with a set number is that you can utilize those set numbers in future searches—combining them with new searches or previous set numbers. This can ultimately save a lot of time and make things a lot less messy.

What do you do when you want to see the items retrieved? There are a few options here:

❋ Displaying results

In KI's command mode, you're provided with a few different ways to see what you found. The basic command to view results is TYPE, followed by the exact set number (e.g., TYPE S2). You're also given a choice to show all, most, or just part of those records. The Long (L) command shows you the full record, Medium (M) provides bibliographic data, and Short (S) the title or name only. You also need to specify *which* records from the set you want to view.

So, for example, if you wanted to view the short format for the first five records of S1, your command to KI would be TYPE 1/S/1-5. You'd then see this display:

```
1/S/1
12633306  DATABASE: CD FILE 275
TITLE: Japan: Matsushita  marketing  blitz  for electronic book player.
(Matsushita Electronics)

1/S/2
12531312  DATABASE: CD FILE 275
TITLE: Sony's recipe: one part hardware, one part software. (Sony Corp.'s
strategy for digital technology)
```

```
1/S/3
11938560  DATABASE: CD FILE 275
TITLE: Sony shows off new hand-held PC: CD-ROM discs allow tiny machine
to play electronic books and other 'multimedia' programs. (Sony Corp.'s
      'bookman') (Technology)

1/S/4
11623568  DATABASE: CD FILE 275
TITLE: A  new  chapter for electronic books. (data bases on Sony Corp.'s
Data Discman) (Software Review) (Commentary column) (Evaluation)

1/S/5
11475335  DATABASE: CD FILE 275
TITLE: Walkman of words: Sony's Data Discman can squeeze into a portable
electronic book. (Wall Street Journal Reports: Technology; special
supplement on computer technology)
```

Note that the three major segments of the TYPE command (set number, format type, and item number) are separated by slashes. You can also instruct KI to print out all the records in the set by simply entering the word *all* in replace of specific item number.

There are a couple of other ways to display results, but I'm going to mention only one very valuable one, especially when searching long fulltext databases. This feature is called KWIC (key word in context) and can be used to replace the L, M, or S portion of the display command.

If you specify K (for KWIC) in your TYPE command (e.g., TYPE S2/K/1-3), the system will display *only the portions of the database records where your search terms were found*. It does this by displaying a 30-word "window" containing approximately 15 words before and after your search term or terms. Here are excerpts from the first three records of S1, when displayed in KWIC format (the search terms are shown in bold):

```
1/K/1
DATABASE: CD FILE 275
TITLE: Japan: Matsushita marketing blitz for electronic book player.
(Matsushita Electronics)
COMPANY NAME(S): Sony Corp

1/K/2
DATABASE: CD FILE 275
ABSTRACT: entertainment and personal communications. Its first offering
is Data Discman, which is a hand-held electronic book player that allows
a user to browse through some 18,000 pages of manuals on...
```

```
Data Discman since it was introduced in 1990. Forthcoming products
include Bookman, a more powerful electronic book player, and
CD-ROM-based video games. Sony's acquisition of Columbia Pictures Inc
enables...
COMPANY NAME(S): Sony Corp

1/K/3
DATABASE: CD FILE 275
TITLE: Sony shows off new hand-held PC: CD-ROM discs allow tiny machine
to play electronic books and other 'multimedia' programs. (Sony Corp.'s
'bookman') (Technology)
ABSTRACT: ROM and multimedia, could be significant in the development of
such multimedia-related technologies as 'electronic books,' educational
software and video games. Microsoft Corp has announced that it plans to
publish software...
COMPANY NAME(S): Sony Corp
```

This command is extremely valuable in helping determine whether a particular record is truly relevant or whether it just happens to use a word in a passing or meaningless manner (for your purposes). So, for instance, say you were researching AIDS and retrieved a 15-page feature article in a magazine database. You might read through hundreds of words just to discover that your search retrieved that item because it matched your search with the phrase . . . if the U.N. aids Bosnia . . . ." But with KWIC, you could immediately see that that record was not relevant for you. (Actually, for a search like this, the smartest thing you could do would be to see if the database used AIDS as a descriptor, and then limit your search to only those records with that descriptor term.

✳ Limiting

Another powerful feature available only under KI's command search mode is *limiting*. The limit command allows you to restrict a search to specific types of database records that match more precisely what you need. For example, say you're doing a search in a magazine database on the word *beef*, but you don't want to be swamped with every story that happens to mention that word somewhere in the text. Instead, you want to make sure that beef is a major focus of the article. With the limit command, you can instruct KI to search only for articles where the word *beef* appears in the piece's headline or title, using a TI command for a major subject term, or DE for a descriptor.

Make sure that the database you've selected uses descriptors. You also need to find out the exact descriptor words it has chosen to describe what you're looking for. A simple way to find this out is to do a preliminary search without using a descriptor, and then study the full format of the records you retrieve. When you come upon a record or records that are on target, look for a row of descriptors and note the specific words used. Then perform *another* search, using those exact descriptors.

Remember, although most databases use the TI and DE limits, the type of limits available for a particular search varies completely by specific database. You need to read KI's database brief or study a sample record to discover which ones are available and whether there are additional limit functions unique to that database.

✳ Ordering documents

Another feature offered by the Knowledge Index is *document ordering*. If your search retrieves an article, report, or some other document, but not in fulltext, you can place an order for that item online. To do so, you need to set up a special separate account with a document delivery company that the Knowledge Index contracts with to carry out this job. This can be a very convenient way to get the fulltext of items you need. Be sure, though, to first check to see that you can't get the article for free at your local library.

Menu vs. command

Is one mode better than the other? Should you choose to search the Knowledge Index by menu or by command? Well, it depends.

If you're a novice searcher, you'd probably be better off starting your searches with the menu method. It's certainly easier, and you'll get a feel for how databases and database searching works.

But although Knowledge Index's menu mode is well designed, it does limit your flexibility and options. Because a menu system is preprogrammed to make certain assumptions about how to group

databases, as well as how to conduct a search, it removes some of your own decision power. Again, that's fine for the beginner, but once you feel fairly capable I'd recommend going for the command method.

KI vs. IQuest

Another important question that CompuServe members need to consider is when to search the Knowledge Index and when to go with the other powerful gateway system, IQuest. Here, briefly, is how the two compare:

	KI	IQuest
# of databases	100+	850+
Easy to search?	Yes	Yes
Menu searching option?	Yes	Yes
Command searching option?	Yes	No
Full Boolean searching?	Yes	Yes
Availability	Evenings & weekends	Anytime
Price range	$24/hour	Varies by file

What's the bottom line? Well, I look at it this way. There seems to be little doubt that the Knowledge Index offers the better deal for the nonprofessional searcher—assuming you can live with its evening/weekend restrictions and aren't using the data in any commercial manner. There just isn't a better bargain anywhere around for easy access to top-notch databases at such a low price. On the other hand, though, you might want to use IQuest for those occasions when a particular database you want to search isn't available on the Knowledge Index. IQuest still has access to a number of specialized databases unavailable on KI.

KI vs. Dialog Direct

Finally, do you give up anything by searching those 100+ Dialog databases on the Knowledge Index versus going directly to Dialog? Yes, you do.

There are certain features and capabilities available from Dialog directly that aren't available for Knowledge Index users (in addition to no time restrictions). One fairly significant one is the ability to search more than one database at a time. On Dialog, this is called its OneSearch feature, and it allows you to specify a series of databases to be searched all together at the same time. This is undoubtedly a powerful feature, and is also a time-saver.

You can't do this on the Knowledge Index (although you can perform a preliminary scan of a group of databases within one of KI's subject categories to get a "hit count" to better determine which of those databases are worth doing a full search on).

There are also a number of special functions that are unavailable on KI, such as the ability to rank and sort your output by various criteria. These are handy features, but for most nonprofessional searchers (and even for some professional ones) they fall under the category of convenient but not crucial.

There's one other thing you give up by not searching Dialog directly. You also give up paying $60 to $115 per hour, with a 50¢- to $2-per-item print charge too!

Overall, what you get from the Knowledge Index is far more than what you trade off. Most people, I think, will be happy to give up a few advanced features to keep many more dollars in their own pocket. Of course, being a Knowledge Index searcher doesn't preclude you from signing up with Dialog directly anyway, so on those rare occasions when you need to go to the source directly, go ahead and do so!

There's more to the Knowledge Index than what I've been able to cover in this section. But this should be more than enough to get you interested. It's obvious that I couldn't recommend this service more highly.

⇨ Special-interest groups

Last but not least are the special-interest groups (SIGs) or, as they're called on CompuServe, the forums. While not as traditional a

reference source as online database, these affinity groups can serve as invaluable information resources and a way to tap into the knowledge of other people online. Most special-interest groups—on CompuServe as well as on the other online services covered in this book—follow the same method of organization and offer similar services. Typically, a SIG contains these elements:

A message board Where members can "post" questions and comments and reply to other members' queries.

A conference board This allows "live" conversation between members.

Libraries A library typically contains both information files with relevant news, facts, advice, and the like as well as useful software that other members have uploaded for their colleagues to use. You can normally browse the library (often by keyword searching) to locate a file that you want, and then download it to your computer.

Often, special-interest groups are used by members simply as a place to just "hang out," to meet others with similar interests and pick up tidbits of useful information. Here's a sample of CompuServe's forums:

AIDS Information	Military
Art Gallery	Motor Sports
Aviation	New Age
Cancer Information	Outdoors
Computer Art	Photography
Computer Hardware (49 forums)	Political Debate
Disabilities	Religion
Electronic Publishing	Sailing
Entrepreneurs	Science Fiction
Gardening	Scuba
Geneology	Seniors
Ham Radio	Software (102 forums)
Health/Fitness	Space/Astronomy
Human Sexuality	Travel
Investors	Working from Home

⇨ Summary and recommendations

Pros CompuServe offers a huge selection of information databases—more than any other consumer-oriented online service. Many databases offer powerful and sophisticated search capabilities. IQuest and Knowledge Index (KI) gateways offer a true window for accessing professional-level global information without knowledge of specialized search commands. Executive News Service is an extremely useful customized news gathering service. CompuServe also contains a large number of diverse special-interest groups. Finally, CompuServe's CIM makes searching the service friendly and efficient.

Cons Some databases, especially on IQuest, are quite expensive, and there's no full Internet access like the kind Delphi offers.

Recommendation If you could choose only one consumer online service to do your research and database searching, you should select CompuServe. It offers by far the most extensive and powerful information files, as compared to any other service covered in this book (except the professionally oriented ones).

3
GEnie

GEnie, like NBC, is another communications company owned by General Electric. GEnie is a large system, offering many different types of services, ranging from games to special-interest groups to reference databases to gateways and other online services offering powerful searchable databases.

Signing up and getting started

To sign on to GEnie, all you need is a basic communications software package and a modem. Unlike Prodigy and America Online (and CompuServe's Information Manager), running GEnie doesn't require any special type of vendor-supplied software. What this means, though, is that since there's no extra software to create friendly graphics, icons, and the like, GEnie isn't a "pretty" service to use. It's just basic, raw text (which GEnie occasionally strains to brighten up by using asterisks or other ordinary type to create designs and headlines). There's a front-end package called Aladdin that makes searching the service easier.

You can navigate GEnie one of two ways. You can use its menus or you can take a shortcut by entering keywords or page numbers that correspond to a particular part of the service. If you want, you can use GEnie's menus to move from product to product.

You do, though, have to get used to GEnie's somewhat arcane technical way of communicating. For example, if you type in an incorrect word at a certain GEnie prompt, you'll get a message informing you of a "bad parameter" or a remark about "system mnemonics." Those definitely aren't user-friendly phrases. A similar warning on America Online would probably say something like "Please enter a keyword or menu item—or check the help menu for assistance." At the other extreme, you might expect the almost Kindergarten-like Prodigy instructions to display something like "Whoops, I think you just made a boo-boo!" (Sorry about the unnecessary Prodigy-bashing. But it is tempting.) When you first log on to GEnie, you'll see the following display:

```
GEnie                     TOP                    Page    1
                  GE Information Services

     1. About GEnie (GE Mail & Chat)
     2. Communications
     3. Computing Services
     4. Travel Services
     5. Finance & Investing Services
     6. Online Shopping Services
     7. News, Sports & Features
     8. Multi-Player Games
     9. Career/Professional Services
    10. Business Services
    11. Leisure Pursuits & Hobbies
    12. Education Services
    13. Entertainment Services
    14. Symposiums on Global Issues
    15. Research & Reference Services
    16. Leave GEnie (Logoff)
```

 # Key information databases

In terms of power and usefulness for the serious researcher, GEnie is second only to CompuServe in its breadth of information sources. Let's take a closer look at what's available for online research in our six special focus areas:

> ➤ Encyclopedias

> ➤ Magazines and journals

> ➤ Health and medical information

> ➤ Business information: news, company directories, company financials, and company and industry analyses

> ➤ Newspapers & newswires

> ➤ College information

Many of GEnie's offerings in these areas are located under its Research and Reference Services section. If you select that category, corresponding to #15 on the Top menu, you'll then be shown the following submenu:

```
GEnie                 RESEARCH                 Page  302
          GEnie Research & Reference Services
 1. About Research & Ref. Services
 2. GEnie BookShelf
 3. Commerce Business Daily
 4. Computer & Electronics Center
 5. Consumer Medicine
 6. Corporate Affiliates Center
 7. Dow Jones News/Retrieval
 8. Dun & Bradstreet (D&B) Databases
 9. Educator's Center
10. Grolier's Encyclopedia
11. Investment ANALY$T
12. Medical Professional's Center
13. GEnie NewsStand
14. Worldwide Patent Center
15. Public Opinion Online
16. GEnie Reference Center
17. TRW Business Credit Profiles
18. Thomas Register
19. Trademark Center
20. Tradenames Database
21. Business Resource Directory
22. Genealogy KB
23. Microsoft KB
24. Newsbytes KB
```

Item #1 simply explains the listed services in more detail. The remainder of the options are various databases, and are one of two major types: GEnie-supplied or gateway databases. A GEnie-supplied database is pretty much as it sounds—one that GEnie directly provides to its own membership. A gateway is different. A *gateway* is an electronic connection made by one online service to another online service for the purpose of accessing other databases not directly stored on the first. In this case, the gateway connections are made between the GEnie system and two professionally oriented

online services: Dialog and Dow Jones News/Retrieval. We'll examine in detail how these gateways work and what you can find from them later in this section.

For now, let's look at the GEnie-supplied databases that correspond to Grolier's Encyclopedia (#10), Business Resource Directory (#21), and Newsbytes (#24).

Grolier's Encyclopedia

This is the same online encyclopedia as the one available on CompuServe, Delphi, and Prodigy. It's the electronic equivalent of *Grolier's Academic American*, 21-volume set, and contains 33,000 articles and 10 million words. The database is updated quarterly.

As on the other services, the Grolier Encyclopedia allows for keyword searching, though nothing that complex. For example, you can't search the actual text of the articles, only the headlines. Also, you can't combine keywords in a very sophisticated manner. Still, it's a quite useful addition to the service.

Business Resource Directory

On the one hand, this business directory database is pretty limited in its scope. It lists information on only very small businesses and, furthermore, it contains information mainly on those small businesses owned or managed by GEnie's own membership. On the other hand, it does allow you to refine your search with some flexibility since you can search by product, service, area code, and other parameters. And the actual directory listing itself is clear and well labeled.

NewsBytes

If you're searching for computer industry news, this is the place to turn. NewsBytes is an independent news-gathering organization set up something along the lines of AP and UPI, but specializing solely in gathering and reporting on news in the computer and high-tech

industry. The stories are typically well researched, clear, and insightful. The database is fulltext, and updated on a daily basis.

Adding further strength to its usefulness is the fact that GEnie, compared to America Online and Delphi's NewsBytes offering, has a much longer searchable backfile, and supports strong Boolean search capabilities. This makes NewsBytes ideal for not only scanning the latest news, but digging for stories and doing some high-level research.

What's also exceptional for a nongatewayed, basic-level database is that not only are you able to use the standard Boolean operators of AND, OR, and NOT, but this database also allows truncation (with an asterisk) and even supports the use of proximity operators.

Here's a sample of a fairly simple search I did recently, looking for articles that discussed Eastman Kodak and its new Photo CD product:

```
GEnie                NEWSBYTES                Page  316
                 Newsbytes News Network

   1.    About Newsbytes
   2.    Newsbytes Instructions
   3.    Today's News Headlines
   4.    Retrieve News by Bureau
   5.    Retrieve News by Subject
   6.    Retrieve News by Story Type
   7.    Download an Issue of Newsbytes
   8.    Full-Text Search Newsbytes
   9.    The Mailbag (Reader Mail)
  10.[*]Send FEEDBACK to Newsbytes

Enter #, <P>revious, or <H>elp? 8

            Search Newsbytes

  1. Search database
  2. Control menu

Enter #, <Q>uit, <H>elp? 1

Query? kodak and photo CD
      49 documents found

         Browse/Retrieval options

  1. Title display
  2. Refine query
```

```
3. Search database
4. Environment display

Enter #, <P>revious, <H>elp, <Q>uit? 1

        Title display

 1. KODAK UNVEILS CD FOR PHOTO STORAGE
 2. RASTEROPS BOARDS FOR KODAK PHOTO CD SYSTEM
 3. KODAK INTROS COLOR IMAGING STRATEGY, NEW PRODUCTS
 4. AUSTRALIA: PHOTO LABS LINK UP VIA MODEM 05/30/91
 5. COMMODORE ANNOUNCES NEW CDTV FEATURES 06/11/91
 6. KODAK TO PUT PERSONAL PHOTOS ON CD DISK 09/18/91
 7. ****Kodak Interfaces Turn Copiers Into Printers 11/19/91
 8. Kodak To Use Macs To Transmit News Photos From Olympics 12/10/91
 9. National Science Foundation Funds Computer Research 12/12/91
10. MCI To Send Out Bills On CD-ROM 12/18/91
11. Kodak, Philips Announce New Photo-CD System Features 01/21/92
12. Philips Intros Low-Cost CD-ROM Creation Systems 03/11/92
13. ****Apple Enhances Laser Printers, Intros CD-ROM Drive 03/28/92
14. ****Intel, WordPerfect, 10 Others Support TWAIN
15. Mac-Based Digital Multimedia Data Organizer Planned By Aldus 07/08/92
```

At this point I could select which if any items of which I wanted to see the fulltext.

All in all, Newsbytes on GEnie is a nearly perfect database. Well, *nearly* perfect. I say this because of one glaring and rather embarrassing flaw. Unlike almost any other properly configured database on any other online system, Newsbytes on GEnie has the unfortunate feature of displaying the oldest news citations first and the newest last, at the end.

This is a cardinal no-no in the online world. It's always better to view the newest citations at the top of the list, since these will almost always be of the highest interest. This backwards approach also forces you to continuously scroll down the displayed list, further and further, until finally arriving at the most recent news items—which can be particularly irksome with very long listings. GEnie's spokesperson admits that this is indeed a flaw, and is due to a problem in their software's ability to interact effectively with Newsbyte's software.

The other section on GEnie where you'll find some good searchable databases is its News, Sports, and Features department, number 9 on GEnie's first (or Top) menu. Here's what this section offers:

```
GEnie                    NEWS                    Page  300
            News, Sports & Features

1.  Reuters Newswires        2.  Newsbytes News Network
3.  Dow Jones News/Retrieval (R)  4.  The Sports Network
5.  GEnie QuikNews (Clipping Svc)  6.  Dialog Database Center
7.  GEnie NewsStand
8.  Columnists & News Features
```

As with the Reference & Research menu, this listing also consists of both GEnie-supplied and Gateway menus. The GEnie-supplied ones of special interest here are:

 # Reuters newswires

You'll see from the above menu listing that Newsbytes, which was listed earlier in GEnie's Reference and Research Menu, is also listed here in its News menu (#2). Placing databases in more than one menu listing is common among online services. It's a good idea because there are many databases whose scope overlaps into more than one subject area, and multiple placements helps ensure that you won't miss finding it.

Most of us have heard of the newswire Reuters. Like the Associated Press (AP) and United Press International (UPI), Reuters is a newswire service staffed by reporters operating out of branch offices around the country and around the world. Their job is to cover and file news stories occurring on their beat. And, like AP and UPI, Reuters stories are normally distributed and picked up by newspapers around the country who run those pieces with a Reuters byline. Unlike AP or UPI, however, Reuters is based in London, and its real strength is in covering world news.

You're fortunate, then, to be able to access Reuters' top-notch news stories online on an inexpensive service like GEnie. GEnie offers two types of Reuters newswires: Reuters World Report and Reuters Business Report. Let's first take a close look at Reuters World Report, which is the broader and more general newswire service.

Once you call up the Reuters World Report, you're offered two ways to find filed stories. One is to simply see the latest news of the day—an up-to-the-minute listing of the headlines of major news stories that Reuters' reporters have filed during the last 12 hours or so. This is an excellent way to immediately see the very latest news stories. Even CNN's headline news doesn't offer this instantaneous level of timeliness. Here, for example, is what I turned up when I did such a search on March 1st, 1993:

```
            Reuters World Report
         Monday, March 01 1993
              16:05EST


 1. All Stories - Last in/First out
 2. Keyword Search

Enter #, <P>revious, or <H>elp? 1

            Reuters World Report
Item Time  Headline
Transmission date: 93/03/01
  1. 16:03 CRISTIANI URGES U.N. PANEL TO DELAY TRUTH REPORT
  2. 15:53 THE HESSE STATE ENVIRONMENTAL MINISTRY REPORTED AFTER
  3. 15:52 VANCE, OWEN MEET BOSNIAN SERB LEADER AS TALKS RESUME
  4. 15:43 LATVIA INTRODUCES NEW CURRENCY ON FRIDAY
  5. 15:33 MAIFREDI FIRED AS GENOA COACH
  6. 15:26 GOUGH AND STEVEN DOUBLE BLOW FOR RANGERS
  7. 15:24 LONDON,  DRAW FOR THE SEMIFINALS OF BRITISH
  8. 15:18 PAKISTAN COURT SENTENCES JOURNALIST FOR CONTEMPT
  9. 15:16 COLOMBIA SWEPT BY REPORTS THAT ESCOBAR'S END IS NEAR
 10. 15:12 TWO CASES OF LEPROSY REPORTED IN NORTHERN ITALY
 11. 15:10 GERMAN ENVIRONMENT MINISTER CRITICISES HOECHST
 12. 15:07 GULF WAR HERO SCHWARZKOPF TO RETURN TO VIETNAM FOR CBS
 13. 15:05 BOSNIAN REFUGEE THREATENS TO BLOW UP BORDER POST
 14. 15:03 HELICOPTER CRASHES IN GREENLAND
 15. 15:03 BOLIVIA UNION LEADERS STAGE HUNGER STRIKE FOR PAY
```

Note that the numbers to the left of the headline signify the time that the story was filed. This database is updated continuously, from Reuters directly to GEnie's computers, so you get the absolute latest news reports.

However, for research purposes, it's rare that you'll want to see only the latest news stories. Instead, you're more likely going to want to be able to search previously filed news stories to collect information on some subject you're researching. For these cases, you'll want to choose the Keyword Search option.

Here's an example of a search I did a day or so after the explosion at New York City's World Trade Center. First, the database asks for the search term, then it states how many stories were found that contained that phrase:

```
Search term? world trade center
Getting WORLD TRADE CENTER stories...

No matches found for WORLD TRADE CENTER.
<RETURN>, <Q>uit ends search
```

You'll note that the search phrase I entered, *world trade center*, didn't turn up any stories. However, it seemed almost impossible to imagine that a day or so after one of the most celebrated bomb explosions in U.S. history there wouldn't be any related news stories! So I was forced to think of other key words that could be used in a story about the explosion. Well, how about *explosion*? That phrase turned up 62 stories, some of which are listed in the following. Remember, as I explained in chapter 1 on database searching, a key to success is the ability to create and experiment with keywords to find the information that might be "hiding" until you come up with the right terms. Just because your search doesn't turn up any results doesn't necessarily mean that there isn't relevant information in the database.

```
Search term? explosion
Getting EXPLOSION stories...

Keyword: EXPLOSION produced 62 stories.
Display headlines? (Y/N)? y

    'EXPLOSION' STORIES
Transmission date: 93/03/01
 1. 14:46 U.S. SPY AGENCIES SIFT FOR POSSIBLE FOREIGN HAND IN BLAST
Transmission date: 93/02/28
 2. 20:58 MEDELLIN DRUG CARTEL POSSIBLE SUSPECT IN BLAST
 3. 18:31 MINISTER SAYS MOSLEM MILITANTS BEHIND CAIRO BOMBING
 4. 16:36 VICTIM OF CAIRO EXPLOSION PLANTED BOMB - MINISTER
 5. 13:37 AUTHORITIES SAY BOMB CAUSED MASSIVE WORLD TRADE CENTRE EXPLOSION
 6. 12:48 ANALYSTS SAY INSURERS LIKELY TO BE HARD-HIT BY NEW YORK BLAST
 7. 11:44 LONDON, FEB 28, REUTER - RESULTS OF BRITISH SOCCER MATCHES
 8. 08:21 FBI AGENT SAYS BOMB CAUSED WORLD TRADE CENTRE EXPLOSION
 9. 08:16 WARNE SPINS AUSTRALIA TO BRINK OF VICTORY
10. 07:25 THE BLAST COINCIDED WITH A MILITARY OPERATION ON NEARBY
11. 05:11 MYSTERY DEEPENS OVER CAIRO COFFEE SHOP BOMB
12. 04:04 AUTHORITIES SAY BOMB CAUSED MASSIVE WORLD TRADE CENTRE EXPLOSION
Transmission date: 93/02/27
13. 23:57 CAFE BOMB COULD MEAN MOSLEM GROUP BREAKING UP
```

```
14. 21:29 BOMBS HIT FRENCH EDUCATION MINISTRY OFFICES
15. 20:35 FBI SUGGESTS POSSIBLE YUGOSLAVIA LINK IN NY BLAST
```

Note that although certain stories in the list clearly relate to the World Trade Center explosion, most do not. (Also note that the search term *world trade center* didn't turn up any stories because of the British spelling of *centre*.) The next step in using this database is to select those headline citations for which you want to see the full article. In this case, I chose number 2:

```
MEDELLIN DRUG CARTEL POSSIBLE SUSPECT IN BLAST
```

```
    NEW YORK, Feb 28, Reuters - The Medellin drug cartel, which has been
threatening to bring its violence to New York, is one of the groups
suspected by authorities for planting the bomb that caused Friday's
massive explosion at the World Trade Centre.
    Authorities say it is too soon to speculate on the specific group
involved in the blast, but federal officials have been concerned for some
time that the cartel might try to stage an attack here.
    James Fox, New York director of the Federal Bureau of Investigation
(FBI), said that while authorities have not reached a final conclusion
that the bomb was planted by a guerrilla group, he said it was unlikely a
lone individual was responsible. "There are drug dealers who are very
upset with the U.S. government who have access to money and explosives
and people who would detonate a bomb," he said on Cable News Network
(CNN).
```

```
(the text continues)
```

You can see how useful this database is. Unfortunately, it also suffers from a major flaw that seriously limits its value for researchers. As with the other online services, Reuters' backfile—the farthest in the past that stories are retained—is only three days. If you're serious about researching news items, you normally want to go back months or even years. Not just three days. For this reason, although Reuters is still an exceptional database, I can't wholly recommend it. The best place to search a newswire like Reuters is on one of the professional services like Dialog—or by using a gateway.

⇨ Other useful databases

Two other databases are worth special mention here: The Sports Network and CASHE.

The Sports Network

Like the Reuters and Newsbytes databases, The Sports Network is an independent news-gathering organization whose reporters file late-breaking stories picked up by daily newspapers around the country. The Sports Network, though, specializes in (drum roll, please) sports!

In addition to providing the latest standings, schedules, and score summaries, The Sports Network also allows keyword searching of previously filed stories.

Like Reuters, The Sports Network is updated continuously, so it's an excellent source for getting timely news. Unfortunately, also like Reuters, it contains only three days of stories, so its value as a research tool is limited.

 # CASHE

CASHE stands for College Aid Sources for Higher Education, and is designed to help prospective college students pinpoint which, if any, of 14,000 different resources of financial aid they might qualify for. It's not really a database you can search yourself, however. Instead, upon logging on you're instructed to fill out an online eligibility application. The CASHE folks then run a search themselves on their financial aid database and inform you, in a written report, which financial aid sources you qualify for. There's an extra cost of $30 per report generated. This could be a useful database for some, but, again, it's not a true research tool.

 # Gateways

GEnie currently provides a gateway to two professional online services: Dialog and Dow Jones News/Retrieval. Both of these are highly regarded systems that offer some of the finest information sources available anywhere online.

Let's first look at the gateway into Dialog. Dialog (described in more detail in chapter 8) is many professional researcher's first choice. Its topic coverage is unsurpassed and its search capabilities are as powerful as they come. So it behooves you to consider the GEnie service for this reason alone.

Virtually all of Dialog's databases are available on GEnie. Here is a listing of how GEnie groups the files:

Commerce Business Daily Published by the U.S. Department of Commerce, the Commerce Business Daily contains information on government procurements, including RFPs (requests for proposals).

Computer & Electronics News Center Product announcements, software and hardware reviews, editorials, and industry trends in the computers and electronics industry.

Consumer Medicine Consumer Medicine is a gateway into The National Library of Medicine's Medline database, which indexes biomedical information from 3,700 international journals published in over 70 countries.

Corporate Affiliates Research Center Contains business profiles and corporate linkage for 100,000 companies worldwide.

D&B Business Locator Descriptive and identification information for 8.7 million U.S. companies.

D&B Canadian Company Profiles A directory file containing key information for over 348,000 Canadian companies.

D&B European Company Profiles A directory file providing detailed information on over 2 million businesses located in 26 European countries.

D&B International Company Profiles A directory file containing key information for parent companies for over 2.4 million Asian, African, European, Indian, and other non-U.S. companies.

D&B U.S. Company Profiles A directory file providing detailed information for over 7.5 million U.S. business establishments.

Educators Center All aspects of education, drawn from several educational databases.

GEnie's Bookshelf Information on over 1 million books in print; can be searched by title, author or subject.

GEnie's NewsStand Contains the fulltext of articles from hundreds of popular magazines and several well-known national newspapers.

GEnie's Reference Center This database is composed of over 20 different databases, covering a wide field of subjects, from computers and education to philosophy, history, and much more.

Investment Analyst A stock-tracking service, providing both current and historical quotes as well as related financial tracking services.

Public Opinion Online (POLL) Contains the fulltext of public-opinion surveys, collected by the Roper Center for Public Opinion Research.

Thomas Register of North American Manufacturers Lists company names and products manufactured for over 194,000 U.S. and Canadian companies.

Trademark Center Contains 1.2 million registered trademarks from the U.S. Patent and Trademark Office, as well as information on trademarks and service marks registered with the Secretaries of State of all 50 U.S. states and Puerto Rico.

Tradenames A worldwide directory of 304,000 consumer brand names and their owners.

TRW Contains payment histories, bankruptcy, tax legal data, banking relationships and related data on 2.5 million firms.

Worldwide Patents Center Can search millions of patents registered at the U.S. Patent Office and at other patent offices around the world.

The names of these databases don't necessarily correspond to the actual names of specific databases on Dialog. Some of these are actually composed of several related databases, all grouped together under one name. For example, GEnie's Medical Professional Service contains these separate Dialog databases:

AGELINE Produced by the American Association of Retired Persons.

AIDSLINE Produced by the U.S. National Library of Medicine.

BIOSIS PREVIEWS Produced by BIOSIS.

CANCERLIT Produced by the U.S. National Cancer Institute.

CONSUMER DRUG INFORMATION FULLTEXT Produced by the American Society of Hospital Pharmacists.

HEALTH DEVICES ALERT & HEALTH DEVICES SOURCEBOOK Produced by ECRI.

HEALTH PLANNING AND ADMINISTRATION Produced by the U.S. National Library of Medicine.

MEDTEXT Produced by the American Medical Association.

That gives you a good picture of the complexity of the online database world. You can see, for example, how one expert organization, such as the U.S. National Cancer Institute, can create an online database of information covering its areas of specialty (CANCERLIT), which then becomes part of a larger system (DIALOG) that offers access to many professional databases. Then, through a gateway, it's available to users of a consumer online service (GENIE).

In fact, there's one more important intermediary not mentioned in the previous paragraph. The gateway connection between GEnie and Dialog is actually performed and carried out by a third-party firm.

There are currently two such third parties doing this for GEnie. One is called Telebase Systems Inc. and the other is Advanced Research Technologies, or ART.

What happens when you want to access a Dialog database? First you select which of the various services you want to search. Let's say you choose to search the Medical Professional Service. GEnie would send a message to its gateway provider (in this case, ART), whose own computer would then ask you to enter your search statement and phrase. You would be permitted to use the basic Boolean connectors of AND, NOT, and OR in creating your search statement. You would also be allowed to truncate if you so desire.

ART would then log onto Dialog and do a preliminary search on all the databases that comprise the Medical Professional Service, and then tell you how many matches it found for each of those databases. You'll also be provided with the option to broaden or narrow your search should you want to do this. You can then choose one or more of those databases to view your results.

If you choose to view your results, you'll be shown the titles or headlines of the first ten items located. You're still allowed the option to modify your search if needed. You can then either look at additional titles, choose to see the fulltext from any of the titles displayed, or begin a new search altogether.

For this gateway privilege, you're charged a fee above and beyond your normal GEnie monthly membership fee. For all ART-supplied gateways (which on GEnie is every Dialog service except Investment Analy$t, Public Opinion Online, and Tradenames) you're charged every time you have what ART calls a *search event*.

A search event, according to ART's definition, occurs each time you view ten titles or choose to view a full record. You pay anywhere from $3.00 to $7.50 for each event you incur, the exact price depending on which database you choose to search. The Medical Professional Center service, for instance, costs $4.50 per event. (One exception to this pricing method is the cost to print a full record from TRW Business Credit Profiles; that database charges you $29.) If no matches are found, you're still billed $1.25 for a "no hit" event.

Is this a good deal? Does it make sense to search Dialog's databases through a GEnie gateway, or would it be more efficient and cost-effective to just log-on to Dialog directly? The answer is "it depends." What are the specific criteria on which you should make your decision? Basically, you need to look at these elements:

➤ Scope of coverage (how many databases can be searched, total number of records)

➤ Ease of searching

➤ Power of searching (I define *power* here as the ability to locate, as specifically as possible, items that most precisely match what you need. That ability is determined by the search software's flexibility and capability to search different sections (fields) of a database, and to support advanced Boolean functions such as truncation and proximity operators).

➤ Value for the dollar

If you compare GEnie's Dialog gateways head to head with Dialog directly, here's what you'll find:

⇨ Scope of coverage

This one's a tie, but with an edge going to Dialog. Up until the middle of 1993 or so, you had to sign up directly with Dialog to be able to tap into the full 400+ files. But GEnie has been adding the missing files to its gateway, so that today its subscribers have virtually the same access as a direct subscriber. Still, you're never quite as secure that you have full access when you search a major system through a gateway, and occasionally there are blocks placed on certain databases. So, for this reason, while access today is virtually identical, you'd still be better off searching Dialog directly if you always want to feel 100% certain that absolutely everything is being made available to you.

⇨ Ease of searching

The winner for this one is Gateway for novice searchers and Dialog for experts. It's in this category where gateways are really supposed

to show their stuff. If you're a beginner in online searching, the menus that a gateway employs make the search process a piece of pie. The way menus work is by presenting a list of options and plain English prompts for key words and search instructions. In contrast, Dialog's system doesn't tell the searcher anything about what to do. You're expected to already know the combination of letters and numbers that instruct the system to choose a certain database, perform a search, and view results. So, while you could with no experience whatsoever conduct an online search on Dialog through a gateway, you couldn't survive in the harsher Dialog environment.

However. However, However! Although consumer online services and gateway producers like to tell people and promote how much easier it is to search their menu system, selflessly protecting innocent users from having to deal with those mean old command systems, their argument goes only so far and, I think, has a pretty good dose of self-serving hype. It's not *that* hard to learn how to search on Dialog (or on most other professional online services). Here's a simple example of just how difficult it is to do a search directly on Dialog:

❶ To select a particular database for searching, read through Dialog's catalog (you can get one free by dialing 800-334-2564), find one that appears suitable, and use its assigned number. So, say you find a database that contains articles published in business management publications called Trade and Industry ASAP, file number 645. To instruct Dialog to open this database, you would key in B 645. B means to begin or open that file, and 645 is the file number. Dialog will locate the database and display a question mark, waiting for your next command.

❷ Enter your search statement. Let's say you want to find published articles on the topic of total quality management in hospitals. You might then key in:

```
Total()Quality()Management AND Hospital?
```

On Dialog, a closed set of parentheses between words signifies that you want Dialog to find items in the database, where those keywords follow in the exact order as you entered. The question mark is the truncation sign, so your search will uncover both *Hospital* and *Hospitals*.

❸ Dialog will search the database and assign this initial search statement a designating set number, S1. Dialog will then tell you that it has found, say, 32 items (records) and then display a question mark to ask you what you'd like to do next.

❹ Say you want to see the first 10 titles. There are four parts to this command. To display anything on Dialog, you always type the letter T. Then you need to tell Dialog which search statement you're referring to. You have only one search statement so far, S1. To tell Dialog that you want to view the title portion of the records only, follow the S1 by a number that corresponds to Dialog's system of designating how much of the record you want to see. The number 6 on most databases will show you titles only. Finally, you need to instruct Dialog which items from the list of 32 records retrieved that you want to view titles. Here you can type a single number, a series of numbers, or a range. So your command to Dialog to view those ten titles would be the following, where each part of the command is separated by a slash, like this: T S1/6/1-10. This is an instruction to Dialog to type (or show me), from my first search statement set (S1), titles only (6), for items one through ten.

❺ Dialog will then display the titles of the first ten items for you to view. Again, you're given a question mark and asked what you want to do.

❻ Say, based on the headlines, you want to see more of items numbers 2 and 6. You'll want to tell Dialog to show you the fulltext of those articles. Again, your first command is T for type/display and S1 to designate which search statement set. But now, instead of entering a 6 for title display, you'll enter a 9, which means fulltext display. And instead of entering 1–10, you'll tell Dialog you want items 2 and 6. So your final command would read T S1/9/2,6. Dialog will display the fulltext of those items and, assuming you're satisfied, you're done.

❼ The final step is to type Logoff.

Now, while this series of commands takes a little getting used to and is clearly not the most intuitive set of statements ever invented, it's also certainly nothing like mastering advanced calculus, or even programming your VCR!

It's true that I've chosen a pretty simple example and, in other instances, you'll need a couple of other tricks up your sleeve—as well as a lot of practice—to conduct a really good search. But these are the basic steps, and you can do a direct search like this on Dialog with knowledge of these basic commands. So the next time someone tries to convince you that these big bad systems are just too complicated for your pretty little head, tell 'em it just ain't true. (Which is a rather long-winded way of saying that gateways are much easier for the novice, but they aren't necessarily any easier then searching directly after you've learned a little bit!)

 # Power of searching

The winner here is Dialog Direct. When you search on a gateway, you automatically give up the ability to perform certain advanced Boolean search functions, which you can do if you search Dialog directly. In addition to these functions, you also give up a couple of other fairly significant capabilities that are possible to perform only directly on Dialog. One is a feature called OneSearch, which allows you to search more than one database simultaneously.

It's important to point out, though, that gateways don't actually ignore proximity operators and field searching. They normally do use these features, but they perform them for you "behind the scenes," based on assumptions the gateway's programmers have made about the type of database you're searching and the most typical ways users would want to use proximity and field searching.

This can be kind of nice. It's like having a set of well-meaning parents backing you up, trying to figure out your needs and actually giving you some extra support and arranging things the way they assume you like them. And Ma and Pop Gateway do a pretty good job of it, too—after all, they've studied what kinds of needs searchers like you have and try to do their best. But, like any well-meaning parents, they're no substitute for doing it yourself. You have unique search needs and you should be the one to figure how you want your proximity operators set up and which fields to search. At some point, you've got to leave the nest!

So, while using these behind-the-scenes manipulations is a useful and helpful way to get a feel for the world of online searching, to truly experience its full power and capabilities you need to be able to control them yourself. Unfortunately, unlike automatic cameras that offer a manual override switch for creative photographers who want to control their own exposures, gateways don't provide such a function. Therefore, you'll need to move to the next level when you're ready.

Value for the dollar

Now for the bottom line: Which service is going to cost you more, and which gives you more bang for the buck? This is a bit tricky, since prices vary so much both on Dialog as well as on gateways. But the winner for this one is GEnie.

As mentioned earlier, ART normally charges you between $3 and $7.50 for each online event incurred. An *event* is defined as a group of 10 titles or each full record displayed. While there's really no such thing as an "average" search, many searches consist of about 10 to 15 minutes of online searching time, displaying of about 7 to 10 titles and viewing the results of 3 or 4 fulltext items. Let's just see how much you'd end up paying for a search like this on a GEnie ART gateway that cost $4.50 per event versus Dialog directly. Consider the following information for Gateway:

Cost per hour of searchtime 0

Cost to display 10 titles $4.50

Cost to display 3 items $11.50

Total charges $16.00

Dialog Direct is where things get really tricky. Every database on Dialog has its own pricing structure and these prices vary widely, so there's no such thing as a "typically" priced database. However, the cost to search many of the business and reference databases typically ranges from about $60 to $130 per hour to search and from 25¢ to

$2 per item to display in full. So just for comparison sake, we'll use a typical reference database that costs $96 per hour to search and $1 per full record to display in full. Here's the corresponding information for Dialog Direct:

Cost per hour of searchtime $24 for 15 minutes and $16 for 10 minutes

Cost to display 10 titles 0

Cost to display 3–4 items $3 to $4

Total charges $19 to $28

The winner here is the gateway service. Of course, it's not possible to illustrate all possible cost comparisons with every possible database. But in general, you'll find that gateways are often cheaper, especially if you spend a lot of time online thinking and trying out different search strategies. (If, though, you happen to be an expert searcher you might find that if you can get on and off Dialog very quickly it can be more cost effective.) You can make your own cost comparisons by substituting the prices of Dialog and ART gateway for specific databases you want to search.

There are a few other aspects of the cost comparison that you should note. The most significant difference is the fact that Dialog charges you on a per-minute basis (the actual fee varies by specific database). In other words, as with phoning your lawyer, the meter is ticking and you pay for every minute you're connected. Another big difference is that Dialog normally doesn't charge you to display titles, but the gateway service does. The gateway also has a somewhat higher price for printing fulltext records. There are, therefore, a couple of ratios to keep in mind here:

➤ The more time online you need, the better deal a gateway is.

➤ The more titles you need, the better deal Dialog is.

➤ The more fulltext printouts you need, the better deal Dialog is.

The strongest and most meaningful ratio is actually the first one—the fact that you aren't charged any hourly fees when using a gateway.

This is important to know—and it's information that you can use to your advantage. So, to cut your online search costs, follow these rules of thumb:

First, if you're unsure about your search and need lots of time to experiment and play around with alternative search statements, trying different databases, and the like, you might consider using a gateway service. (Even expert searchers might consider doing this as a first step to work on search statements and strategies and identify the best databases. Then they can go on to Dialog directly, do a quick search in that file, and print out titles and fulltext records.)

Second, if you know exactly what database you need or are confident in your search strategy, can get on and off the system quickly, and are pretty confident that the search is going to turn up some relevant titles, you can often lower your costs by going directly on Dialog.

Remember, though, that this discussion is limited to price alone. When choosing whether to search Dialog directly or to use a gateway, you also need to consider the importance of other factors mentioned previously, such as scope, ease of search, and power of searching.

So what's the bottom line? Well, if money were no object, then I'd say to learn to use the Dialog command system since it provides a broader scope and allows you to do much more powerful searches. But for some reason I have a feeling that most of you are oddly attached to those little green slips of paper. So gateways can indeed be a cost-effective, albeit somewhat compromised method of power-searching.

Of course, you could have the best of both worlds—a good deal of Dialog's power at even lower costs. That system, called Knowledge Index, is discussed in detail in chapter 2.

The other way you can gateway to Dialog on GEnie is via its other third-party gateway provider, Telebase Systems, Inc. While Telebase does play a minor role on GEnie, offering access to Investment Analy$t, Public Opinion Online (POLL), and Tradenames, the firm plays a much more significant role on CompuServe, and is also discussed in more detail in chapter 2.

What about GEnie's other gateway, to the Dow Jones News/Retrieval system? Dow Jones, as you might expect, is a premier source of business and financial information. This gateway operates a bit differently than the one to Dialog in that there's no intermediary, like ART, managing the connection. When you gateway to Dow Jones, you're connected directly to its own host computer and can search it the same way Dow Jones subscribers do. (You are, however, blocked from three databases available directly to Dow Jones subscribers: Dun & Bradstreet's Financial Records PLUS, Real Time Stock Quotes, and the MCI electronic mail service.)

Because Dow Jones databases are powerful and it can take a while to learn to use them correctly, you should read all search instructions carefully or contact Dow Jones customer service for search assistance. Pricing is tricky too, and is normally based not only on the amount of time you spend online, but how many information units you choose to display (an *information unit* being defined as 1,000 characters of information). Dow Jones customer service number is (800) 522-3567.

 # Special-interest groups

Special-interest groups, as mentioned earlier, while not a typical source of reference information, should not be ignored. These online organizations can be excellent sources for tapping into others' expertise, as well as a place to download relevant information files and software. Here is a sample of GEnie "roundtables"—its name for SIGs.

Air Force	IBM
Apple/Macintosh	Investors
Astrology	Japan
Automotive	Law Enforcement
California/West Coast	Medical
Deutschland	Military
Education	Motorcycling
Family	Music
Food & Wine	Pet-Net
Geneology & History	Photo & Video
Home & Real Estate	Radio & Electronics

Religion & Philosophy	Travel
Science Fiction	Windows
Scuba	WordPerfect
Show Biz	Writer's Ink
Sports	

⇨ Internet access

GEnie supports electronic mail to and from the Internet, but no other functions.

⇨ Pricing

Finally, what does it cost to search GEnie? For basic-service, nonprime-time searching (after 6 PM weekdays and all day weekends, local time), users pay $8.95 per month and receive four hours of usage time. Additional time is billed at $3 per hour. GEnie's professional services, including the Dialog and Dow Jones gateways, cost more, depending on the particular database.

Users are permitted 9,600-bps modems in some locations, but pay a $6-per-hour surcharge at all times.

⇨ Summary and recommendation

Pros NewsBytes, Gateways to Dialog and Dow Jones, SIGs, and low basic charges.

Cons Old-fashioned text-based interface, complex navigation, and few powerful databases on its own system.

Recommendation GEnie is better than most consumer online services in access to online databases. I recommend it particularly for those who need computer news, but it's still not a top choice for serious researchers.

4
Delphi

Delphi is a full-fledged consumer online service, offering a nice mix of useful databases and special-interest groups. Other than its acquisition in 1993 by Rupert Murdoch's media conglomerate News Corp., its biggest claim to fame was to provide members with full access to the Internet. (For details on the Internet and what you can find on it, see chapter 7.) While other online services offer certain kinds of limited Internet access—mainly e-mail and messaging capabilities—as of this writing, Delphi remains the only major consumer online service to offer full access.

Like GEnie and CompuServe, Delphi organizes its services into a series of menus, grouped by category. The following are the items contained in Delphi's main and broadest menu of services:

- ➤ Business and finance
- ➤ News, weather, and sports
- ➤ Computing groups
- ➤ Reference and education
- ➤ Conference
- ➤ Shopping
- ➤ Delphi/Regional
- ➤ Travel and leisure
- ➤ Entertainment and games
- ➤ Using Delphi
- ➤ Groups and clubs
- ➤ Workspace
- ➤ Internet services
- ➤ Mail
- ➤ Member directory

Before examining the details of the specific databases on Delphi, let's first take a closer look at what you'll find when selecting certain Delphi services:

✳ **Business and finance**

➤ UPI Business News

➤ PR Newswire—press releases

➤ Business Wire—press releases

➤ RateGram CD Reports

➤ Commodity Quotes

➤ Register of Public Corporations

➤ Dow Jones Averages

➤ SOS—Stocks & Options Advisors

➤ Financial and Commodity News

➤ Stock Quotes

➤ Forum

➤ Translation Services

➤ Futures Focus

➤ Trendvest Market & Mutual Fund

➤ MarketPulse

➤ Ratings

➤ Money Fund Report from Donaghue

➤ Mortgage Calculator

✳ **News, weather, and sports services**

➤ Newsbrief

➤ National News

➤ Business News

➤ Reuters Newswire

➤ Entertainment News

➤ Views on News

➤ Financial & Commodity News

➤ Weather

- ➤ DataNet Computer News   ➤ Human Interest Stories
- ➤ Sports   ➤ International News

✳ **Reference and education services**

- ➤ CAIN—AIDS Info Network
- ➤ New Parents Network (NPNet)
- ➤ DIALOG Research Library ($)
- ➤ NRPA Network
- ➤ Dictionary of Cultural Literacy
- ➤ NYNEX Electronic Yellow Grolier Encyclopedia
- ➤ Pages
- ➤ HealthNet
- ➤ Online Gourmet
- ➤ Librarian

⇨ Signing up and getting started

Getting going on Delphi is quite straightforward. Unlike Prodigy, America Online, and CompuServe (with its CompuServe Information Manager interface), there's no special front-end graphical interface software. Instead, you use your own communications software to connect to the service. Once you're online you can get to where you want by either navigating through menus or entering the name of a service directly as a shortcut. Delphi's interface and help services, while nothing outstanding, are fairly intuitive and easy to follow.

Now let's take a close look at what Delphi has to offer in the reference information database areas of special focus: encyclopedias, magazines and journals, health and medical information, business information, newspapers and newswires, and college information.

⇨ Encyclopedias

✳ Grolier's Academic American Encyclopedia

Like Prodigy, CompuServe, and Genie, Delphi makes the 32,000-word Grolier's Electronic Academic American Encyclopedia available to members for searching. Searching is quite straightforward, and is done by entering a word or phrase.

As with the other online services, you can choose to view certain sections of the full database and search by a word or a phrase. But you can't use any type of advanced and sophisticated Boolean searching.

⇨ Magazines and journals

✳ T.V. Guide

A new Delphi service is T.V. Guide Online. Users can read and download listings, and also interact with editors. T.V. Guide Online is owned by Delphi's new parent company, News Corp., and analysts expect that other News Corp. periodicals and newspapers (which include *Mirabella*, *Married Woman*, and the *Boston Herald*) will eventually be put online.

⇨ Health and medical information

Delphi offers two useful databases that offer health-related facts and information:

✳ HealthNet

Healthnet is basically an online encyclopedia of health-related information. Although it offers fulltext articles on a variety of topics, you can't perform any keyword searches. Instead, you must use its menu system to choose subject categories and subcategories to narrow down the articles you need. Although this is an okay method

for conducting broad searches, it isn't at all a powerful way to conduct health-related information research. Still, it can be a handy reference. HealthNet is also made available on the CompuServe service.

✳ CAIN

If you're searching for information on AIDS, CAIN is a superb database—and a bargain too, since the cost to search this service is already built into your basic Delphi fees.

CAIN stands for the Computerized Aids Information Network, and is funded by California's Health Services Department. The database indexes and offers abstracts and fulltext for over 3,000 sources of information on AIDS, including data from the Food and Drug Administration (FDA), the National Institutes of Health (NIH), the National Library of Medicine, general-interest and medical journals, and a variety of other government and public data sources.

Searching is very flexible, as CAIN not only supports full Boolean searching, but also allows you to modify searches as you go along by widening and narrowing search statements. In addition, you have the option to perform field searching—a feature rarely found on stand-alone consumer databases. Field searching allows you to specify exactly what portion of each item (record) in the database you want to search. Fields available for searching on CAIN include article titles, name of sources, authors, and publication dates. So, for example, you could instruct the database to locate for you only those records that were published in 1993 and derived from the FDA.

Another plus to CAIN is its very friendly help screens. You receive plain English instructions on how to search the database and what to do if you need more help.

Many sections of the CAIN database are updated daily, while other portions are updated somewhat less frequently, depending on the type of data included. CAIN is available only on Delphi, and currently represents one of the best services available on a consumer online service.

Here's an excerpt of a recent search done on CAIN, where I asked the system to locate any articles that mentioned *chronic fatigue syndrome*:

```
                        Research Library Menu
This database contains abstracts, full text and summaries on the medical,
educational, legal, financial and psychosocial aspects of the HIV virus.

Type the date (example: JAN-93) for a current literature search.
Type DRUG. and the name of the drug for drug information.
Type STATISTICS to search for current surveillance (stats) reports.
Type BASIC for general HIV information and education articles.
Type DAILY. and the day of the week for articles posted today.

Or search for articles by typing:
(your word) Open Keyword      ?      TO IDENTIFY KEYWORD

TI=     Title of article
IMED    To order document
SO=     Source of article        FEEDBACK  Feedback to CAIN
AU=     Author (last name)       HELP!!    Help menu(s)
PY=     Print year               CLEAR     To begin new search

/EXIT    Exit this menu

Search for: chronic fatigue syndrome

2 articles in current collection.
2 articles available.

RESEARCH>(Scan, Read, "?" or Exit): scan

Contents
--------
1  16-FEB    VIRUS VINDICATED IN CHRONIC FATIGUE [UPI]
2   9-FEB    IMMUNE ABNORMALITIES FOUND IN CHRONIC FATIGUE SYND# [NIAID]

RESEARCH>(Scan, Read, "?" or Exit): 1-2

1  16-FEB-1993 13:17  VIRUS VINDICATED IN CHRONIC FATIGUE [UPI]

TI  Virus vindicated in chronic fatigue
SO  UPI News
AU
TX  33 Lines
```

Government scientists have vindicated a virus that had been linked to the chronic fatigue syndrome, leaving the cause of the debilitating illness a mystery. A study involving 21 chronic fatigue syndrome patients found no evidence that the human T-lymphotropic virus type II (HTLV-2) caused the illness, the federal Centers for Disease Control and Prevention in Atlanta reported Sunday.

The findings appear to add HTLV-2 to a growing list of viruses that
were once suspected of causing the disease but were subsequently
vindicated, such as the Epstein-Barr virus and the cytomegalovirus.

(the text continues)

 # Business information: business news

Delphi offers three major business newswires:

✳ PR Newswire

PR Newswire disseminates the fulltext of press releases from
companies and other organizations around the United States. It's well
known in the business information industry, and has a very fine
reputation in its field. The database is updated on a continuous basis,
meaning that the latest news you find online might have been
released only a few minutes ago. You can search the file by a
keyword, company name, or company ticker symbol.

Unfortunately, on Delphi there's a very small backfile of stories
available for searching. Delphi caps the total number of items that can
remain in that file at any one time, so you're unlikely to find an item
older than a few days. So while the service could be useful for scanning
the latest releases, it's much less useful for serious research purposes.

✳ BusinessWire

BusinessWire is actually PR Newswire's major competitor, as it too
specializes in disseminating press and news releases from around the
country. While it's somewhat smaller than PR Newswire,
BusinessWire has developed something of a niche in the high-
technology field.

Searching BusinessWire on Delphi is similar to searching PR
NewsWire, and presents the same problem in its lack of a backfile.

If you think you might be interested in doing more extensive research
on BusinessWire or PR NewsWire, you should consider searching
those files on the Dialog service. Dialog provides a much longer time

period of releases from the two databases. (You can gateway to the Dialog service through Delphi or via another consumer online gateway.)

✳ UPI Business News

This database is not suitable for online research since it's capable of displaying only the latest headlines, and cannot be searched by keyword or any other method. The file could certainly be useful if you want to take a scan at the latest business news, though. But that's all.

 # Business information: company directories

✳ Executive Desk Register

This database provides basic directory data for 5,000 public companies that trade their stock on the New York, American, or NASDAQ exchanges. It's produced by the same firm (Demand Research) that makes its data available on America Online. Each record provides the name of the company, an address, stock ticker symbol, and the name of the CEO or CFO. You can search by keyword, company name, or stock ticker symbol. This is a nice basic source if you just need an address or top contact, but it's hardly a comprehensive company directory. You might find more companies and more detailed information by consulting a library print directory (e.g., Dun's Million Dollar Directory, Standard & Poor's Register, or Ward's) or by using a more comprehensive online company directory.

✳ NYNEX Northeast Access

This is quite a specialized company directory because it provides data only for companies located in the Yellow Pages or Business to Business listings for the states of New York, Connecticut, Maine, Massachusetts, New Hampshire, Rhode Island, and Vermont. The main purpose of a directory such as this one is to locate the names, addresses, and phone numbers of firms who make a particular product or supply a certain service. A total of 1.7 million listings are included in this file, derived from over 300 directories.

Although NYNEX Northeast Access could be pretty useful for certain situations, there are a few problems. First of all, because the database automatically erases your last input, it can be hard to keep track of your own search steps.

Secondly, it can also be difficult to determine which category you should best choose to describe the type of business you're searching for—there's no online help to assist you in determining whether your assumptions correspond to the definitions used by the NYNEX database indexers. Finally, the other obvious limitation is the limited geographic coverage. Delphi has said that it currently has no plans to add similar services for the rest of the country, so if your research requires you to identify businesses from around the nation you would have to look elsewhere. (Note that there are, indeed, a handful of online services and CD-ROM services that do what this database does on a nationwide basis. See chapter 11 of this book, under *Address and phone directories*.)

 Newspapers and newswires

At first glance, it might appear that Delphi offers a lot in the category of newspapers and newswires. Indeed, no fewer than seven fulltext wire services are available:

➤ Newsbrief from UPI

➤ DataNet computer news

➤ Entertainment news

➤ National news

➤ International news

➤ Reuters news

➤ Sports news from UPI

However, each of these databases offers only a headline news service. Not only is there almost nothing of a backfile (usually a couple days at most), but there's no keyword searching. Therefore, these services, while handy for scanning the latest news, aren't going to be useful for real news research.

➡️ College information

Delphi doesn't offer any college-related databases.

➡️ Other databases of interest

A few other databases of special mention are Delphi's Trav-Alerts, Worldline Country Search, Forum, and ParentNet.

✳ Worldline Country Search

Travel information for over 200 countries, including information on customs, visa requirements, and other useful data.

✳ Trav-Alerts

Trav-Alerts provides U.S. state department and other advisories regarding travel in specific countries. While not keyword-searchable, you can search by specific country and the information provided is of high quality and quite useful.

✳ ParentNet

ParentNet is a searchable encyclopedia-type database containing articles on various aspects of parenting. It's produced by a third-party non-profit organization that gathers a wide variety of material from numerous social-service agencies. The database is updated on a daily basis, and has a one-year backfile.

You can search ParentNet by either keyword (no Boolean logic, though) or specified subject headings supplied by the database. ParentNet will display a list of titles of all articles located, from which you can choose to see any in full. If your keyword doesn't result in any articles located, you can browse ParentNet's own index to examine words the database producer has selected to describe their articles. (This capability is a very useful feature, and should be made available in more databases.) Although not a very powerful database, overall ParentNet is a pretty unique and useful service.

 Delphi gateways

Delphi supports a gateway to the full Dialog Information Service. Unlike GEnie and CompuServe, this gateway is not managed by a third party that provides any self-explanatory search menus to guide you in the search. For this reason, you must be knowledgeable in how to search Dialog before using Delphi's gateway.

If you search Dialog through Delphi, you'll be charged Dialog's normal search and print costs (which could range from $40 to over $150 per hour) plus a 35¢-per-minute surcharge by Delphi. For more information on Dialog, see chapter 8.

Special-interest groups

As discussed earlier, special-interest groups can provide you with a different flavor of information, typically that of others' personal experiences, anecdotes, and advice, as well as downloadable files and various software. The following is a list of special interest groups available on Delphi:

Armed Forces	Inventors/Inventions
Aviation	Lesbian
Blended Family Support	Mass Communications
Chess Players	Men
Christian	New Age Network
Classical Music	Nurses
Codependency	Pet Lovers
Comedy	Philosophers
Computer Hardware	Photograph & Video
Environment	Psychic Voyages
Handicaps	Relationships
Health	Science Fiction
Hunting & Shooting	Sports Connection
International Ferret Assoc.	Theology
Internet	Writers

Pricing

Delphi offers two levels of pricing. Both plans are based on weekday searching only. The 10-4 plan costs $10 per month and includes the first four hours of access. Additional online time is billed at $4 per hour. The 20-20 option costs $20 per month, but provides 20 hours of use, and a rate of $1.80 per hour for additional time.

While these are low rates, Delphi boosts them significantly should you choose to do any weekday daytime searching. If you choose to search during those times, you need to add a $9-per-hour surcharge to the standard rates (for both plans). Also, Delphi charges a $3-per-hour premium for accessing the Internet.

Summary and recommendations

Pros Internet access, help menus, and the CAIN Aids Information Database.

Cons Relatively few major reference databases, very short newswire backfiles, mediocre user interface.

Recommendation Delphi makes most sense for researchers who either want a low-cost and easy route into the Internet, or who regularly research AIDS. For other kinds of research, however, it doesn't offer all that much.

5
America Online

America Online is one of the fastest growing consumer online services. In 1992, there were approximately 181,000 subscribers, representing an increase of 39% over the year before. In May of 1993, subscribers topped the 250,000 mark. And by January 1994, America Online hit the half million mark. Growth has been so rapid, in fact, that America Online's computer system has been straining to keep up with the demand. To prevent further strain, the service has even announced that it would try to limit the number of new subscribers!

Much of this growth is the result of creative marketing by the firm, which went public in March of 1992. America Online (AOL) has initiated a variety of special promotions, such as bundling or preinstalling its software with other computer products, entered into various joint ventures, and experimented with regional versions of the service.

⇨ Signing up and getting started

When you sign up with America Online, you're provided with a set of disks. Those disks contain special software that acts as a buffer between you and the America Online's host computer. The software produces various graphic elements, icons, and the like, which make using the service easier and much more friendly (see Fig. 5-1).

Figure 5-1

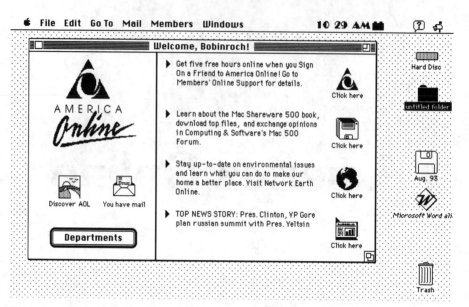

Opening screen for America Online, listing the available online departments.

America Online's interface, in my opinion, is better than another online service known for its graphics, Prodigy. While Prodigy's software produces pretty pictures to accompany and illustrate its services (and advertisements), America Online's graphics are of higher quality and are an integral part of the entire service. It's clear from using AOL that a great deal of thought went into planning and creating a well-designed graphical interface from the bottom up. Mac users in particular will find the interface a dream; it's filled with windows, dialog boxes, menus, scroll bars, and all the other pleasant screen accoutrements that Mac users are accustomed to. (Windows users receive a similarly designed interface.)

Another big plus to America Online is how simple it is to download data and software. When you want to download, all you need to do is open a pull-down window and highlight the download command. It's that simple.

Getting started on America Online is a breeze. The software smoothly guides you step by step through the installation until you've completed it. The whole process takes just a couple of minutes.

You can navigate the service in one of two ways: either by entering a keyword, or by clicking on the appropriate icon and moving through easy-to-follow graphically illustrated "departments." America Online's departments are actually composed of these eight areas of interest:

➤ News and Finance

➤ Entertainment

➤ Travel and Shopping

➤ Computers and Software

➤ People Connection

➤ Lifestyles and Interests

➤ Learning and Reference

➤ Members Online Support

To search one of America Online's databases, you're typically prompted with query boxes and helpful instructions in plain English. Figure 5-2, for example, is what you'd see if you clicked on the

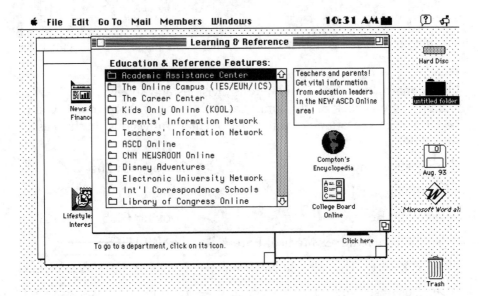

Figure 5-2

Screen for the Learning and Reference department, showing America Online's easy-to-read and helpful instructions.

Learning and Reference department. Then you can select the particular section you want to investigate further. So, for example, if you decided you wanted to go to the encyclopedia, you'd click on the picture of the globe. Then you'd be shown a screen like the one shown in Fig. 5-3.

Figure 5-3

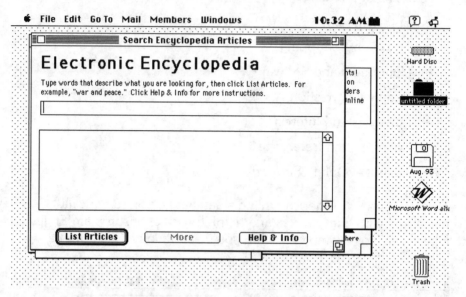

Opening screen for America Online's encyclopedia, prompting you for a search phrase.

Most departments contain numerous divisions and subdivisions. For example, if you click on the Lifestyles and Interests Department, you'd be given a choice of any of a number of smaller divisions. In this case, they'd be:

➤ Astronomy Club

➤ Aviation Club

➤ Baby Boomers

➤ Better Health & Medical Forum

➤ BikeNet—The Bicycle Network

➤ Business Strategies

➤ Business and Finance

➤ Chicago Online

➤ Comedy Club

➤ Cooking Club

➤ disABILITIES

➤ Dolby Audio/Video Forum

➤ Emergency Response Club

➤ Environmental Club

- ➤ Ethics & Religion Club
- ➤ The Exchange
- ➤ Express Yourself
- ➤ Gadget Guru Electronics
- ➤ Gay & Lesbian Forum
- ➤ Genealogy Club
- ➤ The Grandstand
- ➤ HAM Radio Club
- ➤ Issues In Mental Health
- ➤ Kodak Photography Forum
- ➤ Mercury Center
- ➤ Military & Vets Club
- ➤ National Space Society
- ➤ Network Earth
- ➤ Online Gaming Forums
- ➤ Pet Care Forum
- ➤ Radio Control Club
- ➤ Real Estate Online
- ➤ RockLink
- ➤ Scuba Club
- ➤ Science Fiction & Fantasy
- ➤ SeniorNet
- ➤ Student Access Online
- ➤ Sportslink
- ➤ Star Trek
- ➤ Tax Forum
- ➤ Trivia Club
- ➤ Wine & Dine Online
- ➤ Writers' Club

After you click on one of these services, you might find a further sublevel of offerings. Although it can take a bit of digging and clicking to get to where you finally want to go, the graphics and plain English of the system makes the procedure easy to learn.

If you already know where exactly in America Online you want to go, you can type in the keyword, which immediately routes you to precisely that section of the service. So in the previous example, you could also have immediately entered, say, the disabilities forum, simply by entering the keyword *disabilities*.

⇨ Key information databases

Now let's take a look at the kinds of searchable databases available on America Online, examining closely what the service offers in the six key information reference categories we're focusing on:

- ➤ Encyclopedias
- ➤ Magazine and Journal articles
- ➤ Health and Medical Information
- ➤ Business Information
  - Business news
  - Company directories
  - Company financials
  - Company and industry analyses
- ➤ Newspapers and Newswires
- ➤ College information

⇨ Encyclopedias

✳ Compton's Encyclopedia

Compton's is a fully searchable online encyclopedia that contains 5,200 articles and 8.7 million words. Although at first glance this might seem like a great deal of information, it actually isn't that much for a full encyclopedia. In contrast, Grolier's electronic encyclopedia, which is available on GEnie, Delphi, Prodigy, and CompuServe contains 33,000 articles and 10 million words.

To conduct a search on Compton's, simply click on the globe icon labeled Compton's Encyclopedia. A dialog box that instructs you to type in a word or phrase inside that box will appear. Like virtually all of America Online's searchable databases, you're permitted to use the basic Boolean terms AND, OR, and NOT to combine words and phrases. However, you aren't permitted to use more advanced functions, such as truncation or proximity operators, or combine and modify your search statements.

Here's what I found when I instructed the encyclopedia to search for Costa Rica:

COSTA RICA. Renowned for its democratic traditions, the country of Costa Rica differs politically and socially from most of its Latin American neighbors. Wealth is more evenly divided, far more is spent on education than on support for the military, and there is an unmatched respect for freedom of expression and the orderly transfer of government.

Costa Rica is one of seven countries, all republics, in Central America. The average distance from its border with Nicaragua on the northwest to its opposite border with Panama is 200 miles (320 kilometers). Between the Caribbean and Pacific shorelines it ranges between 100 and 150 miles (160 and 240 kilometers) in width. With an area of 19,575 square miles (50,699 square kilometers), it ranks as one of the smaller Central American republics.

In central Costa Rica is a basin area known as the Meseta Central. This intermountain plateau, between 3,000 and 5,000 feet (900 and 1,500 meters) above sea level, is a central feature in the life of the nation. Two volcanic ranges, the Cordillera Central and the Cordillera de Guanacaste, extend northwestward from the Meseta to the Nicaraguan border. Within 15 miles (24 kilometers) of the capital city of San Jose is the active volcano Irazu, 11,253 feet (3,430 meters) high. Extending southeastward from the Meseta toward Panama are the high and rugged mountains of the Cordillera de Talamanca.

Along the Pacific, tropical plains are sandwiched between the interior mountains and two peninsulas that jut into the ocean. Along the Caribbean, the Nicaraguan lake plains extend into northeastern Costa Rica. A narrow plain follows the Caribbean shoreline southward to the Panamanian border.

Costa Rica is a land of many climates. The low-lying coastal plains are hot throughout the year. The Meseta Central has a more moderate climate. At high elevations in the mountains it is cool. More than 120 inches (305 centimeters) of rain falls throughout the year in the coastal regions of southern Costa Rica. The Meseta Central and the northwest get 60 to 80 inches (150 to 200 centimeters) between May and October.

(the text continues)

Although the information provided by Compton's is useful and nicely written, the level of detail is far less than you would receive in most print encyclopedias, and quite a bit less than what's provided in the competing Grolier's online volumes. It serves as a good lesson: Don't assume that what you find online is necessarily superior to—or even equal to—what you find in an equivalent print source.

⇨ Magazines and journals

While America Online doesn't offer any comprehensive, multijournal searchable databases, it has been carving a niche for itself by offering the full text for a select number of popular magazines. While not nearly as powerful a research tool as multiple periodical databases, like CompuServe's Magazine Database Plus, it can be handy for more limited research (and fun, too).

- ➤ Time
- ➤ The Atlantic
- ➤ MacWorld
- ➤ New Republic
- ➤ Stereo Review

- ➤ Worth Magazine
- ➤ Washington Week in Review
- ➤ Wired
- ➤ Popular Photography

⇨ Health and medical information

America Online's major offering in this area is its Better Health and Medical Forum, shown in Fig. 5-4. While the forum contains searchable libraries, it isn't a traditional database of the sort covered in this book.

⇨ Business information: business news

✳ News files

America Online offers a searchable business news service, which is divided into subject specific categories and subcategories. These databases are actually a selection of relevant news items culled from America Online's larger news database called News Search. For a full discussion of that database, see the following section *Newspapers and newswires*. News files are broken down as follows for U.S. business news:

- ➤ Business
- ➤ Market
- ➤ Company actions

- ➤ Company changes
- ➤ Company finance
- ➤ Other

world business news:

> Japan > Mid-East

> Europe > Africa

> Asia > Other

and industry:

> Commodity   > Healthcare

> Consumer and retail > High technology

> Media and leisure   > Transportion

> Financial and business > Other

Figure 5-4

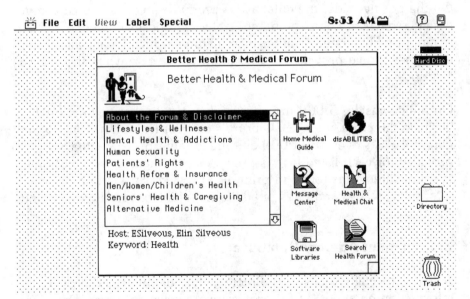

America Online's Better Health and Medical Forum, which contains searchable libraries.

Like most of America Online's searchable databases, you can perform a basic Boolean search to find what you need, but nothing too fancy. The biggest problem with this news service is the shortness of its backfile—just a few days or a week at best. That's fine for

checking the latest headlines and for catching up on recent news, but much too short for any serious research.

Business information: company directories

✳ Employer Contacts

This database contains basic identifying information for about 5,000 U.S. employers. For each firm listed, the file provides a company name, address, industry classification, stock ticker number, and the name of the CEO and/or CFO.

On the positive side, the database is pretty flexible, as you can search by industry class, company name, state, city, ticker number, CEO name, or CFO name. Another nice feature—which ideally all databases should provide—is a notation of the date when the file was last updated.

On the downside, 5,000 firms is hardly a comprehensive national business directory (your local library's copy of *Dun's Million Dollar Directory* lists over 160,000!) and the amount of data actually provided for each listed firm is pretty sparse. (Again, many national business directories found in print also provide extra data such as total sales, names and titles of additional officers, year founded, and so forth.)

✳ Employment Agency Database

This is a specialized business directory that identifies and provides information on about 2,000 professional placement firms. Data provided includes the agency name, address, phone and fax numbers, a contact name, and, where available, the agency's area of specialization. A useful and well-designed help menu makes this database particularly easy to search.

The Employment Agency Database is a special-purpose directory and doesn't really compete with the broader business directories described in this book. However, if you're searching for employment agencies in a certain region of the country or trying to find one that specializes in a certain field, this database would certainly be a worthwhile one to consult.

⇨ Business information: company financials

No databases available.

⇨ Business information: company and industry analyses

No databases available.

⇨ Other useful business services

✳ Microsoft Small Business Center

Probably the largest business information service that America Online offers is its Microsoft Small Business Center (see Fig. 5-5). However, although the Center contains much useful information and business advice, the data isn't fully searchable and therefore isn't really suitable as a powerful research resource.

Still, because there's so much data there, it's still a useful source for locating articles, seminars, software, and expert advice.

⇨ Newspapers and newswires

✳ News Search

America Online offers its users a fine up-to-the-minute searchable news service. The database, continuously updated, is actually supplied by a well-known third-party electronic news-gathering organization

Figure 5-5

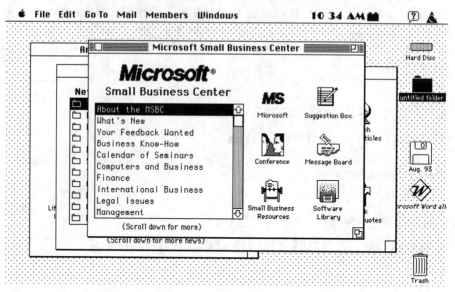

The Microsoft Small Business Center.

called Comtex, which is based in Connecticut. Comtex's news is also available on CompuServe on its NewsGrid service. Figure 5-6 shows the opening screen for this service.

America Online actually splits up this incoming newswire into a number of smaller subwires, organized by broad subject category. So, in addition to the business wires, users also can choose to search Environmental News and SportsLink, which automatically preselects stories relating to those subject areas from the larger newswire.

To search any of these newswires, users have a choice of scanning recent headlines or performing a basic Boolean keyword search. The database is updated on a minute-to-minute basis, so you can, indeed, find out the very latest news—even before you view it on the evening broadcasts or read about it in the next morning's paper.

When conducting a search, the system will first show you just the headlines of the stories retrieved; this allows you to determine which ones appear to be of highest interest and therefore worth seeing in full.

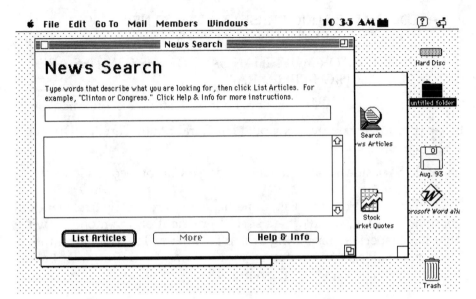

America Online's up-to-the-minute searchable new service, News Search.

Here are the results of a search I did to uncover recent articles on President Clinton's proposed energy tax. To locate relevant articles, I instructed the database to search for any and all news articles that contained the words *Clinton*, *tax*, and *energy*. Here's the list of the citations that were retrieved:

➤ Treasury sees proposed energy tax raising substantial U.S. revenues

➤ Opposition to Clinton's Economic Plan Surfaces in Akron, Ohio

➤ BTU ENERGY TAX WILL HARM THE ECONOMY, UNDERMINE CLINTON'S PROGRAM

➤ Merrill Lynch economist sees steady U.S. growth, stronger dollar

➤ Economists say fiscal boost not needed but back some Clinton plans

➤ KR ANALYSIS: Clinton plan faces hurdles, but gains crucial support

> ➤ EDISON ELECTRIC PRESENTATION AT NEW YORK SOCIETY OF SECURITY ANALYSTS

> ➤ U.S. SENATOR MOYNIHAN SAYS OPPORTUNITIES ARE RIPE FOR HIGH-SPEED RAIL

> ➤ U.S. business, labor leaders endorse Clinton's economic plan

> ➤ Proposed Energy Tax Could Hit Rural South Carolina Drivers Hard

> ➤ U.S. business, labor leaders endorse Clinton economic plan

As you can see from this list, some headlines are clearly irrelevant or marginally useful, while others seem to be right on the money. Two that look especially promising are "BTU Energy Tax Will Harm the Economy, Undermine Clinton's Program" and "U.S. Business, Labor Leaders Endorse Clinton's Economic Plan."

The next step is to instruct the database to print out the fulltext of those two promising items. Here are excerpts from both:

```
BTU ENERGY TAX WILL HARM THE ECONOMY, UNDERMINE CLINTON'S PROGRAM, SAYS
NAM WASHINGTON (FEB. 24) PR NEWSWIRE - "The administration's proposed BTU
energy tax would slow economic growth, push prices up, retard business
investment and cost the country over 600,000 jobs. It should be replaced
with a broad-based consumption tax such as the VAT," National Association
of Manufacturers President Jerry Jasinowski told Congress today.

"By all major economic criteria, a broad-based consumption tax appears to
be a superior way to gain revenue and maintain growth," he testified
before the Senate Committee on Energy and Natural Resources.

"Although the BTU tax appears to be a well-intentioned attempt to tax
consumption, in reality a third of it would fall on industrial
production. Because manufacturing is more energy intensive, the loss in
industrial production would be 30 percent higher than the loss in GDP,"
he said.

"Industries that would be particularly adversely affected include primary
metals, aluminum, chemicals, paper, cement, fertilizers, transportation
and the energy sector itself."

Jasinowski warned that the BTU tax also would harm the competitiveness of
U.S.-produced goods in foreign markets, significantly reducing exports
which have accounted for 30-40 percent of U.S. economic growth.

(the text continues)

- - - - - - - - -
```

```
U.S. business, labor leaders endorse Clinton's economic plan

    Knight-Ridder

    Washington--Feb 25--President Bill Clinton's plan to cut the nation's
budget deficit and stimulate the economy today won endorsements from the
heads of several large US corporations and labor unions.
    The White House lined up more than 20 labor and industry leaders this
morning to announce their support for Clinton's economic package, which
includes the goal of reducing the annual deficit by 140 billion dlrs in 4
years.
    "We all agree the growing federal deficit is a threat to the welfare
of the nation," said Lodwrick Cook, chairman and chief executive officer
of Atlantic Richfield Co. (NYSE:ARC), who also said the plan's broad-
based energy tax hike was "essential."
    Cook called Clinton's economic proposal an "even-handed plan," and a
"gutsy step" intended to "signal to the world that America is serious
about putting its economic house in order."

(the text continues)
```

While News Search is a nice service, keep in mind that the file retains stories for only about a week. So while it can be fine for locating the most recent news stories, it's not appropriate for in-depth research, where you need to go further back in time.

This case study on President Clinton's proposed energy tax provides an excellent example of the importance of taking the time to carefully examine the source of online news stories. If you read these two news items, you'll see that each one arrives at an opposite conclusion regarding the impact of the proposed energy tax on business. The first reports that the tax will "harm the economy," while the second claims that business and labor leaders are "endorsing" the plan. What gives?

There are a couple of important considerations here. The first is the original source of the stories. America Online contracts with Comtex, a third-party organization, to receive its news stories; Comtex, in turn, obtains its news items from a variety of organizations. The first article, for instance, was derived from an organization called PR Newswire (as is noted immediately following the February 24 filing date). The second story was drawn from Knight-Ridder, the publishing and news-gathering firm.

The difference between the two sources is important. PR Newswire is not a typical news-gathering operation. It's a firm that disseminates

press releases from companies and organizations who contract with it and pay a fee to get their news out in an electronic forum. So the first point you need to keep in mind when reading an item from PR Newswire is that, for the purposes of that organization, *news* is defined as information that a client company pays to be released to the public. That's quite different than the definition of news a traditional newspaper or wire service might use. Knight Ridder, in contrast, like a typical news-gathering organization, hires reporters who specialize in different areas and report what they feel is newsworthy on their beat.

The second crucial point to consider when evaluating these stories is the credibility of the person or entity making the claim. In the PR Newswire article, the charge that the BTU energy tax would be bad for the economy was made by a trade organization called the National Association of Manufacturers. In the Knight-Ridder piece, the plan was endorsed by cited business leaders.

Does this mean that Clinton's proposed energy tax really is supported by business and that you should ignore the PR Newswire article? Hardly. If you read the Knight-Ridder article carefully, you'll see that the "support" of the plan is only based on "more than 20" labor and industry leaders. Headlines themselves can be notoriously misleading. Since the person who writes headlines is rarely the same individual who wrote the story, there is oftentimes a misunderstanding on the part of the headline writer of the nature of a story, or a misleading concentration on one aspect of the piece to the exclusion of other relevant factors, lending an inaccurate tone.

Secondly, while the legitimacy of the claims made by the trade association quoted in the PR Newswire article must be viewed with some caution, it's a fact that this influential trade group has testified against the bill, thereby lending credence to the view that some in business do believe that the proposed tax will be bad for the economy.

The point is to always analyze your news items carefully, since no two news stories are alike. Furthermore, these stories would be just the beginning of your research! You'd need to do a lot more digging and reading before coming up with your own conclusion on the likely impact of the tax on the economy.

I don't want to leave you with a negative impression of PR Newswire. It (as well as competing press-release distribution wires) can be superb sources for tracking company news, finding out about newly released products, and keeping up with certain industry developments. You just need to remind yourself that you're reading something that a company has paid a fee to distribute. As true with all information sources (including traditional newspapers, network broadcasts, and the like), if you know where a source is coming from—what its interests, priorities, and points of view are—you can evaluate its items within that context and be a more informed news consumer.

Unfortunately, like many consumer online services, the extent of America Online's news database's backfile coverage is very limited— usually just a couple of days. So while it's a very nice headline-monitoring database, it's not really appropriate for true research purposes.

✳ NewsBytes

NewsBytes is the premiere computer news-gathering organization in the country. Like general-interest newswire services such as Reuters, AP, and UPI, the NewsBytes organization employs correspondents around the country whose job is to track industry developments and file stories.

As with most America Online newswires, you have the choice of scanning the latest headline news or conducting a search of the wire by inputting keywords or phrases into a dialog box and using the basic Boolean operators AND, OR, and NOT. See Fig. 5-7 for the opening screen of NewsBytes.

The NewsBytes database is updated continuously, so you can find out about computer developments occurring as recently as a few minutes ago. Unfortunately, like most of America Online's news databases, the NewsBytes file only extends back a few days, making it less desirable for research purposes. (In comparison, the NewsBytes database on the GEnie service extends back much further in time, making it that much more valuable.)

Figure 5-7

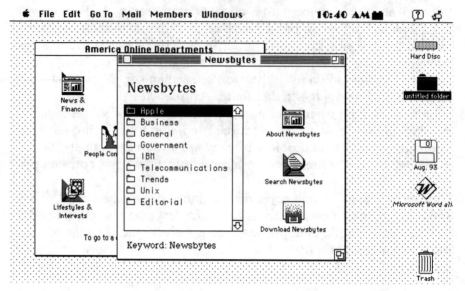

The opening screen of Newsbytes.

✳ White House Forum

While not technically a traditional database, this is a really unique information service. The White House Forum contains a searchable database of all of the White House Office of Media affairs (*see* Fig. 5-8). These are the same releases and transcripts that the major newspapers rely on for news from the Oval Office.

You can perform basic Boolean searches to locate what you need. Here, for example, is a greatly edited version of what I turned up when I instructed the database to locate any release that contained the phrase *information superhighway* (the term used by Vice President Gore and others to describe a proposed nationwide electronic data network):

```
Press Release on Technology Announcements 2.22.93

THE WHITE HOUSE
OFFICE OF THE PRESS SECRETARY
FOR IMMEDIATE RELEASE

MONDAY, FEBRUARY 22, 1993

PRESIDENT OUTLINES COMPREHENSIVE NEW TECHNOLOGY INITIATIVE:
```

Technology to Create Jobs, Protect the Environment, Improve Government
Bold Changes Proposed to Redirect, Focus U.S. Efforts

SAN JOSE, CA — Offering bold and dramatic changes to harness technology
to drive economic growth and job creation, President Bill Clinton and
Vice President Al Gore today (2/22) unveiled a comprehensive new
technology initiative to move America forward to a stronger economy, a
cleaner environment, more competitive businesses, more effective
government, better educational programs and technological leadership in
critical fields.

"In order to revitalize our economy, it is time for a dramatically new
approach that recognizes the strength and potential of America's
scientific and technological resources to change and improve the quality
of our lives," President Clinton said.

The new initiative: Technology for America's Economic Growth, A New
Direction to Build Economic Strength offers a comprehensive blueprint to
focus American technology around three central goals:

— Long-term economic growth that creates jobs and protects the
environment; — Making government more efficient and more responsive; —
World leadership in basic science, mathematics, and engineering.

"We face new challenges, from our competitors around the world and from
the people we serve here at home, that demand new solutions and creative
thinking. Technology offers new opportunities for jobs, for a cleaner
environment, for better schools, for high-quality health care and for
scores of other advances. We must move to seize these opportunities,"
said Vice President Gore, who the President has asked to play a
leadership role in implementing these new initiatives.

(the text continues)

In addition to searching White House press releases by keyword, you
can also browse and retrieve the latest releases. Here's an excerpt of
what I found for March 13, 1993:

President's Remarks at Press Availability: Conn. 3.13.93

THE WHITE HOUSE
OFFICE OF THE PRESS SECRETARY
FOR IMMEDIATE RELEASE

March 13, 1993

INTERVIEW BY THE PRESIDENT WITH CONNECTICUT MEDIA
The Cabinet Room
11:42 A.M. EST

THE PRESIDENT: I'm sorry I'm a little late, but I'm trying to make sure
we're doing what we need to do about the storm, which, as you know, is
moving up the coast with winds very heavy now in the South Carolina area.

And the center of the storm is projected to reach here as late as 7:00 p.m. tonight, so it will come to you sometime in the middle of the night. And we're working hard, but I wanted to get an update and see what FEMA was doing. And we're going to be talking today about what other resources we ought to make available.

But the winds are of great concern. And so I would just -- whatever you can do to make sure your people know that there are winds coming, and unless this storm dissipates, they can be serious, that would call for them to exercise great caution as the center of the storm approaches -- which will be sometime late, late tonight for you -- I'd appreciate it.

Questions?

Q   Yes, sir. Can we talk about the defense cutbacks in Connecticut?

THE PRESIDENT: Sure.

Q   In your -- you have a $1.7 billion plan for retraining and dual use technology. You've got $350 billion set aside for FY '93. I guess the bottom line is, when we hear in Connecticut, for example, Pratt & Whitney, they're going to be laying off 7,000 people -- sir, for people that are going -- are facing unemployment, the people who are unemployed,

(the text continues)

Figure 5-8

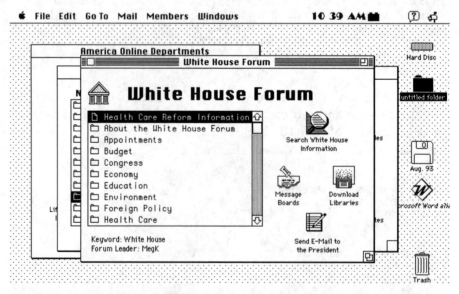

The White House Forum, which contains a searchable database of all of the White House Office of Media affairs.

Kind of fun, isn't it? To make things even more interesting, you can use this forum to send electronic mail messages directly to the President. So if you feel like dropping Bill and Hillary a line, feel free.

⇨ College information

✳ College Board

This database allows you to search an online version of the equivalent 2,000-page print guidebook to colleges, published by the College Board (see Fig. 5-9). For each school located, you obtain a long descriptive listing that contains data on matters such as the college's major academic programs, type of students attending, and admission requirements. If you know the name of the school you want to find out about, you can simply key in its name; otherwise, you can enter phrases and words with basic Boolean commands to find certain types of schools. For example, you could instruct the database to locate all schools that contain the words *Florida*, *Sociology*, and *coed*.

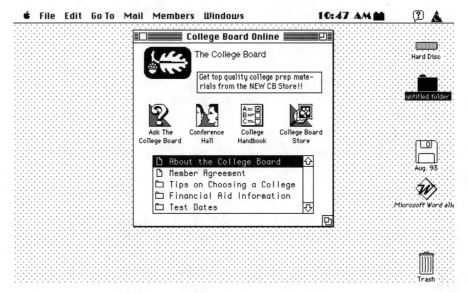

Figure 5-9

America Online's College Board Online database.

The College Board database, like most of America Online's databases, doesn't provide any kind of controlled vocabulary, i.e., predetermined and consistently employed index terms that you can look over to ensure that you use the best keywords when making a search.

Without a controlled vocabulary, it can be hard to ensure that the terms you choose to search will match up with those used in the database. One way to help resolve this problem is to simply scan a few random database records before doing a full search and note the words used. Then you can use these words yourself in your next search to try to obtain more matches and better results.

Other college board information services available on America Online include tips on choosing a college and types of available financial aid. As of this writing, America Online has announced, but not yet installed a Barrons online database. This database will provide an electronic version of the well-known Barrons college guide.

Other useful databases

The following is a listing and short description of other searchable databases that America Online offers, which will be of interest and use for those with specialized research needs:

B&B Guide This is a very handy and nicely constructed database that lists data for about 9,000 bed and breakfast accommodations.

The Bible Yes, even the bible is online. In this case, it's the King James version. You can enter keywords and phrases in basic Boolean format to locate relevant passages and text.

Chicago Online This unusual service is actually a joint venture between America Online and The Chicago Tribune. It provides online news, features, entertainment, sports, and other information reported in the Chicago Tribune. While it will probably be of highest interest to users in the Chicago area, much of it would be of national relevance as well.

David Horowitz This well-known consumer advocate's advice and reports can be searched and read online.

Job Listings America Online makes three different services available for persons interested in finding employment opportunities:

E-Span Contains electronic classifieds, placed by firms around the country who are searching for candidates to fill open positions. The database is updated weekly.

Help Wanted-USA Contains similar postings and is broken down into two separate files: one contains employment ads uploaded during the current week, and the other contains ads from the previous week. This database is also updated weekly.

Classifieds Bulletin Board Allows users to place their own ads or read ads placed by other America Online members.

Kidsnet This unusual database allows parents, teachers, and other interested users to locate information on television shows geared specifically for children. Significantly, the database not only supports basic Boolean searching, but also allows users to narrow searches by several criteria: specific date of airing, grade level appropriateness, availability of educational support materials, and specific network.

Home Video Update/Movie Reviews Reviews of current and older videos and movies, searchable by menu.

KnowledgeBase Microsoft has created this database to provide users with advice and help in using their software. Products covered include Works, Word, and Excel, among others. A total of 32,000 articles are available.

Network Earth This database covers topics such as population, energy, wastes and toxics, land use and misuse, biodiversity and habitat preservation, air quality and climate, and oceans and aquatic life.

Parents Information Network Offers parents interactive forums on issues of importance to them, bibliographic citations to articles

from major educational periodicals, databases, real-time conferencing, guides to other parts of the America Online service, and more.

Educational Magazines Bibliographic information on over 300 different educational magazines, journals, newsletters, annual reports and guides, and periodicals ranging from *Highlights* to *American Educator* to *Nature* to *National Geographic*.

WineBase This is definitely a niche service, but it's a very good one—and a lot of fun. See Fig. 5-10 to see what the opening screen looks like. The database contains information and ratings on thousands of different wines. What's neat about WineBase is the precise and useful way it has been designed to be searched. You can,

Figure 5-10

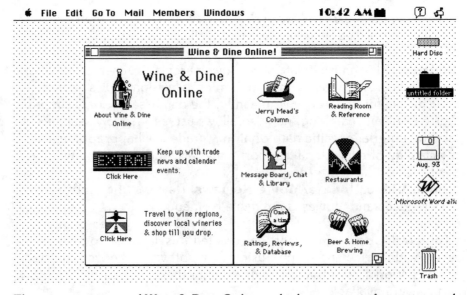

The opening screen of Wine & Dine Online, which contains information and ratings on thousands of different wines.

for instance, instruct the file to find and list all wines that are of a certain vintage, price range, and so forth. When you then call up the full record, you're provided with a nice description of the wine. Here is the result of a search I conducted to find a top-rated white zinfandel:

```
Glen Ellen 1990 White Zinfandel (92)

Updated: 92-01-15
Document ID:

WINE TYPE: Pink
RESIDUAL SWEETNESS: 3%
PRICE CATEGORY: Inexpensive
PRICE AT THE WINERY: $4.99/750 ml
BRAND NAME: Glen Ellen
VINTAGE: 1990
VARIETAL: White Zinfandel
SPECIAL DESIGNATION: Proprietor's Reserve
WINERY IS IN: Calif.
CASES PRODUCED: 160,000
REVIEWED BY: American Wine Competition
DATE REVIEWED: 06/91
SCORE (50-100): 92
AWARD: Gold Medal
OTHER AWARDS: Best American and Best Buy
```

 # Internet access

At the end of 1993, America Online launched its Internet Center service, offering selected access to the Internet. Features include e-mail and special utility programs called Gopher and WAIS (see chapter 7). However, unlike Delphi, America Online (as of this writing) has not made full Internet access available, which allows users to log onto remote computers and download data. America Online's philosophy is to take things slowly while introducing the Internet, because it's such a complex system.

 # Special-interest groups

America Online has a lot to offer when it comes to special-interest groups. As mentioned earlier, while SIGs are quite different than databases, they can still be valuable online information resources and could provide certain insights not normally available from traditional online databases. For example, while browsing in America Online's Issues in Mental Health folder, I came across a group of members

discussing in great detail and with great emotion a psychological disorder known as *borderline personality disorder*.

It was fascinating to "listen in" on these people's sharing of experiences, whether it be the problems of living with persons who have the disorder or working on recovery. It was clear that the people who were participating in this dialog were learning a great deal from each other simply by sharing their experiences and insights.

Although SIGs don't typically offer searchable databases, SIGs on America Online normally do contain a library feature where members can, by navigating hierarchical menus, browse and obtain hundreds or thousands of articles and reports as well as download tons of useful software programs. Again, while not nearly as efficient a research resource as a searchable database, SIGs can play a role in uncovering information—especially where personal experiences are relevant to your research.

Here is a sample of America Online's special-interest groups:

Astronomy	Home Office Computing
Aviation	Horoscopes
Baby Boomers	Investors
Bicycle Network	Mental Health
Book Bestsellers	Military & Vets
Business & Finance	Movie Reviews & News
Comedy	Multiple Sclerosis
Cooking	Music Notes
Desktop publishing	Pet Care
Disabilities	Real Estate
Dolby Audio/Video	Science Fiction
Education	Scuba
Emergency Response	Seniors
Environmental	Space
Ethics & Religion	Taxes
Gay & Lesbian	Technology
Geneology	Television
Grateful Dead	Trivia
Ham Radio	Wine & Dine
Hardware	Writers

⇨ Pricing

Your first month of usage on America Online is free, and covers up to 10 hours worth of use. If you use more than that amount, you pay $3.50 per hour. After the first month, America Online charges you $9.95 per month, which includes 5 hours of online time. Again, any extra time is charged at a rate of $3.50 per hour.

⇨ Summary and recommendations

Pros Outstanding user interface, newly formed Internet Center, a growing selection of electronic magazines, innovative and forward-looking company, lots of downloadable files (plus lots of useful software). All services available for the same basic price.

Cons Weak in the number and substance of searchable research databases. Mediocre search capabilities and assistance.

Recommendation If you want to join the online world but don't have much interest in conducting in-depth and powerful research, America Online is a great choice. But if you're looking for a service that can offer substantive and powerful information sources, you'd be better off with CompuServe.

6
Prodigy

Prodigy has a number of interesting qualities and some unique characteristics. Among them are:

➤ The firm claims that it's the largest of the consumer online services—with membership allegedly hovering close to 2 million.

➤ It's jointly owned by two corporate giants—IBM and Sears.

➤ Its interface, or screen, continually displays a variety of pleasant graphic images and pictures to make for a friendly and visually stimulating environment.

However, there's one thing Prodigy is not—it is not a service for the serious researcher. (Maybe not even for the lighthearted and silly researcher.)

Prodigy says that it's designed to have "broad consumer appeal." And, like network sitcoms, Pepsi-Cola, and Sunday supplements, it certainly does. But by appealing to the average American family (whatever that is these days), Prodigy cannot and does not offer enough depth or substance for anyone who really needs to dig for facts and hard information.

Not that there isn't anything of substance on Prodigy. In fact, there's a very decent selection of personal investment and financial services, articles from the popular *Consumer Reports* magazine, and a perfectly fine online encyclopedia. There's also a headline news service, though it's not searchable. But Prodigy is really geared for people who have decided to go online for reasons other than to do research—that is, to join chat clubs, send and receive electronic mail, check the weather, make travel arrangements, play games, and go shopping.

In particular, go shopping. Prodigy, as a true American service run by two consumer-oriented American institutions, really stresses the shopping services. In fact, you might even say that Prodigy pushes the shopping angle. Not only does the service offer numerous online "shops" where users can read about products and place orders online, but the Prodigy screen continually displays little running graphical commercials. These ads pop up all over the screen, all the time—there's no such thing as a commercial break!

Signing up and getting started

Joining Prodigy is a simple and painless procedure. After you inform the company whether you're using an IBM (or compatible) or a Macintosh, you're mailed a package of disks that contain the Prodigy software. Installation is a snap. The software guides you step by step into the system until you're officially registered and online.

Getting around and navigating Prodigy is equally easy. The quickest way to move from service to service is by keying in special "jump" words, which instruct Prodigy to take you from, say, Groliers Encyclopedia to The Cooking Club to Jokes from Our Members. See Fig. 6-1 for an opening Prodigy screen.

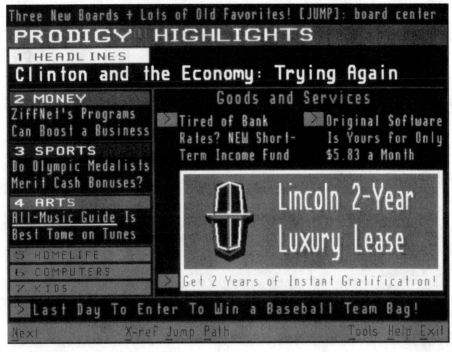

Figure 6-1

Opening Prodigy screen.

Key information databases

Here's what you can find in the key reference areas:

Encyclopedias

❊ **Grolier's Academic American Encyclopedia**

This is probably Prodigy's strongest reference resource. Grolier's Academic American Encyclopedia contains 32,000 articles, fully searchable via a single phrase (see Fig. 6-2). You can download the data onto your disk for later printing. One drawback to searching Grolier's on Prodigy, though, is that because the system displays type so large you can't see much more than a few lines on your screen at

Figure 6-2

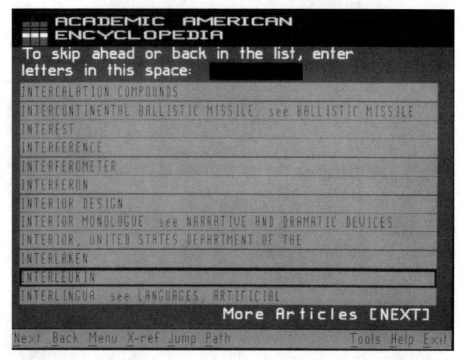

Grolier's Academic American Encyclopedia, available through Prodigy.

any one time. This makes for some pretty slow going when trying to get through a complete article, though they can be printed offline to speed things up. Grolier's is updated quarterly.

⇨ Magazines and journals

✳ Consumer Reports

The fulltext of recent *Consumer Reports* issues is available on Prodigy (see Fig. 6-3). However (as with the Consumer Reports file on many other online services), you can't perform keyword searches; instead, a menu system displays categories of products that you choose from to highlight what you want to read. While not a very powerful service, it's a handy one that some people will find useful. (Though not necessarily all that much easier than going to the library and asking for the recent *Consumer Reports* index!)

Figure 6-3

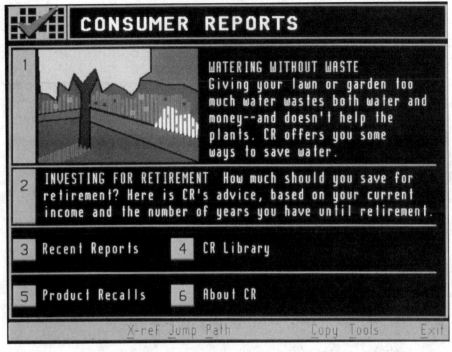

The Consumer Reports database, which offers the fulltext of recent issues of Consumer Reports.

⇨ Health and medical information

No searchable databases.

⇨ Business information: business news

✳ Business News

Under this category, Prodigy offers a modest service provided by Dow Jones News/Retrieval that locates the fulltext of business news stories that were filed during the last seven days. Users can search by company name, industry category (from a list of 75), news category, or stock symbol. It's a handy service, though the shortish backfile makes it more useful as a headline alert tool rather than a real research resource.

➡️ Business information: company directories

While Prodigy doesn't currently offer any online company directories, it has announced that, by the end of 1994, it will team up with Nynex Corp. to offer yellow page directory information for New York and New England.

➡️ Business information: company financials

No searchable databases.

➡️ Business information: company and industry analysis

No searchable databases.

➡️ Newspapers and newswires

Headline news services only—not searchable.

➡️ College information

No searchable databases.

➡️ Other databases

Since it's clear that Prodigy's offerings for the serious researcher is pretty limited—and since I've been giving it something of a hard time—I'm going to cut it a little slack and mention a few of its databases that are actually pretty useful, even though this book doesn't really concentrate on these areas:

❋ Magill's Movie Guide

This neat little database, shown in Fig. 6-4, is one of the best on
Prodigy. It contains 13,000 movie reviews, which have been drawn
from the print version of Magill's movie guide. What's appealing
about this database is that you can search it by several criteria: title,
genre, star, director, or year. In addition, you can combine those
terms. So, for example, you could instruct the database to find
names—and reviews—of any and all movies in which John Huston
directed and Humphrey Bogart starred. Or which movies Dustin
Hoffman starred in that were released in 1973. And so on. What's
significant about this database—and what distinguishes it from one
that's just okay or gimmicky—is that these kinds of multiple,
combined keyword searches are something you can't do when
consulting the equivalent print version. It significantly improves the
way you can find what you need. And that's what a database is
supposed to do!

Figure 6-4

Magill's Movie Guide database.

✳ Software Guide

This is another winner on the Prodigy service: a database containing all of *Home Office Computing* magazine's critical reviews of software packages, published since 1988. Like Magill's, the big plus to this service is the number of relevant criteria that you can search on. In this case, they're: type of computer, category (communications, database, desktop publishing, education, etc.), and rating (poor, fair, good, excellent). So, for example, you could instruct the database to find all published reviews on communications software for the Macintosh that received an excellent rating. You can also search by title.

Although this is a nice service, keep in mind that you're scanning only a single publication's software reviews. You could hardly consider this a comprehensive literature search!

✳ Zagat Restaurant Survey

Okay, I know that it's pushing it to include restaurant reviews in a book that's supposed to be for serious researchers (okay, it's not pushing it—it's over the line), but hey, I'm trying to give Prodigy a break here and I support useful databases like this one. The Zagat print guidebook is one of the leading, if not the leading, guide to restaurants in major cities across the country. This database is particularly helpful since you first choose a major city and then conduct a search for restaurants based on one or more of several selection criteria: type of cuisine, special features, Zagat ratings, and price. If you were, say, travelling to New York City and wanted to go to an Indian restaurant that rated very highly but was only moderately expensive, you could key in those criteria and get a listing, review, and rating. Or, alternatively, if you were considering a specific restaurant, you could just enter its name, see if it has been covered, and, if so, read Zagat's review. (While we're on the topic of food, Prodigy also has a Cookbook Shelf database, where you can search 3,300 recipes by category of food, type of cuisine, and ingredients.)

⇨ The rest of Prodigy

The following services, while they're all databases of one type or another, aren't as powerful or well designed as those previously mentioned. Still, they could come in handy in a pinch:

✳ **Mobil Travel Guide**

This popular series of guides to food and lodging in 3,300 cities around the country isn't a bad database, but it's updated only annually and is *very* slow. Personally, I would find it a lot quicker—as well as more enjoyable—to flip through a library or bookstore print copy.

✳ **Parenting Guide**

This database contains 600 articles covering a number of basic issues that are of concern to parents. However, you can search only by a broad menu system, not by keywords. Furthermore, 600 articles is a very small database, and you're going to find only the broadest most basic advice here (e.g., how to deal with adolescents), and are unlikely to be able to zero in on specific problems.

✳ **Petcare Guide**

Like the parenting guide, this database is also menu-only, and doesn't support any kind of keyword searching. It's not bad, though, if you want basic encylopedic-type information on the major health and related issues that you might confront as a pet owner.

✳ **City Guides**

This is an unusual database, as it has been created and derived from Prodigy's own members' comments on what to do and see in major cities around the U.S. You can, for example, get a sprinkling of off-the-cuff comments on attractions such as museums, outdoor recreation, restaurants, weather, and other aspects of a city.

⮕ Pricing

Prodigy's start-up kit costs $49.95. This provides six I.D.s and one month of service. After that, the standard plan costs $14.95 per month to access core services and two hours of the plus services (or $16.95 per month if you're using a 9,600-bps modem) and $4 for each extra hour searched. There are a small number of premium-cost files, which are mostly geared for investment and stock-tracking services.

⮕ Summary and recommendations

Pros Very quick to start up, easy to use, attractive graphics, home investor services, Grolier's Encyclopedia, and Consumer Reports.

Cons Almost no powerful online databases, no gateways, slow communications, annoying advertisements.

Recommendation If you're looking for a friendly and inexpensive online service that your kids might have fun playing with and learning from, if you just want a low-cost way to do some personal investment tracking and light analysis, or if you enjoy electronic shopping, you'll probably like the Prodigy service. But if you're a student, businessperson, or consumer who wants in-depth information, you'll need to look elsewhere.

Much maligned Prodigy has managed to build a reputation as the giant that can't do anything right. In addition to offering few powerful research databases, it has alienated its members with poor management and pricing decisions, been ridiculed for its annoying online ads, and, according to *Forbes* magazine, managed to lose over $1 billion for parents IBM and Sears. Some analysts have predicted that the days of Prodigy as a player in the online world must surely be coming to an end.

But in late 1993, there were signs that the firm might finally be starting to right itself. Under a new management team, Prodigy began

signing up more powerful information providers, including Dun & Bradstreet and Infonautics' Homework Helper. It also began exploring new mediums of interactive delivery via cable TV, and revamped its software to be compatible with Windows and high-quality photos. And—is it Christmas already?—announced that its obnoxious advertisements would be relegated to "background" status. I get the sense that all of a sudden a lot is happening. If it's not too late, this still unrealized Prodigy might just make its parents happy.

7

The Internet

For years now, people have been claiming that the planet is shrinking, that barriers between nations are breaking down, and that the globalization of the international economy has made the world borderless. If you've remained skeptical about these claims, look no further than the Internet computer network to lay your doubts to rest.

What is the Internet? Like Prodigy, CompuServe, and the other services described earlier, it's an online network that allows users to exchange electronic mail, locate information, and participate in special-interest groups. But the Internet isn't just another online service—it's a vast international "network of networks." The mother of all networks. And once you've hooked yourself up, you leave the physical place that you call home and enter a borderless electronic world populated by 20 million people from over 50 countries.

Let's take a closer look at what the Internet is and what you can do with it. The Internet isn't just a single network. It's actually a "web" of about 15,000 existing computer networks, located at over 120,000 different sites around the world. It's estimated that about 2 million separate computers are connected to the Internet—ranging from PCs in the home to minicomputers, mainframes, and even supercomputers. If you know anything about computers, you can appreciate the difficulty of networking together all these diverse types of systems. It's possible on the Internet by use of a special communications protocol called TCP/IP.

One other thing you need to understand about the Internet is that no one person or organization is in charge. That's right, nobody runs the thing! There's some oversight by the U.S. Government's National Science Foundation, but there are no centrally managed services, no customer service center, and no central operations center. When you enter the Internet, you step into frontier territory—the Wild West of the electronic information age—and it's everyone for himself or herself.

What this means is that, like the Wild West, riding into Internet territory is exciting, adventuresome—and a bit dangerous. You're on your own and you get by on your wits! You might find that panning for information turns up a gold mine of data to carry back home, or you can just as easily end up wandering around lost in the Internet, regretting that you ever ventured far from good ol' America Online or CompuServe.

Where do these networks come from, and who actually creates them? The Internet contains an amazingly diverse number of *host sites*. Universities, research laboratories, corporations, government agencies, libraries, political activist groups, commercial database vendors, and many other types of organizations have connected to the Internet and, in many cases, have added (or *uploaded*) their data on the network to make it freely accessible to everyone else on the Internet.

But what exactly is available on these networks, and what can you do? Let me first tell you that if this entire book was devoted to the resources available on the Internet, it still wouldn't begin to cover everything there! But let me tell you very broadly what you can do, and what you can find. On the Internet you can:

> ➤ Send electronic mail

> ➤ Receive electronic mail

> ➤ Read electronic journals

> ➤ Take online courses

> ➤ Access hundreds of library cards

> ➤ Join discussion groups

> ➤ Exchange your views with the world
> ➤ Search online databases
> ➤ Obtain software, graphics, and video
> ➤ "Listen" to electronic radio broadcasts

Because this book is devoted to the topic of finding facts and information, I'll concentrate mainly on how to locate online databases. However, as discussed earlier in the book, an online database is not the only place you can find answers—some of the best information comes from directly querying other people. And the Internet is swarming with knowledgeable people from around the world, whose fields of expertise range from abacus collecting to Zaire's economy—and almost everything in between. One of the best—and most enjoyable—ways to get an answer to your question is to "throw out," or *post*, your query over the Internet's electronic mail, and then sit back and wait for an answer. Most of the time you'll receive a reply; in fact, you'll often get several.

One incident that illustrates this particularly powerful aspect of the Internet was related by two business librarians, Sharyn Ladnyr of The University of Miami Richter Library and Hope N. Tillman at Babson College, in an article on the Internet published in the January 1993 issue of *Online* magazine:

> In a news forum concerned with books, I asked about the source of a quote from Einstein. One response said that it was attributed to Einstein in a book by Marvin Minsky, without an indicated source. The next response was from Marvin Minsky, indicating that he had heard Einstein make the remark in class!
>
> **David Davis, Librarian**
> **Concurrent Computer Co.**

So remember, even if you're concentrating on how to find and query an organized and systematized body of knowledge called a database, some of the most fruitful answers on the Internet will be derived by your questioning the disorganized, decentralized, and even chaotic mass of ordinary people with whom you share your electronic space.

What sorts of databases and organized collections of information are available on the Internet? Well, there's good news and bad news. The good news (I assume you want the good news first—that's the traditional way) is that the Internet is jammed full of books, magazines, newspapers, hundreds of library card catalogs, commercial online services, and thousands of special-interest databases. On the Internet, you can find such diverse and useful resources as:

> Online books and journals

> University library card catalogs

> Government information

> Daily news headlines

> Downloadable software

> Agricultural statistics

> Geographic information

> Internet user guides

> Legal information

> Health and medical reports

> Online music listings

> AIDS information

> News from NASA

> Sports schedules and standings

> Transcripts from the Supreme Court

> Weather-related data and maps

. . . and, of course, countless other bits of information. One special type of Internet resource is called *usenet newsgroups*. These are electronic affinity groups (like the consumer online service's special-interest groups or forums) that allow users to read and share information, and discuss and debate issues on scores of different subjects, ranging from high-tech and technical subjects to political and social problems to professional matters.

In addition to smaller, "homemade," and lesser-known information
databases, there's an increasing trend for the major information
database powerhouses to offer their high-octane data services over
the Internet. Big players like Dialog, Mead, and Dow Jones have all
recently made their fee-based services available. However, unlike
most of the more freely distributed information resources on the
Internet, these large commercial services charge fairly hefty fees to
search their files.

Oh yes, there's still the matter of the bad news. There's no single
source that lists and identifies all of this information. That's right—
not one, at least as of this writing. One observer described viewing
the structure of the Internet as looking at a place where "someone
dumped an entire library's worth of books on the floor in front of you
in no particular order." A word that might come to mind immediately
is *frustrating*.

Fortunately, there have been attempts by some individuals to solve
this problem, at least to a degree. Certain altruistic Internet users
regularly create their own information directories of databases, which
they post for other users to read and download. One such generous
soul is Scott Yanoff, whose "Yanoff list" is one of the more frequently
consulted compilations of Internet resources.

A recent Yanoff list contained resources on these subjects, among
others:

Agricultural Information	Handicap Resources
AIDS & Gay Resources	History
Amateur Radio	Infrared Weather Maps
Archeology	Law
Astronomy & Space Report	Legislative Information
Aviation	Math & Statistical Data
Breaking News Stories	Movie Information
Cancer Information	Movie Charts & Reviews
Education	Nielsen T.V. Ratings
Food & Nutrition	Philosophy
Games	Sports Schedules
Genetics	Stock Market Reports
Geography	Sunspot Reports

Supreme Court Rulings	Webster's Dictionary
The Bible	White House Press Releases
Tropical Storm Forecasts	

That's a lot of stuff! And it barely scratches the surface. Yanoff's address on the Internet is Yanoff@csd4.csd.uwm.edu. Although it's well beyond the scope of this chapter to provide details on the specific files and databases available on the Internet, one that stands out in particular that could be of immense value to data researchers is a database called Uncover. Uncover allows users to search for information on more than 3 million articles published in over 12,000 journals and magazines since 1988. You can also order fax copies of most articles with a credit card (most articles cost about $7 to $12 each). To access Uncover, enter this command:

```
telnet uncover.carl.org
```

then select Uncover from the menu displayed. These strings of seemingly random letters, dots, and/or numbers. These strings correspond to the "home address" of each resource, i.e., the identifying location of the particular computer where that resource resides. Every host computer on the Internet has both a unique identification number and a unique identification name. Normally, you use the name to connect to a host computer, but you can use the numerical address too.

In either case, the number or name consists of words or numbers separated by periods or dots. The addresses are actually coded abbreviations, which are simpler to understand than they first appear. Each part of the address identifies something about the host computer: the type of sponsoring organization, the name of the computer at that organization, the particular division or sublevel of that computer where that resource is located, and sometimes a country-of-origin code.

At the broadest level are the codes that identify the type of sponsoring organization, which are found at the very end of the address. Some of the abbreviations are:

com. Commercial, private organization, or business

edu. Educational organization

gov. Governmental organization

mil. Military organization

net. Networking organization

To illustrate how these addresses work, say I decided that my company should become an Internet provider and make available a file that provides a listing of tips on how to effectively search consumer databases. The address for that file would be derived from the type of organization, computer, and specific file. Working from the broadest level first, my company is a commercial organization, so the last part of my address would be .com.

My computer that's linked to the Internet would need an identifying name, so let's say I then applied for a domain name (usually the company name), which I could abbreviate as InfoAdv. Working backwards, then, my Internet address would read .infoadv.com. Finally, say I called the computer that housed the database of search tips infotips. So, finally, the full-word address on the Internet for this resource would be infotips.infoadv.com. (Sometimes you'll also see a two-letter country code at the end of an Internet address.) I would also be assigned a unique numerical address, as well.

One recent development has been an effort to actually compile a white-page and yellow-page-like directory of resources on the Internet. This online directory was created by AT&T as part of a cooperative Internet information service provider organization called InterNIC, funded by the National Science Foundation. The idea behind this directory is to provide a "one-stop" resource where even beginners can find what they need on the Internet. Another product catching on is called Mosaic, created by the National Center for Supercomputing Applications in Champaign-Urbana, Illinois, which allows users to point and click, and search via Hypertext.

You can link up yourself to this "directory of directories" on the Internet by connecting to the address ds.internic.net (login as guest if you're a first-time user) or call directly at 1-800-444-4345.

⇨ Getting around the Internet

It's vital to know the basic methods and commands for getting around the Internet. Although the Internet itself, as I've mentioned, is big, complicated, and composed of varying interfaces, there are actually just a few basic commands that you can use at any time while online. These are the primary tools you can use to find and retrieve information. Here are the commands and their uses:

⇨ Telnet

Telnet is the command to use whenever you want to log on to a remote computer somewhere on the Internet. In other words, this function allows you to communicate with any computer anywhere on the system as if you were an already networked terminal. Once you've "telneted" onto a particular computer, you can then use the Gopher, Archie, or other utilities described below to start locating what you need.

⇨ FTP

This is the other basic command on the Internet. Like Telnet, the FTP command allows you to log onto other computers on the Internet. However, FTP goes a step further and also allows you to copy (download) actual files from those computers to your own. Those files could be reports, newspaper articles, book citations, software programs, graphic images, and so on.

While using these commands sound simple—and in some ways they are—remember the catch is that you always have to know what computer you want to communicate with and what its Internet address is.

One of the most important things you need to know in order to find what you need on the Internet is the use of special electronic information-finding applications that have been created specifically to assist Internet users in browsing through the massive network and finding what they need. All of these are freely available for all Internet searchers. Let's examine each:

 Gopher and Veronica

The Gopher application might be the most basic of the Internet search utilities. It's a protocol that allows you to browse servers of information, organized in a menu format. A closely related function to the Gopher utility is one called Veronica. Veronica allows you to customize the Gopher menus with keywords; this is a powerful method for uncovering files and documents that cover topics in which you're interested. Using Veronica results in a menu display.

Gopher and Veronica work hand in hand. To use either function you must first be connected to a Gopher server. Here are the names of a few that are open to anyone:

Host name	IP #
consultant.micro.umn.edu	134.84.132.4 (login as gopher)
gopher.uiuc.edu	128.174.33.160 (login as gopher)
panda.uiowa.edu	128.255.40.201 (login as panda)

Archie

Archie, an interface to a catalog of publicly available information, allows you to search for a particular file or document across the Internet. Tracy LaQuey, author of *The Internet Companion* (Addison-Wesley, 1993), compares the Archie utility to a PC's "find file" utility program. Of course, you need to know the name of the file you're looking for before you can use this function. It is not, therefore, a way to perform any kind of subject information search, but a tool to help you locate a file you know already exists.

World Wide Web

The World Wide Web (WWW) utility lets you explore related documents by using hypertext—an application that links together files

and documents that contain the same words or phrases. So if you highlight a word in one document, the World Wide Web will locate other documents in that file or elsewhere on the Internet that also contains that word or words.

 # Wide Area Information Service

The Wide Area Information Service (WAIS) is probably the most important utility program for Internet users who want to conduct subject information searches. WAIS allows you to perform keyword searching on a selected number of databases on the Internet. In order to be searchable through the WAIS utility, a file or document must be created in the WAIS format. Currently, there are over 450 databases and information resources that can be searched via WAIS.

How can you obtain access to these search utilities? Once you're already on the Internet, in order to use any of them you need to electronically sign up (or "telnet") with a utility provider on the Internet. This is a very simple procedure; there are scores of providers for each of these applications, and their addresses can be found in a variety of directories, such as the Yanoff listing on Delphi's (or other Internet providers') auto-connect and help menus or in appendices of Internet reference books, such as LaQuey's *The Internet Companion*.

Signing up and getting started

Now that you know just a bit about what the Internet is and what it can do for you (other than sometimes drive you batty), you'll need to know what exactly your options are for signing up and getting online. There are basically three major routes for connecting with the Internet:

➢ If you're associated with a university, research institution, or other organization already on the Internet, you can usually get automatic access just by requesting an account. If you're lucky enough to have this option available, you should be able to sign on for free.

➤ You can sign on with one of the consumer online services described earlier in this book that offer Internet access. Be warned, though, that as of this writing only Delphi offers full Internet access. Other providers, if they offer any access at all, offer only limited access—mainly sending and receiving electronic mail.

➤ You can sign on with one of the many, many, independent Internet access providers located throughout the country. The number of organizations offering full Internet access has mushroomed over the last year. A few leading providers are:

California Education & Research Federation Network (CERFnet)
P.O. Box 85608, San Diego, CA 92186
(619) 455-3900

NEARnet
10 Moulton St., Cambridge, MA 02138
(617) 873-8730

OARnet
1224 Kinnear Road, Columbus, OH 43212
(614) 292-8100

Performance Systems International (PSI)
11800 Sunrise Valley Dr., Suite 1100, Reston VA 22091
(703) 620-6651

You can find a discussion of how to choose the most appropriate provider, along with a much longer contact list, by obtaining a copy of *Connecting to the Internet: A Buyer's Guide*, which compares and reviews over 70 different Internet providers (the book was written by Susan Estrada and published by Wiley).

Because there are so many ways to sign on to the Internet, it's wise to do some shopping around and select a provider that offers you the most. In selecting one, you should find out and get answers to the following questions:

➤ Does the provider offer full or only limited Internet access? Although most people will probably want full access, if you

want just electronic mail capabilities, you might get a better price from an organization that offers just that function.

➤ What is the provider's user interface like to use? Are there help screens guiding you step by step? See if you can arrange a short trial period to evaluate the service.

➤ What are you charged for access? Does the provider charge a flat monthly fee, an hourly rate, or a combination of the two? Pricing methods and approaches vary widely, so it's smart to do some price-comparison shopping. Many charge just a flat monthly fee, which could range, say, anywhere from $5 to $20 depending on what you get. The best way to determine which pricing plan will work best for you is to try to estimate how many hours per month you're going to be using the Internet and then plug in the various providers' fees to see which one works out to be the best deal for you. If, once you've been on the Internet for a while, you find that your actual usage varies from what you thought it originally would be, you'll probably need to revise your comparison list and see if you should choose another provider.

One provider that merits extra attention is Delphi. As of this writing, Delphi is the only major consumer online service that offers full Internet access. As a total Internet novice, I personally find Delphi's series of help screens, menus, and hand-holding practice files an immeasurable help in getting me going. Although I've made a number of errors when online and have often found myself lost, without those helpful guidelines I don't think I would have been able to get as far into the Internet as I did. So if you're interested in joining the Internet but have no experience, I'd strongly recommend trying Delphi as one way to get that extra help.

Once you've selected a provider and have entered the Internet, be prepared for some rough going. Author Tracy LaQuey advises new users to be patient and not give up too soon. She says that the only way you'll ever get comfortable working on the Internet is through trial and error. You can't, she advises, just log on to the Internet and expect that everything you want is going to be there waiting for you. Unfortunately, some people get onto the Internet, have trouble navigating and finding what they need, and assume that they're not

cut out for the challenge. But if you feel this way, remember that you're not the only one.

Let me put it this way—if you're a skier, do you remember the first time you ventured out on the slopes? Do you recall struggling off the chair lift, tangling yourself up in your own skis, and falling every few feet on the way down? As other joyful men and women—and, worst of all, those eight-year-old superbrats—insultingly whizzed past you, weren't you convinced then and there that you and skiing were just not meant to be? And just what in hell do people really see in the sport anyway? But those brave souls who decided to go up again, and again, and then again finally learned—one way or another—how to get down the slope in one piece and even enjoy the process. And others who practiced even more became one of those joyful experts who really mastered the sport. Well, like skiing, you've got to go easy on yourself, be patient, and just keep going until you get it right. And you *will* get it right!

Where does the Internet stand today? First, it continues to grow at an enormous rate and is being discussed with increasing frequency in the popular media. The Internet is also adding more and more commercial, as opposed to nonprofit, services. This is causing some growing pains and controversies, since the Internet was initially conceived as a noncommercial forum strictly for academic and research purposes. However, as its popularity has grown, the Internet has begun allowing some "gray area" services that straddle the academic and commercial worlds. That crack in the electronic door has widened, and now the commercial area of the Internet is growing more rapidly than any other segment. Although all sites still have to conform to an "acceptable use" policy, the trend is clearly to allow more for-profit services that charge a fee for their services.

There are other concerns too. Some are worried that the Internet is getting so popular that the network will soon run out of possible addresses and won't be able to add any more users. However, other experts are confident that this will be resolved by the technicians just as the phone company was able to overcome their worry of running out of phone numbers. Another issue is the ongoing difficulty most people have in learning how to get around the Internet. Again, though, my feeling is that as the Internet's popularity increases, there

will be more and more guidebooks, directories, and providers creating simpler methods and approaches for helping users get around the Internet and finding what they need.

⇨ Quality control concerns?

A final issue that I personally see as a potential concern is information quality control. This is really a broader issue that relates more to where the data on online systems comes from and how users view this data, but the Internet is probably a prime example of where the problem can be the most dangerous. Because there's no centralized control, anyone and everyone on the Internet can upload (or *post*) his own information files and offer it as authoritative advice or data any particular subject. This presents some obvious problems with reliability and accuracy of the information.

The problem isn't really so much that all those opinions, informal collections of facts, and homemade databases are out there for others to find and access. If you think about it, when we need advice or answers to ordinary questions in our day-to-day lives, we normally ask family members, friends, and colleagues. "Hey, do you know where there's a good Chinese restaurant?" or "Can you recommend a decent dentist?" or "What's the latest on the hostage problem?" or "I'm wondering if my mother has Alzheimer's—is forgetting names a symptom?" And so on. There's nothing wrong with this; it's the most natural way we gather information, and most of the time we learn and benefit from what we find out.

A problem arises, however, if you go online with a query, retrieve some informal advice or access a homemade database, and assume that you've just completed a thorough information search and treat the results as an authoritative answer. Remember, information from your computer isn't any more reliable than any other type of information. If you view what you receive online as just another viewpoint or opinion, you'll be on the right track.

Still, remember that even when you query your electronic colleagues online, you're missing a number of cues and helpful information that

you normally have when you ask friends for advice and answers. For instance, when you need advice on, say, what to do about your child's underachievement in school, it's likely that there are certain people at your office whose opinions you'd value and others whose views you'd never want to solicit. This intuition is incredibly valuable. But when you look for answers online and retrieve some anonymously volunteered discussion and analysis, you have to be careful.

You might ask, then, if you can't always trust the information you find on the Internet or other online services, what kind of information can you trust? Or is it just that some information is trustworthy and others less so? That is a complex question—and a full discussion is beyond the scope of this book. However, here is some broad and basic advice to ask yourself whenever you retrieve information online:

What exactly did you retrieve? Is it a commercially produced online database, part of a research center's document collection, a business' in-house study, a doctoral thesis, a fellow user's advice, what? While no one type of information is always inherently superior to another, it's clear that some must pass higher levels of scrutiny. For example, you wouldn't view an article published in a peer-reviewed medical journal on treatments for back pain the same way you'd view Joe Online's musings about how he cured his backache by having someone rub prune juice on it.

For any type of information you find, it's always useful to find out who created the information, what their credentials are, and why it's online. Practically speaking, you're not going to have the time to spend to do this every time you retrieve some piece of information. But for any research that's significant or can significantly impact your life in some way or another, you'll want to investigate the source.

A cardinal rule for researchers, as well as journalists, is always to get more than one source. This is an important one, folks, so I'm going to repeat it: always get more than one source. I'd feel a lot more inclined to take a second look at Joe Online's advice if a half dozen other online users logged on to confirm that their experiences were the same! In fact, I'd also feel more confident in believing the medical

journal's conclusions if its views were replicated by a few other researchers.

And once you get an answer, don't just swallow it and keep it to yourself. Throw it out online again, and ask for others' feedback.

Try to get your information from a variety of sources. What do the newspapers say—both the major dailies as well as smaller, independent, and alternative newspapers? How about researchers, scientists, businesspeople, and professors? What has been your neighbor down the block's experience? All these sources can offer a uniquely valuable perspective, all holding some element of the full picture that can help you put together your own picture.

Of course, you're not going to be able to do exhaustive research every time you need some answers. Maybe you'll be lucky and, when Joe Online tells you that rubbing prune juice on your back works, all you have to do is to try it to find out that—hey, it really does help. But what if Joe Online's advice is to spend $1,000 for some expensive herbal remedy or to do some contorting exercise that will throw your back out even further? You've got to consider what you're risking by following a single source's advice and what the ramifications are if it turns out to be wrong. Learn the art of evaluating information and critical thinking. The subject of information quality and reliability is covered in much more detail in a book I wrote on research techniques, *Find It Fast* (Harper Collins, 1994).

8

Professional and alternative online services

As I've discussed previously, there are thousands of individual databases and scores of online services. The main goal of this book is to cover the handful of major consumer online services. But there is a whole lot more out there in the online world worth knowing about. While it's impossible to cover everything in the online world in any detail, I do want to give you at least a flavor of some services that might potentially be of high interest and great value to you.

This chapter is divided into two sections. Part one takes a quick look at professional online services. The second part takes a look at a selected group of what I call "alternative" online services. These are lesser known, but are intriguing or potentially significant enough to be worth discussing. Of course, there are many, many other online services that exist that aren't covered in this book. To get a feel for some of them, I'd suggest taking a look at a book called *The Electronic Traveller*, written by Elizabeth Crowe and available from Windcrest/McGraw-Hill. Or just browse through a library copy of Gale's *Directory of Databases*.

→ Professional systems

It's important that you be aware of the kinds of professional online services that exist, why and how you might access them, and what each has to offer you.

First, you might ask what exactly distinguishes a so-called professional online service from a consumer-oriented one. While there's no "official" criteria, I believe that professional online systems can, for the most part, be distinguished by the following six characteristics:

> Professional systems concentrate on providing information databases almost exclusively. There are few, if any, extra services such as games, special-interest groups, clubs, and so forth.

> The individual databases themselves found on the system are typically top of the line in terms of research value, that is they often contain in-depth specialized information, are very large (some contain over a million items of information), offer a very long backfile, and are updated frequently.

> Conducting a search on a professional-level service is normally more complex than on a consumer-oriented one. New users usually need training and practice in conducting effective online searches.

> Searching on a professional system also allows for a high level of flexibility, and users can conduct sophisticated searches in order to more precisely locate exactly the kind of information required.

> The cost to search a professional database can run quite high. For example, spending $20 to $30 for a 15-minute search isn't uncommon.

> The vendors of these systems market them mainly to professional researchers. While the types of individuals that compose the professional research field vary widely, it might include, for example, librarians and information specialists, market researchers, research scientists, lawyers, journalists, and financial analysts.

There are a number of online services that fall under this category. But there are really only a handful, five to be precise, that have truly made a major impact and a name for themselves in the professional research community.

The following sections provides a short description of these five major broad-based professional online hosts.

 # DataStar

Swiss-based DataStar is well known in the professional online community for its highly respected European and international databases, as well as its innovative and forward-looking approach to searching. In 1993, DataStar was purchased by Dialog Information Services (see the following section), which has stated its intention of keeping DataStar operating as a separate and independent entity. The following is a partial listing of DataStar databases (the four-letter code following each database is its label):

✳ Aerospace

Flightline—Aviation (FLIG)
Frost & Sullivan Market Research (FSMR)
DRT European Business Report (DRTE)
ICC Stockbroker Research (ICBR)
INVESTEXT Broker Report (INVE)
Predicasts: Aerospace/Defense Markets & Technology (PTDT)
Predicasts: Newsletters (PTBN)
Predicasts: PROMT—Markets & Technology (PTSP)
Reuter Textline (TXLN)
Trade and Industry Database (INDY)

✳ Healthcare

Ärzte Zeitung Online (AEZT)
British Medical Association: Press Cuttings (BMAP)
CAB Abstracts (CABI)
DHSS-DATA—Health Administration (DHSS)
Medical Toxicology and Health (DHMT)

General Practitioner (GPGP)
Health Periodicals (HLTH)
Health Planning and Administration (HLPA)
HESLINE—Health & Safety (HSLI)
Magazine Database (MAGS)
Nursing & Allied Health (NAHL)
Predicasts: PharmaBiomed (PTPB)
Sports—Sports Medicine (SPOR)

✳ News

British Medical Association: Press Cuttings (BMAP)
German Business Statistics (FAKT)
FINF-TEXT—German Company News (FITT)
IL Sole 24 Ore (SOLE/SOLD)
Japan News wire (JPNW/JPND)
Jerusalem Post Electronic Edition (JEPO)
KYODO Japanese News Service (KYOP/KYOD)
Russian and CIS News (SVNW/SVND)
Swiss News Agency Wire Service, French version (ATSA/ATSD)
Swiss News Agency, German version (SDAA/SDAD)
Swiss News Agency, Italian version (AGZA/AGZD)
Reuter Textline Daily, today's news (TXLD)
Reuter Textline, news archive (TXLN)
USA Today Database (USAA/USAD)
De Financieel Ekonomische TIJD (DFET)
Mondo Economico, L'Impresa (MNDO)
The Independent (IDPT)
Moneyclips—Middle East Newsfile (CLIP)
Neue Zeurcher Zeitung (NZZA/NZZD)

⇨ Dialog Information Services

Probably the most popular system among professional researchers, Dialog offers more individual databases—over 400—than any other online vendor anywhere in the world. Its offerings are amazingly diverse, covering subjects ranging from aeronautics to zoology and most everything in between. A subset of over 100 of Dialog's databases called Knowledge Index is available through the

CompuServe system. The following are the database subject groups available through Dialog:

Business—Business & Industry
Business—Business Statistics
Business—International Directories & Company Financials
Business—Product Information
Business—U.S. Directories & Company Financials
Dialog Files
Law & Government
Multidisciplinary—Books
Multidisciplinary—General Information
Multidisciplinary—Reference
News—Newspaper Indexes
News—U.S. Newspapers Fulltext
News—Worldwide News
Patents, Trademarks, & Copyright
Science—Agriculture & Nutrition
Science—Chemistry
Science—Computer Technology
Science—Energy & Environment
Science—Medicine & Biosciences
Science—Pharmaceuticals
Science—Science, Technology, Engineering, Social Sciences, and Humanities

And here is a sampling of the individual databases available under some of those categories:

✳ Business—Product Information

Trade Names Database (116)
Thomas Register Online (535)
Thomas New Industrial Products (536)
Piers Exports (U.S. Ports) Current—3 mo. (571)
Piers Exports (U.S. Ports) Current—15 mo. (572)
Piers Imports (U.S. Ports) Current—3 mo. (573)
Piers Imports (U.S. Ports) Current—15 mo. (574)
PTS New Product Announcements (621)
Consumer Reports Fulltext (646)

✳ Law & Government

NCJRS (21)
PAIS International (49)
GPO Monthly Catalog (66)
U.S. Political Science Documents (93)
CIS (Congressional Information Service) (101)
ASI (American Statistics Index) (102)
Congressional Record Abstracts (135)
Federal Register Abstracts (136)
Legal Resource Index (150)
GPO Publications Reference File (166)
Criminal Justice Periodical Index (171)
British Official Publications (HMSO) (227)
LaborLaw II (243)
LaborLaw I (closed) (244)
Tax Notes Today (TNT) (650)
BNA Daily News (BNADAILY) (655)
Federal Register (669)

✳ Science—Computer Technology

Microcomputer Index (233)
Buyer's Guide to Micro Software (soft) (237)
Business Software Database (256)
Computer Database (275)
Microcomputer Software Guide (278)
Computer News Fulltext (674)
Computer ASAP (675)
DataPro Software Directory (751)

⇨ Dow Jones News/Retrieval Service

The leader in financial, commodity, and stock information, Dow Jones News/Retrieval also offers several top-notch news and general-information databases. Dow Jones has recently been experimenting with a new service called DowVision, which is designed to provide a

more natural English-like searching environment, geared to nonprofessionals with little search experience. All but three of Dow Jones databases are also made available by an electronic gateway on the GEnie service (see chapter 3). Dow Jones recently introduced a new flat-rate-priced service called Market Monitor, which provides daily and historical news, quotes, forecasts, and analyses for $29.95 per month. The following is a partial listing and explanation of databases available through Dow Jones:

✳ Business & World Newswires, //WIRES

Dow Jones News Stories from Dow Jones News Service, *The Wall Street Journal*, and *Barron's*.

Dow Jones International News News from Dow Jones' international newswires as well as *The Wall Street Journal*, *The Wall Street Journal Europe*, and *The Asian Wall Street Journal*.

Professional Investor Report Unusual intraday trading activity on more than 5,000 stocks traded on the N.Y. and American exchanges and the OTC National Market System (15-minute delay).

Dow Jones Capital Markets Report Comprehensive coverage of world-wide fixed-income and financial-futures markets.

Federal Filings Notices and analyses of significant SEC filings, bankruptcy, and high-yield activity.

Business Wire, Canada NewsWire, and PR Newswire Press releases on corporations, government agencies, industry associations, labor unions, and stock exchanges.

Japan Economic Newswire Same-day coverage of Japanese business, economic, political, and financial market news from Kyodo News Service.

Investext Abstracts Analyst-report abstracts from Investext. Includes easy access to full report.

✳ Company/Industry Information

//CANADA, Corporate Canada Online News and financial data on 2,200 public, private, and government-owned Canadian companies.

//DB, Duns Financial Records PLUS Financial reports and business information from Dun & Bradstreet on 1.5 million private and public companies.

//DMI, D&B Dun's Market Identifiers Company and market identification data on 7.2 million U.S. companies—98% of them private. Directory information useful for market research, competitive analysis, prospecting, etc.

//DSCLO, Disclosure Database 10K extracts, company profiles, etc., on 12,000 publicly held companies from SEC filings.

//EPS, Zacks Corporate Earnings Estimator Earnings-per-share estimates and P/E ratio forecasts for 3,500 companies and 100 industries.

//INVEST, Investext Fulltext of 50,000 research reports covering 5,000 U.S. and international companies and industries. Search by company name or text search. Abstracts also available.

//MG, Media General Financial Services Financial and statistical information on 6,200 companies and 180 industries. Compare company to industry, two companies, or two industries.

//QUICK, Dow Jones QuickSearch One command gathers information from eight databases: the latest news, current stock quotes, financial overviews, income statements, company vs. industry performances, and more.

//SEC, SEC Online Fulltext of 10Ks, 10Qs, annual reports, proxy filings, and 20Fs for more than 5,600 NYSE, AMEX, and selected NASDAQ-listed companies.

//SP, Standard & Poor's Online 4,700 company financial profiles: dividend and market figure, earnings, and estimates.

//WATCH, Corporate Ownership Watch Insider trading activity on 8,000 publicly held companies and 80,000 individuals (officers, directors, or owners of over 10% of a class of company stock).

//WORLDSCOPE, Worldscope International reports on 5,500 corporations in 25 countries. Includes corporate profiles, operating summaries, balance sheets, income statements, financial ratios, stock data, and more.

⇨ Mead Data Central's Lexis and Nexis

Mead Data Central's claim to fame includes its Lexis system, an enormously popular professional legal research tool, as well as its Nexis service, which was the first major online system to offer the fulltext (not just bibliographic citations or summary abstracts) of articles and news items. Today, Nexis is still the only online service that offers a full backfile of the fulltext of *The New York Times*, and remains the online service of choice for many expert searchers and librarians. The following is a partial listing of Nexis databases (the code following the source title is the LIBRARY;FILE):

✳ Automotive

Automotive Engineering (TRAN;AUTENG)
Automotive Industries (TRAN;AUTOIN)
Automotive Marketing (TRAN;AUTOMK)
Automotive News (TRAN;AUTONW
AutoWeek (TRAN;AUTOWK)
Car & Driver (TRAN;CARDRV)
Motor Age (TRAN;MTRAGE)
Ward's Auto World (TRAN;WARDS)
Ziff Transportation Industry, Newsletters 1 (TRAN;ZTP1)

✳ Chemicals/Pharmaceuticals

Biotechnology Newswatch, McGraw-Hill's (NEXIS;BIOTEC)
Chemical Engineering (NEXIS;CHEMEN)
Chemical Marketing Reporter (NEXIS;CHMMKT)
Chemical Week (NEXIS;CHEMWK)
COMLINE Daily News, Chemicals and Materials (NEXIS;JPNCHM)
Cosmetics and Toiletries (NEXIS;CSMTLT)
Cosmetics International (NEXIS;CSMINT)
Drug and Cosmetic Industry (NEXIS;DRGCOS)
Drug Store News (NEXIS;DRUGST)
Drug Topics (NEXIS;DRUGTP)
FDA Consumer (EXEC;FDA)
International Petrochemical Report (ENRGY;PETCHM)
Pharmaceutical Business News (NEXIS;PBNWS)
Plastics World (NEXIS;PLSWLD)
Soap, Cosmetics, and Chemical Specialities (NEXIS;SOAP)
Soap Perfumery & Cosmetics (NEXIS;SPCSM)

✳ Electronics

Advanced Manufacturing Technology (NEXIS;ADMANF)
COMLINE Daily News Electronics (NEXIS;JPNELE)
Consumer Electronics Newsletter (CONSUM;CNSMEL)
Electronic Business (CMPCOM;ELCBUS)
Electronic Learning (CMPCOM;ELCNWS)
Electronic News (CMPCOM;ELECTR)
Hewlett-Packard Journal (CMPCOM;HPJNL)
Information Today (CMPCOM;INFTDY)
Inside R&D (CMPCOM;INRD)
Stereo Review (NEXIS;STEREO)

NewsNet

NewsNet is a relatively small online service, but it has made quite a
name for itself by providing fulltext access to specialized technical
industry newsletters. These newsletters often contain "insider"
information, and can cost hundreds of dollars (or sometimes more) to
subscribe to in print. However, on NewsNet users can selectively

search and access just the data they need, thereby obtaining the needed information without having to pay for a print subscription. The following shows some of the databases available through NewsNet:

✳ Advertising and Marketing (AD)

American Marketplace (AD13)
Boomer Report, The (AD14)
Green Market Alert (AD21)
Green Marketing Report (AD16)
Marketing Research Review (AD06)
PR News (AD23)
Video Marketing News (AD07)

✳ Food and Beverage (FB)

Agweek (FB11)
Emerging Food R&D Report (FB13)
Food Channel, The (FB05)
Food Chemical News (FB07)
Food Labeling News (FB10)
Ice Cream Reporter (FB04)
Kane's Beverage Week (FB06)
Kosher Business (FB09)
Washington Beverage Insight (FB02)
Wine Business Insider (FB08)

✳ Research and Development (RD)

Battery & EV Technology (RD30)
Electronic Materials Technology News (RD31)
Federal Technology Report (RD46)
Flame Retardancy News (RD40)
Futuretech (RD34)
Innovator's Digest (RD09)
Inside R&D (RD28)
Japan Science Scan (RD29)
New Technology Week (RD23)
Technology Access Report (RD38)

Earlier in this book I discussed how some of these professional databases can be accessed and searched through the electronic gateways set up by the consumer online services. This can be a convenient and comfortable way to do an occasional high-octane search. But this more limited approach won't be appropriate for all research situations.

Under what kinds of circumstances might you want to choose to sign up directly with a professional online service? I can think of several instances when you might seriously consider doing so.

One would be if you're working on a long-range project that regularly requires you to have the best possible access to the most comprehensive and timeliest sources of information available anywhere. Another would be if you have a specialized information need that you haven't been able to satisfy on any of the consumer online services.

Finally, you might want to sign up with one or more professional systems if you're simply interested in gaining expertise in how to conduct high-level database searches. That kind of a skill can be of great value in a number of professions today. (For instance, market research, investment and stock analysis, news reporting, and of course library science are all fields where the ability to search professional databases is either a major advantage or a required skill.)

What else do you need to know about professional online services? There's a good deal of intricacy to searching these systems. For example, each system has its own methods for displaying and organizing the results of a search, and usually offers a variety of features to make displaying search results more useful. Just to give you one example, Dialog recently introduced a command called Rank, where users can sort and perform statistical analyses on the results of their search in a variety of ways.

Then there's the matter of pricing. Generally speaking, the way you pay for searching professional databases is by paying a per-minute fee for every minute you're online. These rates vary widely, and can range from a low of about 65¢ per minute to around $3 or even more. An "average" professional database per-minute cost usually

ranges from $1 to $2. On top of these fees, you're also often charged a fee for each item in the database that was located and that you want to view on your screen or print out. Again, these fees vary greatly by specific database and can range from about 25¢ to $3 per item. Finally, some online services also charge a one-time sign-up fee, a yearly or monthly subscription charge, or both. Pricing is further muddled when you factor in various rate changes depending on the time of day you make your calls, occasional volume discount plans, and other kinds of special pricing considerations.

Many professional researchers feel that the online industry's pricing method is simply a mess. There's a growing movement in the industry to simplify the pricing method and move away from the per-minute "ticking clock" plan to a more predictable and traditional flat-rate price plan.

The best way to find out about specific pricing and special search features is to contact the vendor or vendors of your choice and ask to be sent a new user's guide. There's also a customer service number you can call to get answers to your search questions.

Contact information for all of these professional online services can be found in the second part of appendix C.

⇨ Alternative online services

As I've discussed, there are scores and scores of smaller and specialized online services. For example, there are specialty online services devoted just to banking, Belgium, dancing, NATO, pesticides, teenage sexuality, Vienna, wildlife, and thousands more. To give you a feel for what's available, I've selected a few that I thought would be of particular interest to the greatest number of lay-searchers.

⇨ U.S. government databases

The United States federal government is one of the largest publishers in the world. Departments and agencies are constantly churning out

countless reports, research studies, periodicals, news bulletins, statistical analyses, pamphlets, and other information on almost any conceivable topic you can imagine. Whether it's aeronautical research, economic statistics, home-buying tips, or wind-energy analyses, if you have a query on a topic, you're likely to find someone studying the subject in Washington.

During the last ten years or so, government departments and agencies have been converting their paper files and publications to electronic format. And since the government must offer public access to almost all of these papers, free and inexpensive online services have been created and offered to the public as another means for them to find and gather all of this good stuff.

Where can you go to locate all of this government material? There are hundreds of individual databases available from the government, each with its own access policies, search protocols, and individual quirks. Luckily, though, in 1993 an electronic gateway providing immediate access to over 100 government databases was initiated by the U.S. National Technical Information Service (NTIS), a branch of the Department of Commerce. A "one-stop shopping" service, called FedWorld, allows any user to dial a phone number and then directly tap into electronic bulletin boards, files, and other information available on these 100+ services. These include, for example, databases from the Library of Congress, U.S. Bureau of the Census, National Science Foundation, Environmental Protection Agency, and many other services and data files.

To get online with FedWorld, all you need to do is set your communications software to dial (703) 321-8020. Set parity to none, data bits to 8, and stop bit to 1. Terminal emulation should be set to ANSI or VT-100. If you have questions, you can call on a voice line at (703) 487-4608. (For information on locating CD-ROM products produced by the federal government, see chapter 9.)

PeaceNet/EcoNet

The Institute for Global Communications (IGS) is the force behind several alternative online services that have gathered quite a following

in the last few years. PeaceNet, EcoNet, and related online alternative services offer an information exchange for people interested in promoting peace, social justice and environmental awareness. IGS is also the home of an electronic "salon" sponsored by *Utne Reader*, where users exchange ideas and converse on a wide variety of political, philosophical, and social issues. To find out more or to sign up, you can contact the Institute at:

18 De Boom Street
San Francisco, CA 94107
(415) 442-0220

⇨ The Well

Another left-leaning online service, one with a West Coast flavor, is the Well, which stands for the Whole Earth 'Lectronic Link. It's also a popular hang-out spot for those wanting to muse and share thoughts about social and political issues, as well as delve into a wide range of other thought-provoking issues, ranging from high technology to dreams, ethics, San Francisco Bay area issues, and much more. You can reach The Well at:

27 Gate Five Road
Sausalito, CA 94965
(415) 332-4335

⇨ National Videotex

A relatively new entry to the consumer online information scene is National Videotex, a service of Houston-based U.S. Videotel. The service looks potentially promising, as it combines low search rates with well-designed gateways (provided by Advanced Research Technologies) to a number of high-level, powerful business files. Contact National Videotex at:

5555 San Felipe, Suite 1200
Houston, TX 77056
(713) 840-9777

⇨ Homework Helper

A new twist to the online scene is being offered by a company called Infonautics, a firm whose founders were involved in the creation of the Telebase Systems Inc. gateway described earlier in this book. Homework Helper is an online information service designed to help junior and senior high school students with their studies, and is expected to be launched sometime in 1994. According to Infonautics, participants and information providers include a number of well-known publishers and information companies, such as Prentice Hall's General Reference, Gannett, RR Bowker, Compton's New Media, EBSCO Publishing, Forbes, LA Times, Reuters, Time Magazine, and others.

The idea behind the service is to offer an easy-to-use online service that can be searched by using regular English words and phrases. The student enters his or her query and then receives a list of articles, ranked in order of relevancy, to help answer the proposed question. The service is expected to cost under $20 per month. Contact:

Infonautics
435 Devon Park Drive, Suite 600
Wayne, PA 19087
(215) 293-4770

Again, while I've chosen to highlight what I feel to be some of the most intriguing and useful of the online services, there are a lot more out there in the electronic world for you to discover. You can learn more by checking some of the books listed in appendix C.

9

Consumer CD-ROM databases

A single CD-ROM can store up to 550MB or more. And 550MB of information is equivalent to:

- ➤ 250,000 typewritten pages
- ➤ An entire encyclopedia volume set
- ➤ 20 four-drawer file cabinets

That's a fair bit of information to be able to put on a disc, slip into your computer, and manipulate. (Note that compact discs, both audio and data, are spelled *disc*, to distinguish them from hard and floppy computer *disks*.) The last few years have seen an enormous growth in the numbers and types of CD-ROM information databases, especially lower-priced discs geared to consumers. These discs contain:

- ➤ Thousands of articles from hundreds of popular magazines
- ➤ The complete 21-volume *Grolier's Encyclopedia*
- ➤ Statistics from the U.S. 1990 Census
- ➤ Phone directories covering the entire country

> ➤ Government environmental regulations

> ➤ A map of every street in the United States, with demographic data

> ➤ The *Physician's Desk Reference Manual*

> ➤ Hundreds of thousands of sports statistics

> ➤ Movie and video reviews

> ➤ Names and addresses of millions of U.S. companies

> ➤ Herb and gardening facts and advice

> ➤ Facts and travel data on major cities around the world

> ➤ A sourcebook of American history

And, oh, about a couple thousand more. A much longer and detailed list can be found in chapter 11. But before we look in detail at what kinds of CD-ROMs exist and how to choose the right one, let's take a look at the history of these amazing little devices.

A CD-ROM is a shiny 4.75-inch hard aluminum disc, and it looks exactly like the audio CDs we're all familiar with. The main difference, though, is that audio CDs are encoded with and designed to play music and sounds, while CD-ROMs contain and can "play" data and information (as well as audio). But the technology is the same. Each are created by lasers, which create tiny pitted areas in the disc that encode the music or information. Those impressions can then be "read" and "played" when inserted into an appropriate player, or for CD-ROMs, an appropriate CD-ROM drive.

CD-ROMs have actually been around for several years—but it wasn't until about 1990 or so that they really took off. One leading directory of these CD-ROMs, *Gale Directory of Databases*, illustrates this growth in its January 1994 edition by listing the number of CD-ROM products it has covered since 1989: in 1989, 433; in 1990, 715; in 1991, 1019; in 1992, 1321; and 1993, 1433.

And those numbers reflect only information-oriented, searchable CD-ROMs. If you count all types, you'll find over 5,000 different CD-ROMs!

Why such a recent growth? There are a few reasons. Probably the biggest is the recent decline in price. As late as 1989, the cost of the average CD-ROM data disc (as opposed to audio disc) was well into the upper hundreds of dollars. But by January 1994, many CD-ROMs were being sold for less than $100. Some, in fact, can now be found for under $50. And the trend towards even lower prices continues as of this writing.

Related to this trend, and probably just as important, has been the increase in the number of personal computers being sold already equipped with a CD-ROM drive. In early 1993, it was estimated (by InfoCorp of Santa Clara, California) that approximately 2 million computers were equipped with CD-ROM drives—that's about double the number from the end of 1991. And it's forecast that by the end of 1993 about 2.6 million such drives were shipped. The Boston-based research firm Delphi Consulting has predicted that, by the year 2000, the total number of CD-ROM drives shipped will be 36 million.

For a number of years, the CD-ROM industry was stuck in a classic "chicken and egg" dilemma: there weren't enough CD-ROM drives out there for CD-ROM title producers to justify mass-producing inexpensive titles, but there also weren't enough CD-ROM titles around to justify the mass production of more drives. Each manufacturer waited for the other product to take off. But eventually production of both drives and titles increased, sales steadily improved, and today there are lots of chickens, lots of eggs, and the industry merrily clucks along.

⇨ Different CD formats

Unfortunately, while the CD-ROM industry might have solved its chicken-and-egg problem, consumers still have a problem: a lack of standards. Or more properly, a confusing set of multiple formats and accompanying standards. If you follow this industry for any length of time, it's not too long before you're practically buried under a small mountain of odd-sounding abbreviations: CD-ROM, CD, CD-I, CD-R,

CD-DA, CD-ROM XA, CD-WO, photo CD, etc. Here, then, is a succinct explanation of what all of those terms stand for:

CD Compact disc. This is the broadest term, and refers to the great majority of laser-encoded discs.

CD-A Compact disc audio. This is the technical term for the music CDs you insert into your CD player. The abbreviation isn't used too often; most of the time audio CDs are simply called CDs.

CD-ROM Compact disc, read-only memory. CD-ROMs are, by far, the most common type of information CDs. The ROM stands for *read-only memory*, which means that although you can "read" and use the information encoded on those discs, you can't add any of your own information. So, unlike a computer's hard disk or floppy disks, you can't create and save your own information.

CD-R and CD-WO Compact disc recordable and compact disc write once. These two abbreviations refer to the same type of compact disc. Unlike CD-ROMs, you can add or "write" information onto the disc; however, it can be done only once. You're unlikely to encounter this technology when shopping for a CD product for your computer. Instead, CD-Rs and CD-WOs are typically used by institutions and organizations who want to store or transfer their internal documents onto space-saving CDs, instead of on traditional storage mediums like paper or microfilm.

CD-I Compact disc interactive. CD-Is, unlike other compact discs, aren't a PC peripheral, but a single-purpose, all-in-one computer and CD, used as an extension to the television. These have most frequently been associated with the electronic firm Philips and entertainment-oriented CDs.

CD-ROM XA Compact disc, read-only memory, extended architecture. This is an enhanced version of the CD-ROM standard, and was created by Sony and Microsoft. A CD-ROM XA is capable of sophisticated audio, and permits the interleaving of sound and video in a synchronized and smooth manner.

Photo CD Photo CDs are a special type of compact disc, created by Eastman Kodak and designed to record and display still photographs.

A single Photo CD can store up to 100 photos. One of this format's significant features is its ability to allow users to make multiple recordings on the disc, called *multisessioning*. Photo CDs can be used on Photo CD players.

Multimedia CDs Multimedia CDs offer users the ability to display more than one type of media—not only data, or only music, or only photographs, but a combination: e.g., data and music, data and photographs, or data and music and photographs. Other types of media include video and animation. Multimedia CDs are a very "hot" product right now, and are covered in more detail later in this chapter.

These aren't the only compact disc formats in existence. Manufacturers like Sega and Nintendo have created their own types of CDs for use with their video games. And Sony introduced a smaller sized, nonstandard CD for its Data Discman.

As you can see, when it comes to standards and formats, there's certainly no shortage. As one observer recently remarked about them, "the nice thing about standards is that we have so many to choose from!"

Purchasing considerations

Confusing standards aren't the only difficult aspect to buying CD-ROMs. When you go to buy a CD-ROM title, there are a number of areas you must examine closely, including the following:

➤ Technical compatibility

➤ General content quality

➤ Data quality control

Let's look at each of these:

Technical compatibility

The CD-ROM that you're evaluating must, of course, be able to run on your CD-ROM drive. Traditional text-only CD-ROMs (technically

known as the High Sierra or ISO 9660 standard) will work on any CD-ROM drive. But if that disc was created in a different format, such as CD-ROM XA, is nonstandard in some way, or incorporates multimedia technology, your drive might not be equipped to play it.

A technology introduced in the Spring of 1993 by Compton's New Media, called M.O.S.T. (Multiple Operating Systems Technology) should ease some compatibility issues. The technology is designed to allow the same disc to operate on a variety of platforms, such as DOS, Windows, Macintosh, and Sony's own MMCD format. In other words, the CD's operating system is independent of the drive.

⇨ General content quality

Here there are two major considerations: original source data and any data created or added by the CD-ROM vendor.

The quality of the original source data will, of course, be a primary consideration in a decision to buy a particular CD-ROM. No matter how snazzy and powerful a disc is, it cannot truly alter the reliability and usefulness of the original data. You can't transform a bad reference book into a good one by putting it on a disc. If, for example, you're debating between Compton's and Grolier's encyclopedia on CD-ROM, you might want to first take a look at their latest print versions at a nearby large library, and find out which you prefer.

The point here is that you need to be convinced that the original publisher of the information is credible and has created a solid information source. Sometimes, though, there's no original print source; certain CD-ROM data is created for the first time in electronic form. For these, you can't look at a print equivalent. However, you should try to go to a retail store and, if possible, take the disc for a "test drive" before you buy so you can judge the data quality yourself.

The other general product content issue is what, if anything, the CD-ROM vendor has done to enhance or add usefulness to the original data. This might be newly created subject headings, indexes and codes for easy access to the data, summaries and abstracts from the original information, and so on.

 Data quality control

Determining the quality of a CD-ROM's data is a crucial, though often overlooked, part of the product selection process. One reason it's often overlooked is that ascertaining the quality of information isn't as easy as, say, determining the quality of an automobile. But there's no question that the quality of information products varies just as much as other consumer items such as a car, a phone, or a suit. The trick, of course, is figuring out what constitutes data quality and how to measure it.

One of the biggest data quality problems plaguing CD-ROM databases is indexing. To know why this is such a problem, you need to understand how a fulltext, searchable CD-ROM is typically created. To allow the CD-ROM's search software to find specific words in the text (which might be derived from journals, newspaper articles, research reports, or whatever the original source items are), indexers create a master list containing all the important words on the disc. When a user conducts a keyword search, the CD-ROM's search software compares those words to the master listing to check for any matches. If a match is found, the software then (typically) locates where that word came from and retrieves the original source.

However, any typos or errors in that master index list will cause a problem. What happens in such cases is that even though the searcher enters his or her keyword(s) correctly, the system might come back with a response that no such words exist in the database—since the indexer misspelled the word and no match was made! Similarly, if indexers spell a word correctly some of the time but incorrectly other times, the searcher will be alerted to only those instances where the word is spelled correctly.

The upshot is frighteningly simple: you can't rely on a database to inform you whether certain words and phrases are, indeed, in that database. And this is a fundamental error; it defeats the entire reason for database searching—to be able to locate information.

The next logical question to ask, then, is just how widespread is this problem of inaccurate indexing. One expert who has spoken and

written on the topic is Professor Peter Jacso, of the University of Hawaii. Professor Jacso has performed various computer-assisted analyses of very sophisticated professional library CD-ROMs, and discovered a horrendous level of errors. And these tests were conducted on expensive professional systems. One can only wonder what might be found on a $39.95 consumer CD-ROM! (Professor Jacso's book on CD-ROM selection, titled *CD-ROM Software, DataWare and Hardware: Evaluation, Selection and Installation* is listed in appendix C.)

As a buyer, therefore, you must be ever vigilant and take nothing for granted. One of the best ways to locate and detect possible errors is by browsing through a CD-ROM's internal index. Many, though not all, CD-ROMs will allow you to do this.

Creating the CD-ROM

I've already gone over two fundamental quality areas: that of the original source data and any enhancements or "value added" extras that the CD-ROM producer might have made. Now, though, we should look at the CD-ROM product and creation procedure itself in more detail. These can be broken down into these areas:

> ➤ Completeness

> ➤ Currency

> ➤ Accuracy

One useful way to look at these areas is to apply them to a hypothetical CD-ROM, similar to many you can find on the market today. So let's say that you're browsing through a CD-ROM vendor's catalog, and come across this advertisement and promotional copy:

Home Health & Medical Bookshelf

Now you can have instant access to the same in-depth information that doctors and other medical professionals rely on! The new Home Health & Medical Bookshelf is a simple to use CD-ROM that consists of the fulltext of articles from 300 leading international health-related trade publications, plus the fulltext of the renowned Home Physicians Reference Guide. Locate precisely the facts you need by using powerful and advanced keyword searching. Not only do you have access to the very latest issues

of these journals, but you can also retrieve stories all the way back to
1980. The price is just $95—and, for an extra $45, we'll automatically
send you an update disc every other month containing the latest journal
articles!

Are you ready to begin a little dissection? Good. Let's take these
claims one by one, starting from the top:

Claim: "instant access"

Analysis: No problem here. It's certainly true that searching a CD-
ROM for information normally takes just seconds. So far, so good.

Claim: ". . . the same in-depth information that doctors and other
medical professionals rely on!"

Analysis: Really? Says who? And if that is true, you'd better watch
out: professional and scholarly journals read by doctors and medical
personnel would be way too technical for most people to make much
sense of. More likely (and hopefully), these are journals written for
the interested layperson.

Advice: Find out the names of some of the journals. Go to your local
library and scan a few. Ask yourself if these are the kinds of
magazines that contain the information you want. If so, fine. If not,
the product is not right for you.

Claim: "simple to use"

Analysis: Simple compared to what? Compared to professional
desktop-publishing software, sure. But simple compared to other CD-
ROMs on the market? We'll see. The simplest and most effective
products offer desirable features such as:

A menu and command search mode to choose from Menus
are best when learning how to use the product, while commands are
normally a more efficient approach once you've become a proficient
searcher. The best systems offer a choice and let the searcher easily
switch between the two.

Graphical interfaces The latest and most desirable CD-ROMs have built-in Macintosh-like graphics, employing features like dialog boxes, windows, pull-down menus, and icons.

Intuitive feel This is a more subjective feature, but no less crucial. When you sit down to use the product, ask yourself if you feel lost and unsure what to do, or if you feel like you're being guided in a friendly and logical manner into the system. When you need help, is there a convenient and obvious way to get help, and is it really helpful? Remember this rule: if you feel confused when searching a CD-ROM database, it isn't your fault. It means the CD-ROM vendor hasn't done its job in creating an easy-to-use product!

Advice: The only way to find out how easy and intuitive it is to use a CD-ROM is to try it. See if you can arrange to try it at a retail store or on a trial basis.

Claim: ". . . consists of the fulltext of . . ."

Analysis: Fulltext is in the eye of the database producer. In other words, what's fulltext to one might not be fulltext to another. Some vendors call their periodical databases fulltext even if they omit items like letters to the editor, product briefs, short articles, and classified ads. But, hey, who wants to write marketing copy for a product proclaiming "almost fulltext!"

Advice: Determine for yourself how crucial it is for you to get the "full" fulltext. If it is, before ordering the product call the database producer and ask for an explanation of the company's policy on fulltext, and whether it's 100% fulltext or selective fulltext. If it's selective, what type of information is omitted?

Claim: "300 leading international health-related trade publications"

Analysis: International, huh? Hmmm . . . Ever since my local airport started daily flights into Canada it's been billing itself as an "international airport." Technically, quite correct. But not what most of us assume when we think of the word *international*. The same is true for some databases claiming international coverage. International might mean one Canadian or Mexican journal, or it could mean 25%

of the publications originate from Europe, Japan, and around the world.

Advice: If a product claims global coverage and that feature is important to you, ask for a list of periodicals included and examine them closely to determine for yourself just how many are international and exactly where they originate.

Claim: "the renowned Home Physicians Reference Guide"

Analysis: Renowned? By whom, the copywriter's mother?

Advice: Forget "renowned." See if this title was first published in print form, go to a library or bookstore, and browse through it to determine for yourself if it's what you want.

Claim: "powerful and advanced keyword searching"

Analysis: Yes, keyword searching can be a powerful way to find the information you want. But there are many levels of keyword searching capabilities. And these days, any self-respecting information CD-ROM database will have some kind of keyword search software built in. But you wouldn't assume a car was unusually powerful because its brochure proudly proclaimed that it had a "powerful internal combustion engine"—you'd need to find out how many cylinders, its horsepower, cc capacity, and so on. Similarly, you also need to get the details about what this particular "search engine" is capable of.

Advice: Find out, either by asking the database producer or by conducting your own tests, if the keyword search software allows:

Truncation The ability to search the root or a portion of a word by using a special symbol (? and * are common). For example, to search for occurrences of the words *infect*, *infection*, *infections*, and *infected*, you could enter a truncated search command like *infect**. Advanced truncation systems even allow you to place a symbol at the beginning or middle of a word to pick up variations.

Proximity searching Can you search for words located not only next to each other, but within a specified number of words? For example, can you instruct the system to not just find instances of *market share*, but also locate records where the word *market* is within, say, three words of the word *share*? This feature allows you to find occurrences of a phrase like *share of the market*.

Field searching and limiting Can you find words not just in the body of the text, but also in specified sections known as *fields*? Field searching allows you to pinpoint more precisely the type of records you need. Fields include author names, headline or title of an article, journal title, and subject descriptor.

Set reuse and combining After you've run a search, does the system assign a number to that search statement and let you use it again later? The ability to reuse and combine past search statements with new ones is a powerful feature.

Index browsing Does the database allow you to browse through its internal index so you can see and identify the specific words the database staffers have used to index the material? This is very important since, when you know which words the database uses, you can then select those same words for your search statement and view the number of postings and cross references. This step increases the odds that you'll be able to locate what you need.

Claim: "access to the very latest issues"

Analysis: The very latest? That's pretty dubious, and probably impossible even under the best of circumstances. Say, for example, that you're sent an update disc for your Home Health & Medical Bookshelf every other month. You might assume that if you were to get a disc, say, in January, that it would contain magazine issues published through that month. Unfortunately, this is rarely if ever the case. It typically takes a number of weeks for a CD-ROM producer to obtain, scan/input, and process a new issue onto its disc. So by the time one reaches you, the "latest" information on that disc is likely to already be a couple of months old. It can even be older if an issue was published immediately after the CD-ROM producer's cut-off date or if there are less frequent updates.

Advice: The best way to find out just how current a CD-ROM actually is, is to perform a few hands-on tests. Look up a recent news event and see if it's included. Or look up a common topic that's reported in almost every issue and see what the most recent dates are. Or, if the database permits (you can ask the producer or check the user's manual), search a date field and find out how many items were entered into the database since a particular point in time. Sometimes, if you just browse around the file you'll be able to tell just how recent the latest entries are.

As discussed earlier, keep in mind that when database producers promote their update frequency that this interval isn't the same as their lag time. The *update frequency* refers to how often the database producer loads new information onto its disc and sends it to its users (weekly, monthly, quarterly, annually, etc.). *Lag time* refers to the amount of time that elapses between the publication of a journal (or another type of dated information source) and the time it takes for the producer to get that data into its system. So, even if you receive an update disc in January, it's possible that the latest issue entered was back in October or November.

Claim: ". . . retrieve stories all the way back to 1980 . . ."

Analysis: That certainly might be true, but then again it could be misleading. The key issue to find out is how many of each of those 300 covered publications is covered back to 1980. Sometimes CD-ROM databases include all of the most recent years' articles and items, but are more selective for older items.

Advice: Determine for yourself just how crucial it is that you have complete coverage of older as well as newer items. If it's important, you'll need to call the CD-ROM producer and ask about coverage, since this type of information is almost never published. In fact, the database producer might not even be able to tell you the answer. In that case, you'll just have to conduct some tests on the disc yourself.

Remember, whenever you have a detailed question about a database, you're not likely to get much help from the customer service department or ordering department from a catalog or retailer. Instead, you'll need to call the actual database producer itself. You

can find these company's phone numbers by asking either the catalog or the retailer for it, or by looking up the name in a library copy of the *Gale Directory of Databases* (see appendix C).

The bottom line is that you must look extremely carefully at vendors' claims, which means not just reading the "fine print" but reading what's beyond what the product literature states by asking detailed questions and performing hands-on tests.

Other key selection criteria

In addition to all the information previously discussed, you should also check for:

> ➤ Warranty

> ➤ Vendor support

> ➤ Networking capability

And, of course, there's always cost! Many vendors are selling the same titles these days and are often bundling them with other titles or a CD-ROM player. Make sure you shop around, and don't be afraid to tell a vendor how another has priced the item. Finally, be on guard for "shovelware"—batches of cheap, public-domain programs bundled together without rhyme or reason and sold in a great big jumble. The price might seem attractive, but you can end up buried in junk.

Ultimately, of course, it's unlikely that you'll have the time or the inclination to conduct an intensive battery of tests on CDs you're considering buying—especially if they're very inexpensive. But if you're thinking about buying a product costing much over $100, you really should try to check it against as many of these factors as possible. And even with very inexpensive CDs, you might still be able to weed out the least useful ones by asking just one or two key questions or performing a short trial. In many cases, you can get some useful information on more popular CD-ROMs by checking popular computer magazines for product reviews. In fact, this book identifies a few online and CD-ROM databases that contain these kinds of articles and reports (e.g., Computer Library, NewsBytes, ComputerSelect, and Computer Database).

⇨ Multimedia CD-ROMs

Did I seem a little cynical in the way I analyzed CD-ROM vendors' product claims? Well, for multimedia titles, I can only say "Be afraid . . . be very afraid . . ."

Right off the bat, we need to define some terms. What exactly is a *multimedia* CD-ROM? Depending on who you speak to, you're likely to get varying definitions. Technically, *media* is the form and format of communication, and includes straight text, audio, still photographic images, animation, or video. And all *multimedia* really means is "more than one" form of media. So a CD-ROM (or any electronic information product) that contains, say, both text and sound, would quite appropriately be a multimedia product.

In the more popular sense, though, the label *multimedia* is typically used to describe electronic information products that have three, four, five, or more types of media included.

What significance does multimedia have for the serious researcher? Some of the most recent multimedia releases have been nothing less than breathtaking in their high-tech dazzle and capabilities. However, as of this writing, except for the encyclopedias, most multimedia titles currently on the market are geared more toward games, entertainment, and teaching aids. The "serious" information titles are still mainly text only. But this is likely to change.

If you do decide to buy a multimedia CD-ROM, all of the earlier "buyer beware" cautions hold true—and then some. The biggest potential pitfall for serious researchers is to be sold on a multimedia's sizzle, but then finding there's no beef. When considering a multimedia product, you need to be doubly sure of the integral quality of the original data sources and the capability of the search software, since it's so easy to be distracted by the shine of the product's technology.

You might also be tempted to think that all this multimedia stuff is only a lot of marketing and technology hype. I wouldn't blame you for thinking that and, to tell the truth, this was my initial reaction.

But there really is more to it than just a lot of buzzwords and press-release prose.

For example, multimedia is already starting to have a pretty significant—and positive—impact on how children are being taught. Some reports have indicated that certain kids who would never take a second look at a print encyclopedia are using, enjoying, and learning from a computerized multimedia disc. Encyclopedias are particularly suitable for multimedia, because an encyclopedia's mission is to provide users with as complete and true an understanding as possible of a particular concept or phenomena. So, for example, a multimedia encyclopedia will not only show a picture of a flute, but play a few notes; not just describe the space shuttle, but display a video of its takeoff!

And just as magazines, journals, and newspapers are enhanced by the use of photographs, charts, and graphs, so will a CD-ROM that's capable of displaying these images along with text. New uses for reference-oriented multimedia will also undoubtedly emerge for applications that don't yet exist.

As these new information multimedia titles begin to emerge, though, it's important to remember the fundamentals—the quality and credibility of the original source, how powerful and flexible the search engine is, how easy the product is to use, and how comprehensive and timely the product is. After you're satisfied that you can answer these questions in the affirmative, you can then go on to appreciate the additional benefits that a well-designed multimedia product can offer.

The other key point to keep in mind when considering multimedia CD-ROMs is the capability of the CD-ROM drive. Running multimedia titles—or at least running them effectively—requires a more powerful and complex drive (in addition to a stronger base computer system). These issues are covered in more detail later in this chapter.

Special focus: encyclopedias and reference tools

Of all the searchable information CD-ROMs on the market, the encyclopedia has probably met with the most acceptance and acclaim. Let's take a closer look at the encyclopedia CD-ROM.

If you think about it, an encyclopedia really is an ideal type of source to put onto a CD-ROM, especially a multimedia one. Take, for example, the popular *Grolier's American Academic Encyclopedia*. In print form, the set consists of 21 full volumes and weighs 62 pounds. But that same information on a CD-ROM fits onto a single disc and weighs just .6 ounce. So already, just from a storage and space standpoint, the product makes sense.

Secondly, an encyclopedia is pure information, and therefore perfectly suited to powerful keyword Boolean searching that can't be done with a printed product. Third, print encyclopedias are very expensive to buy and, while the CD-ROM versions aren't cheap, they're typically much less expensive. Finally, because the mission of an encyclopedia is to illustrate, as closely as possible, the true meaning and substance of various phenomena, the use of sound, video, and other media can greatly advance that objective.

Currently there are only a few encyclopedias on the market on CD-ROM. The two that have made the biggest impact are The New Grolier Electronic Encyclopedia (sometimes marketed under the name Software Toolworks) and Compton's. Grolier's contains 33,000 articles and 10 million words, and includes not just text but digitized video and animation, thousands of color and black-and-white pictures, and high-quality audio. Compton's product is also multimedia, and contains 9 million words. It also features something called a *virtual workspace*, where users can open as many windows as they want simultaneously to lay out materials as needed, cull them, and move information from one pile to another. Another multimedia

encyclopedia is MicroSoft Corporation's Encarta, a Windows-based multimedia CD-ROM encyclopedia, which combines text, sound, photographs, and animation. It's based on the Funk & Wagnall's *New Encyclopedia* and provides 21,000 articles, over seven hours of sound, and more than 7,000 photographs and graphical images.

How do you know which electronic encyclopedia is right for you? In addition to considering price, the best way to make a choice is to try them out and see how you like using them. How easy are they to use? How intuitive is the searching? What types of keyword and Boolean searching can you do? How realistic and impressive are the multimedia capabilities? You might be able to arrange to get a demo by going to a large computer retail outlet close to you.

What are some other reference guides that would make a good CD-ROM? Large dictionaries, such as the *Oxford English Dictionary*, have been put on disc, and again cost much less in electronic form than on print and take up much less room. Other reference guides that are being marketed on CD-ROM include writing aids such as thesauruses, quotation books, style guides, and the New York Public Library Desk Reference. One of the most popular and widely acclaimed reference CD has been MicroSoft's Bookshelf, which is composed of a variety of writing and research aids. Other related reference titles that have found a niche include the McGraw-Hill Science and Technical Reference Set and Random House's Webster's Electronic Dictionary.

The huge capacity of the CD-ROM has also opened the door to the creation of other useful reference titles. For example, a product called Street Atlas USA contains mapping and address information for every street in the U.S. And there have recently been several firms who've introduced national phone directories. Some of these allow for powerful searches such as reverse searching, where the user inputs the phone number and the disc finds and displays the address. (See chapter 11 for a listing of these CD-ROMs.)

Finally, I should mention that one of the largest producers of reference CD-ROMs is the United States government. Currently, the federal government creates and produces countless reports, manuals, books, and studies in print form. However, there's a movement to convert much of this print publishing to CD-ROM. In fact, an organization in the federal government, made up of people who have an interest in CD-ROM creation and distribution (called SIGCAT, which stands for the Special Interest Group on CD-ROM Applications and Technology), published a directory in April 1993 called the SIGCAT CD-ROM Compendium. It lists about 300 CD-ROM titles produced by the federal government, on topics ranging from acid rain to zip-code display mapping. To get a copy of this $11, 175-page softcover book, contact:

U.S. Government Printing Office
Superintendent of Documents
Washington, DC 20402
(202) 783-3238
(Stock No. 021-006-00153-8)

Or to find out more about this organization, you can contact SIGCAT yourself at:

P.O. Box 3706
Reston, VA 22090
(703) 648-4452

 Selecting a CD-ROM drive

If you don't already own one, a crucial step in acquiring a collection of CD-ROM titles is choosing a CD-ROM drive for your computer. If you also haven't bought a computer, when you do select one be sure to buy one with as much memory and power you can afford, since CD-ROM applications—and especially multimedia applications—require a lot of horsepower. In general, if you're buying a DOS-based (IBM-compatible) computer, you should try and get one that uses a 386 or higher processor with at least 4MB (preferably 8MB) of RAM and a minimum of an 80MB hard drive. Mac users would be best off with an LCIII or higher, with the same kind of memory and hard disk configuration. That's pretty much a standard as of early 1994, but recommendations change quickly with the introduction of more power-hungry applications, new technologies, and faster and more powerful computers.

Assuming you already have your computer, you'll need to decide what kind of CD-ROM drive to buy. In the last few years, prices have plummeted drastically, from a couple thousand dollars to a few hundred. A number of vendors are "bundling" selected CD-ROM titles with a drive, and offering particularly attractive package deals. Here are key areas you should look at when deciding which one to buy (listed in order of importance).

 # Compatibility with your computer

This is clearly a basic. If you're a Mac user, you'll need a drive designed to work with the Macintosh. If your computer is a PC, you need to make sure that the CD-ROM's interface (or *controller card*) is compatible with your system's architecture, which might be ISA, EISA, or MCA. The vendor should be able to help you with this particular issue. (Drives that come with SCSI controller cards are generally compatible with the most systems, though you still need to choose a SCSI drive with an appropriate adaptor, depending on the architecture of your computer.)

Compatibility with particular CD-ROM titles

This is another important consideration. As I mentioned earlier, there currently exist a slew of different CD-ROM formats. You won't automatically be able to read a CD-ROM title created in, say, a CD-ROM XA format in an ordinary CD-ROM drive, which is designed to read the original High Sierra/ISO 9660 formats. And if you want to be able to play disc photographs taken under Eastman Kodak's own Photo CD format, you must also check to see if a particular drive has that capability.

If, however, you think you're going to use your CD-ROM for only ordinary, text-only applications, and have no plans to use those incorporating advanced sound and video, format compatibility isn't a major issue.

 Speed of the CD-ROM

Once you've determined that a particular drive will work with your computer and that you'll be able to use the titles you want, the next step is to examine the features and capabilities of the CD-ROM itself. Probably the biggest feature that separates one drive from another is speed. Even though CD-ROMs represent the latest popular technology for data storage, they're still a fair bit slower than a typical computer's hard disk. And a slow CD-ROM can be slow indeed (at least relative to our expectations in using computers—it might make you wait a few seconds to access its data).

There are two major ways to measure CD-ROM drive speed: access time and transfer rate. *Access time* measures the amount of time it takes for the drive to get to the data, and *transfer rate* is how quickly the drive can move the data to your computer.

Of the two, access time is the major determinant of the overall CD-ROM speed, and is measured in milliseconds (ms). Today's drives typically have a speed ranging from about 180 ms (fastest) to about 800 ms (slowest). You should try and select a drive no slower than 350 ms. Transfer rate is measured in kilobytes per second (KB/s), and traditionally has been 150KB/s. However, the latest drives use *multispin* technology, which rotates the disc two or three times as quickly. These more desirable drives have a transfer rate of 300–450 KB/S.

Additional features

Some other desirable CD-ROM drive features are a buffer memory, disc caching, and optimizing software. The other key considerations, as with any consumer purchase are, of course, vendor support, warranty, and price. The key here is to shop around and make your own comparisons. Finally, the last thing you should do before buying a drive, if possible, is to test out any discs you have in that drive to see how well they work.

 Vendors

Here is a list of the names and phone numbers of some of the leading vendors of CD-ROM drives:

Apple Computer   Tandy
(408) 996-1010   (817) 390-3700

Chinon   Hitachi
(800) 441-0222   (800) 448-2244

Pioneer   JVC
(800) 228-7221   (800) 882-2345

Eastman Kodak   NEC
(800) 242-2424   (800) 338-9549

Because this technology changes so quickly, it's impossible for a book to advise which particular model or models currently offer the best deal. Your best bet is to read the major computer trade magazines (*PC Magazine*, *Byte*, *PC Week*, *MacWorld*, *MacUser*, etc.) that regularly test and evaluate these devices and provide purchasing recommendations.

The future of CD-ROMs

What can I say about the future of a technology that already seems futuristic? Much of what is going to happen hasn't even been dreamed of, and will depend on as yet undetermined technological and social events. But one thing that seems pretty certain is that the number of CD-ROMs—especially multimedia titles—will continue to soar in the foreseeable future.

10
CD-ROMs for free at your library

Did you know that tens of thousands of dollars worth of some of the finest, state-of-the-art CD-ROM databases are available to you at no charge? And that these systems can be used day or night with virtually unlimited printing privileges? If this sounds too good to be true, it isn't. And you can thank none other than your public library system for this saintly service, which (along with the Sunday *New York Times* and 99¢ breakfast specials) remains one of the last great bargains in America.

What's even more amazing is that although more and more people are discovering these treasures inside library walls, many others are completely unaware of their existence. But these information riches were meant to be shared, so I'm going to shed some light right here.

⇨ Some background

First, here's a little background on how all of this came to be. Over the last ten years or so—and particularly during the last 3 to 5 years—libraries around the country have been purchasing CD-ROM databases and providing access to their patrons. They've been quite enthusiastic about adding these products to their collection, and the number of CD-ROMs made available in libraries has grown rapidly.

One reason why libraries are so enthusiastic about CD-ROMs is that, previous to their availability, the only way libraries could fully participate in the information age and offer electronic information searches was to offer access to online databases. However, professional online services are very expensive and, furthermore, the costs are unpredictable since vendors charge on a per-minute basis and libraries cannot predict how long a search will last. Most cash-strapped libraries just couldn't justify or bear paying these fees. Although some resolved that problem by charging clients for online searches, this solution rubbed many professionals the wrong way since a primary mission of a public library is to offer free access to information, regardless of a patron's economic abilities. The policy of charging for an online service puts a library in the uncomfortable position of offering access to powerful information services only to those with enough money to afford it. But CD-ROMs, while not cheap, are normally less expensive over the long run, and, even more importantly for institutional purposes, offer a fixed price that can be budgeted for irrespective of usage.

So when you sit down to use a CD-ROM, remember that you're not just helping yourself, you're also helping reduce the number of guilt-plagued librarians. A worthy goal indeed!

Tip: Don't get CD-ROM databases confused with a library's electronic card catalog! Today, many libraries have replaced or supplemented their traditional pull-out card catalogs with a searchable online system. While these are designed to tell you which books (and sometimes which journals) the library holds, they aren't the searchable information databases discussed in this chapter. Make sure you know what kind of system you're using when you sit down at a terminal!

⇨ Different types of CD-ROMs

What kinds of CD-ROMs can you find in a library? And what might you use them for? To answer this question properly, I must first determine what the role of a library index is, since the heart of a CD-ROM is simply an index, albeit a very powerful one. So I'm going to take a short detour here and provide a little background.

Starting with the basics, we all know why periodical indexes are an essential thing: they save us from the nearly impossible task of trying to actually read through stacks of back issues of magazines to find the articles we need. In libraries, the most well-known and popular periodical index is the familiar green volumes of the *Readers' Guide to Periodicals*, which most of us started using when we wrote our first school paper. And although libraries still keep this hardcopy mainstay on hand (and for good reason, since coverage goes back for many years), this reference suffers from the same limitations as all print indexes: it's slow because it takes time to flip through the volumes to look up a subject; it doesn't allow searching by phrases or complex word combinations; and, since physical volume size is necessarily limited, coverage dates are spread out over a series of books, making it necessary to consult more than one volume to do cumulative research.

Some of the drawbacks of the print index were conquered with the introduction, in the late 1970s, of an automated microfilm index, which indexed articles from hundreds of popular periodicals. This product (created by Information Access Company of Culver City, California) allowed users to push a button on a terminal and quickly scan through an alphabetical microfilm index of five years' worth of articles. But while this system helped overcome the speed and convenience limitations of print indexes, it didn't allow the use of keywords and phrase searching. Furthermore, microfilm itself, while a blessing for many libraries with storage problems, has never been one of the more pleasant formats to work with. (Though at least with Information Access' system, the microfilm was preloaded and ready to use. No need, then, to wrestle with ornery film tape on those confounded microfilm readers. Compared to those dastardly devices, even a library's old photocopier seemed as easy to use as a toothbrush. Don't get me started on microfilm readers.)

So while print periodical indexes—and for a short heyday microfilm indexes—have been of incalculable value to library researchers, neither matched the capabilities of the first truly broad-based consumer-oriented CD-ROM index, introduced in 1986. This system, called InfoTrak, was created by Information Access Company, the same firm that produced the microfilm index. A few years later, another powerful consumer CD-ROM system was introduced. This

one was called ProQuest, and was produced by University Microfilms Inc. of Ann Arbor, Michigan. It would be no exaggeration to state that the introduction of these systems has changed—and is changing—the ways libraries operate and how patrons use libraries to find information.

What exactly, then, do these systems offer and how do they differ? It's worth first pointing out that, while InfoTrak and ProQuest offer different information databases and use different techniques to conduct searches, there are similarities between the two. Both are composed of the same basic hardware: a PC, an attached CD-ROM reader, the CD database disks themselves, and usually a printer. And, in both cases, to use the product, you sit down at the PC and enter keywords or phrases to instruct the system to search for and locate relevant citations.

Let's now take a close look at both of these popular systems, InfoTrak and ProQuest, in more detail.

InfoTrak

InfoTrak is the brand name for a collection of CD-ROM databases produced by Information Access Company. InfoTrak is actually not a single product, but a series of different CD-ROM databases—any one or more of which can be found at many libraries. Note that each of those databases can be categorized as one of four major types:

Index databases An index database tells you where and when an article was published. It provides only the basic information (bibliographic data) that you need to locate the magazine or newspaper article yourself. That data typically includes a title or headline of the article, the name of the periodical, the date of the publication, and page numbers. You're always provided with subject hearings, and sometimes you're also provided with a volume number and author's name.

Index and abstract databases Index and abstract databases include the same indexing information described in the previous category, but also offer a short summary (abstract) of the original

article. Typically, abstracts run about one long paragraph, though they can be as short as a couple of lines and as long as a few paragraphs. Sometimes what you learn from reading an abstract is enough information to satisfy your needs. Other times, though, you'll decide that you'd still like to obtain and read the full piece.

Fulltext databases Fulltext databases reprint the entire original text (in ASCII) right on the screen. When you use a fulltext database, you don't normally have to track down the original piece since you can read (and typically print out) the complete article. Sometimes, though, you might still want to track down the original piece because most CD-ROMs can't reproduce graphs, headlines, and other graphical items. Also, some fulltext databases omit certain short items, advertisements, and other exempt items, depending on the policy of the database producer.

Combined databases A combined CD-ROM database is a combination of more than one type of item. One database, therefore, might contain indexed, abstract, and fulltext items.

The following list is a short description of each of InfoTrak's current CD-ROM databases. Each of its products are updated on a monthly basis. Note that databases followed by the letter A are found mainly in academic and university libraries.

✲ Academic Index (A)

Indexes approximately 400 scholarly and general-interest journals, including substantial abstracts for most titles. Also provides six months' coverage of the *New York Times*. Subject areas covered include the arts, education, history, literature, popular science, psychology, economics, and cultural studies.

✲ Academic Index, Expanded (A)

Indexes approximately 1,500 journals with substantial abstracts for most titles, plus the current six months' coverage of the *New York Times*. Subject areas covered include humanities, social sciences, science and technology, communication studies, computer education, environmental studies, and health and women studies.

✳ Business & Company ProFile

A combination of the Business Index and Company ProFile databases.

✳ Business Index/Public Library Edition

Abstracts 700 journals, plus the *Wall Street Journal*, *New York Times*, *Asian Wall Street Journal*, and *Financial Times of Canada*. Coverage extends back four years.

✳ Business Index/Academic Edition (A)

Abstracts 850 journals, plus the *Wall Street Journal*, *New York Times*, *Asian Wall Street Journal*, and *Financial Times of Canada*. Coverage extends back four years. This system uses more powerful search software than the Public Library version (see the section later in this chapter, *Search methods*, for more details).

✳ Business ASAP

Provides the fulltext of articles found in 350 journals selected from the Business Index. Coverage goes back two years, in addition to the current year.

✳ Company ProFile

Combines directory information and the text of newswires for over 140,000 private and public companies. Emphasis is on hard-to-find private company information. Includes newswire releases for the most current six months. Coverage extends back three years.

✳ General BusinessFile

All of the information contained in the Business Index, Company ProFile, and Investext (public and academic library versions).

✳ General Periodicals Index

Indexes and abstracts 1,100 business and general-interest periodicals, as well as the *New York Times*, *Wall Street Journal*, and *Christian*

Science Monitor. Subjects covered are broad and of a popular nature. Coverage extends back four years for periodicals and two months for newspapers.

✳ Government Publications Index

An index to the monthly catalog of the government printing office. Includes indexing to public documents generated by legislative and executive branches of the U.S. government.

✳ Health Index

An index to over 160 core publications on health, fitness, nutrition, and medicine. Also includes health-related articles from approximately 3,000 other magazines and newspapers.

✳ Health Reference Center

Provides the fulltext of 150 titles on health, fitness, nutrition, and medical issues. Includes 100 consumer-oriented magazines and 500 medical educational pamphlets. Also provides the fulltext of five leading medical reference books.

✳ Investext

Indexing and the fulltext of company and industry research reports prepared by over 60 leading Wall Street firms, as well as regional and international brokerage and financial firms. Reports cover over 8,000 U.S. companies and over 2,000 publicly-held foreign companies.

✳ LegalTrac

An index to over 800 legal publications. Sources include all major law reviews, seven legal newspapers, law specialty publications and Bar Association journals. Coverage begins in 1980.

✳ Magazine Index Plus

Indexing of the 400 general-interest magazines most frequently found in public libraries, plus the current two months of the *New York*

Times and *Wall Street Journal*. Subject areas covered include current affairs, consumer information, travel, arts, and entertainment.

✳ Magazine ASAP Plus

Provides the fulltext of articles found in 100 titles selected from Magazine Index Plus. Coverage is for a total of two years.

✳ Magazine ASAP Select

Provides the fulltext of 50 titles selected from Magazine Index Plus. Covers two years.

✳ National Newspaper Index

Indexing of five national newspapers combined in one source. Covers indexing of the *New York Times*, *Wall Street Journal*, *Christian Science Monitor*, *Washington Post*, and *Los Angeles Times*.

⇨ UMI's ProQuest

The following list is a short description of UMI ProQuest's CD-ROM databases:

✳ ABI/INFORM

Provides 150 word abstracts from articles published in major leading business periodicals. Two versions are available. One scans 900 journals and coverage extends back five years; the other scans 100 journals and also extends back five years. Some libraries might also subscribe to the ABI/Inform Backfile system: one contains indexes for the years 1971 to 1980 and the other covers 1981 to 1986.

✳ Business Dateline

Provides the fulltext of articles from 350 regional business journals. Coverage extends back to 1985. Regional business journals include titles such as *Crain's New York Business* and *Kansas City Business Journal*.

✳ Newspaper Abstracts

Provides indexing (and brief abstracts) for eight major national newspapers: the *New York Times*, *Atlanta Constitution*, *Boston Globe*, *Chicago Tribune*, *Christian Science Monitor*, *Los Angeles Times*, *Wall Street Journal*, and *Washington Post*. Coverage extends back to 1985.

✳ Newspapers Fulltext

This database provides the fulltext of *American Banker*, *Atlanta Constitution*, *Atlanta Journal*, *Christian Science Monitor*, *New York Times*, *San Francisco Chronicle*, *USA Today*, *Wall Street Journal*, and *Washington Post*. Coverage extends back two years.

✳ New York Times Ondisc

Provides the fulltext of articles printed in the *New York Times*. Updated monthly.

✳ Periodical Abstracts

Abstracts hundreds of popular magazine articles. There are three versions of this database. One abstracts 1,500 journals, extends back to 1986, and also includes the last six months of the *New York Times* and *Wall Street Journal*; a second version contains abstracts from 950 journals and also extends back to 1986; and the third version abstracts 500 journals back to 1986 and covers six months of the *New York Times* and *USA Today*.

✳ Resource One

This small system provides abstracts of articles from 140 periodicals extending back to 1986, *USA Today* to 1991, and includes a selection of articles from the *New York Times*.

ProQuest also produces the following databases, which aren't quite as frequently encountered by the general public as the ones listed previously:

➤ Dissertation abstracts (abstracts of doctoral dissertations)

➤ Inspec (abstracts from journals covering IEE journals of electrical engineering, physics, and computing)

Finally, UMI's newest series of databases are what it calls *full-image CD-ROMs*. Unlike ordinary CD-ROMs, these discs are able to reproduce exact replicas of the original print source, including headlines, graphs, and images. As of this writing, few public libraries have these newer and more expensive systems installed. If you come across one, however, I'd recommend using it. They're quite impressive and provide results that are much more aesthetically pleasing than text-only CD-ROMs. Figure 10-1 shows the difference between ordinary fulltext and an image-based product, from an advertisement by UMI.

Figure 10-1

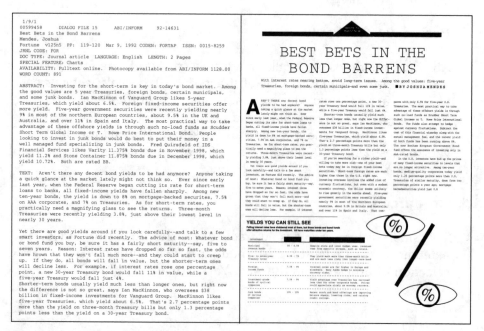

Reprint of a UMI advertisement, showing the difference between ordinary fulltext and an image-based product. University Microfilms Inc., Ann Arbor, MI, 1993

Currently, UMI offers the following full-image CD-ROMs:

> ➤ Business periodicals
> ➤ General periodicals
> ➤ IEEE/IEE publications
> ➤ Magazine express
> ➤ Social science index

Most of those titles correspond directly to one of UMI's ordinary text-only CD-ROM databases and are designed to work in tandem with them. The way these systems typically work is that the search itself is not done on the full image, but on a companion file containing just titles, subject headings, or abstracts of the item. Once a match is made, the system locates that article on the image CD-ROM, retrieves it, and displays it on the screen. It's then available for printing on an attached laser printer.

How do you know which library near you has one or more of these InfoTrak or ProQuest CD-ROMs? The simplest way is to call your local libraries and ask. If you live near a college or university, you'll probably find that these institutions will have a larger selection (since they usually have more money).

As you can see from the previous listings, all CD-ROM databases are certainly not alike! Novice users sometimes mistakenly believe otherwise if, for example, they've used an InfoTrak system at one library. It's easy to assume that another InfoTrak terminal at another library (or even in another section of the same library) would contain the same type of data.

Such an assumption could cause a major problem. Clearly, if you're doing business research, you'd want to make sure you're searching one of the business databases. So be sure that whenever you sit down at a CD-ROM workstation you find out which database or databases are actually available and loaded onto the system. You can usually find this out by looking for a sign next to the computer that identifies and describes the database, or by looking right on the opening screen

for the information. If you can't find either of these identifiers, just ask the closest librarian.

Not only do the various CD-ROMs provide information on different subjects, but they also differ in other significant ways: by type of database (index, abstract, or fulltext) and comprehensiveness (usually measured by the number of periodicals scanned and numbers of years covered). These differences can be extremely significant. For example, if you're searching for articles about an incident that happened three years ago but the CD-ROM database you're using covers only two years worth of articles, you're not going to get too far. Similarly, if you need to conduct a comprehensive search for articles published in the popular press but the database you've selected scans only 50 publications, clearly you had better not end your research work there.

The other crucial issue to keep in mind when choosing and using a CD-ROM system is whether or not it's current. There are really two distinct matters relevant here: update frequency and lag time. See the previous chapter for an explanation of these two terms, near the end of the section *Data quality control*.

Search methods

There's one other important distinction between CD-ROM databases, which relates to the method and flexibility each provides in searching the database. This distinction is significant because it directly determines how you locate information and how precise you can be in instructing the system to find what you need.

InfoTrak currently offers a number of different types of search software for its CD-ROM databases, which vary greatly in their power and capabilities. Because it's often up to the library that purchases the product to decide which level of search software to select with the product, you usually can't know ahead of time exactly which type you're going to find. Virtually all of InfoTrak's search software, though, can be roughly categorized as falling into one of these categories:

Subject index scan

This was InfoTrak's original and most basic search software. It's a very easy and very fast method for conducting a search. You type in a word (or short phrase) that best describes your subject and the system then displays its own internal index to show whether it has indexed any items with that word or short phrase. If so, the system will also display the number of articles it has indexed under that term. You're then able to retrieve those actual citations. If a match isn't made, you can browse the system's index (forward and backward through its alphabetical list) to see if a different term might be suitable.

The biggest disadvantage to the subject index scan approach (when used alone) is that it isn't very powerful; you can't combine words or terms, use Boolean logic, or instruct the system to conduct searches of words in the abstracts or text of the articles themselves. You can only try to match up your word with the system's own index. However, this approach can still be quite useful for less complicated searches, and it can work particularly well when used as the initial step to help you better determine the best words to use in a full keyword search.

 # Expanded subject searching

Some of InfoTrak's databases come equipped with what the company calls its expanded search capabilities, which let you combine terms and concepts and use a controlled keyword search. This is more powerful than the above search method, but it's still quite a bit less powerful than Boolean searching.

Keyword Boolean searching

InfoTrak databases that have EF software installed allow keyword and Boolean searching. Basic keyword searching allows you to enter a single word or phrase that you choose to describe your subject, and use the AND, NOT, and OR Boolean operators.

 # PowerTrak

InfoTrak's PowerTrak systems allow you to enter your own commands rather than following a predesigned menu. You can use Boolean operators, field searching, and combine sets, and conduct powerful searching just as if you were using a command-based professional online system.

If you're a pretty proficient searcher, you'll probably prefer the more advanced software because it allows you to more precisely target your searches. However, the easier systems can still be quite useful, especially if you don't feel too confident in constructing keyword searches. A key point to remember, though, when searching InfoTrak databases is to find out what kind of searching the particular workstation you're using allows. If you can't tell by looking at the screen, look for any instruction manuals placed near the terminal or ask a nearby librarian for assistance.

ProQuest

Unlike InfoTrak, ProQuest uses the same search methodology for all of its databases. Each database supports full Boolean searching, including advanced features like proximity operators, truncation, field searching, modifying and combining of search sets, and reuse of search strategies.

These are quite sophisticated capabilities for a consumer-oriented library system. The obvious advantage to using this search system is that you can pinpoint much more precisely and efficiently the exact type of articles you need. If you're skilled at searching, this makes for a very powerful and useful database. If you aren't comfortable in conducting these types of searches, however, you could be walking into something of an information minefield. One wrong move and you could be in real trouble. This brings us, then, to the next section: conducting efficient and effective searches.

Strategies for successful searching

Although the emergence of library CD-ROMs has been a bonanza for serious and amateur researchers alike, they haven't arrived without their share of difficulties. The biggest problem seems to be new and inexperienced users who attempt to sit down at a terminal and conduct a search on the fly—and end up with poor results. Not too long ago, one librarian recounted a story where she noticed a young woman working on a CD-ROM system who became overwhelmed when her search for articles on school and drugs resulted in her retrieving over 800 citations. In other cases, novice searchers have had the opposite problem, ending up with no citations whatsoever.

The biggest danger in the latter scenario is that a user might be tempted to assume that if he or she didn't find anything, then the database must not contain any items on that subject or that such information doesn't exist. What's more likely, however, is that the user either used ineffective search words or entered them in the wrong order or format, causing the system to miss the relevant citations.

Unfortunately, there's very little formal instruction for the general public on how to be a better CD-ROM searcher. The vendors of the systems do try to publish easy-to-understand documentation and have been working on creating CD-ROMs that are as self-explanatory and easy to use as possible. In fact, ProQuest and InfoTrak's EF systems both use nice pop-up help screens that provide instant tutorials that address users' questions as they occur. But as useful as these features are, they're no substitute for hands-on training or classes. Librarians, who would be excellent candidates for giving such classes, are usually too time-strapped to add an extra duty to their schedules. The result is that you need to educate yourself.

What can you do to ensure that your search strategy is a good one? Appendix B is devoted specifically to the topic of conducting keyword and Boolean searches. I'd recommend reading it before trying any

advanced Boolean searches. In addition, follow these general guidelines:

➤ Always read the descriptive literature that's posted next to the system. This usually consists of a stand-up card or small booklet that describes the databases and explains how to conduct a search.

➤ Fool around with the system. Practice with different words and word combinations. Notice what seems to work and what doesn't. Take notes.

➤ When you feel pretty comfortable with a system, take a few minutes out to think about and write down your search strategy. This is what you're going to enter into the computer to locate relevant articles.

➤ If your search is unsuccessful (if you received too many, too few, or irrelevant citations), don't give up. Consider asking a nearby librarian for help in creating a search statement. These people are experienced at conducting online searches and should be able to tell you how to modify what you've come up with to obtain better results. Getting help from a librarian will also be useful in furthering your education in learning how to modify a search and understanding what makes for a good search statement.

➤ If you've had success in your search and found one or more useful articles—congratulations! To get really proficient at conducting searches, you now need to practice, practice, practice. Like everything else (except maybe flossing), the more you do it the better you'll get and the more you enjoy it.

Is one system better than another? Should you choose one CD-ROM product over the other? The biggest selection criterion is subject coverage—you've got to be sure that the system you've selected covers your particular field of interest.

Another distinction is the typical trade-off between power and simplicity. InfoTrak's ordinary index-only browsing databases, for example, aren't very powerful, but their simplicity can be appealing even for advanced researchers who want to do a quick basic search. The more advanced Boolean search systems provide superb pinpointing search capabilities, but can be slower and tricky to

navigate. Overall, though, all of InfoTrak's and UMI's products are well designed and can serve you very well. The key in either case is to know how the system and specific database products you choose to use works—its rules, its quirks, and its own ways of operating. The more familiar you become with any one of them, the more you'll find it will work well for you.

⇨ Other CD-ROMs

So far in this chapter, I've focused specifically on the ProQuest and InfoTrak CD-ROMs since they're most frequently encountered and provide the broadest and most wide-ranging information. However, there are other very useful and highly regarded CD-ROMs that you should be aware of.

One of the most widely accessible and popular systems are those produced by H.W. Wilson Company, a company well known for its print reference indexes and other library materials. The following is a list of current key Wilson Disc products you might find at your library:

- ➤ Applied Science and Technology Index
- ➤ Art Index
- ➤ Biography Index
- ➤ Biological & Agricultural Index
- ➤ Book Review Digest
- ➤ Business Periodicals Index
- ➤ Cumulative Book Index
- ➤ Education Index
- ➤ General Science Index
- ➤ Humanities Index
- ➤ Index to Legal Periodicals
- ➤ Library Literature
- ➤ MLA International Bibliography

> Readers' Guide to Periodical Literature
> Readers' Guide Abstracts
> Readers' Guide Abstracts/Select Edition
> Social Science Index
> Wilson Business Abstracts

Here is a list of other CD-ROMs you might find at a library. Some of the more specialized ones are most likely to be encountered at libraries or sections of a library that concentrate on a particular subject field (e.g., a university's business school or a governmental research center). This list is not comprehensive, by any means, but it does illustrate the breadth of products available. For more information, see chapter 11 of this book.

Agricola Agriculture, forestry, soils, ecology, flora, and fauna.

American History & Life U.S. and Canadian history, current affairs, and folklore.

Biological & Agricultural Index Indexes over 225 trade periodicals covering agricultural chemicals, engineering, biotechnology, food science, soil, genetics, and more.

Books in Print Plus Corresponding to the well-known standard print volumes, this CD-ROM provides descriptive and identifying information for all books currently in print.

CASSIS (Patent Data Library Program) U.S. Patent Office data on five million+ U.S. and non-U.S. patents. 1969 to 1989.

College Blue Book Guide to undergraduate and graduate college and university programs in the U.S., searchable by degrees offered, subject major, size, cost, geographic region, state, etc. Also indexes scholarships and loans by topic, education level, and sponsor.

Compact Disclosure U.S. Financial data on 11,000 U.S. companies.

Compact Disclosure/World Financial data on companies worldwide.

Compendex Plus (Engineering Index) Primary database for engineering and technology literature worldwide. 1986+.

Computer Select Fulltext of articles from 65 major computer journals.

Congressional Masterfile 2 Index to U.S. congressional activities. 1970+.

Earth Sciences Indexes books, journals, dissertations, etc., on all earth sciences and technology topics. 1975+.

EconLit Comprehensive, indexed bibliography with selected abstract of the world's economic literature. 1969+.

ERIC All aspects of education.

Ethnic NewsWatch Index and fulltext of newspapers and magazines from the ethnic and minority press in America. Fall 91+.

F&S Index Plus Text Indexes, abstracts, and in some cases provides the fulltext of recent articles from over 1,000 sources on companies and industries.

GeoRef Earth science information.

Historical Abstracts World history except U.S. and Canada since 1450.

Life Sciences Collection Indexes and abstracts worldwide in life sciences literature. 1986+.

MathSci Math, statistics, and computer science.

Monthly Catalog of US Govt. Publications Primary database of U.S. government publications. 1976+.

NTIS U.S. government research and development reports.

PAIS Primary database for public policy questions. 1972+.

PsycLIT Primary database for psychology and behavioral sciences. 1974+

Science Citation Index Primary database for citations to articles in 3,300 science journals. 1985+.

Sociofile Primary database for sociology (1974+) plus social policy and planning (1980+).

Sport Discus Sports psychology, exercise, coaching, and training.

USA Counties Statistics on U.S. counties.

U.S. Statistical Abstract All types of U.S.-oriented statistics.

U.S. Census Bureau CD-ROMs Economic censuses, county business patterns, and censuses of agriculture, of population and housing, and of import and exports. Check dates of coverage.

Another popular distributor of CD-ROMs in libraries is a firm called SilverPlatter, based in Norwood, Massachusetts. A number of its most popular CDs are listed in chapter 11.

11
The consumer database finder

This chapter is designed to help you locate online databases and CD-ROMs to answer your questions and solve your information problems. The databases listed are organized into 40 broad topic areas:

➤ Address and phone directories

➤ Agriculture

➤ Animals and wildlife

➤ Art and music

➤ Astronomy and space

➤ Biographical information

➤ Business and company information
  - General business information
  - Business and company news
  - U.S. company directories
  - International company directories
  - Company financials
  - Company and industry analyses

- College information
- Computers and consumer electronics
- Consumer advice
- Country and geographic information
- Demographics and statistics
- Drugs and pharmaceuticals
- Economics
- Education
- Employment and careers
- Encyclopedias
- Entertainment
- Environment
- Ethnic and minority information
- Food and diet
- Gardening and plants
- General reference and writing aids
- Government information
- Health and medical information
- History
- Law and legal information
- Literature
- Magazines and journals (popular)
- Meteorology and weather
- Military
- News
- Parenting
- Patents and trademarks

➤ Political news and reports

➤ Religion

➤ Science and engineering

➤ Social sciences and humanities

➤ Sports

➤ Travel

➡ Database selection

For each category, this section lists the three major types of electronic databases covered in this book: consumer CD-ROMs, CD-ROMs found in libraries, and online services. This section is *not* comprehensive; it cannot and does not include every online database and CD-ROM in existence. There are specialized directories that you can find in a library that attempt to do that job. What this section provides, however, is a quick look up and contact information for many of the most broadly useful and popular electronic databases that are geared to consumers and the general public. The following is an explanation of the criteria employed for determining which CD-ROM and online databases I included:

Consumer CD-ROMs Includes every CD-ROM I could locate that met the following criteria:

➤ Covered a subject corresponding to one of this book's major topic categories.

➤ Was a *searchable*, reference-oriented, information database (e.g., no games, pure audio or video CDs).

➤ Was priced at $200 or less. This was the cut-off I chose to reasonably designate a product that was geared to consumers. I did, however, make an exception for encyclopedias and address and phone-directory CD-ROMs since these're typically more expensive.

Library CD-ROMs Includes every library CD-ROM described in this book, as well as a selection of others that I determined to be of broad use and likely to be found in a public or academic library.

Online databases Includes every online database mentioned in this book, *including* all gateway databases described. On CompuServe, IQuest-seeded databases specifically highlighted in this book are covered, but those not mentioned are not. Does not cover databases available on nonconsumer services (Dialog, Nexis, etc.) that aren't available through a consumer gateway. (Also not included are any pure stock, commodity-tracking, or trading databases mentioned peripherally in the book.)

Each topic category provides the following information:

➤ Typical questions that the listed databases could be used to find answers to. These are just sample queries to give you an idea how the databases can be helpful. Your questions, of course, will be unique to your information problems.

➤ Names of online database or CD-ROMs.

➤ For databases, on which online service the file can be located.

➤ For CD-ROMs, the producer or vendor of the product. (Note that in some cases there might be additional vendors of the same CD-ROM product. For example, government information CDs are often made available by several vendors, all of whom have created their own product but use the same original data.)

➤ A short description of the databases.

At the end of the chapter, you'll find a listing of contact names and addresses for the producers, vendors, distributors, and retail outlets for the consumer CD-ROMs listed. If you're interested in purchasing a CD-ROM, remember to first ask whether it's designed to run on a PC (IBM-compatible) or Macintosh, and what its RAM, storage space, and other hardware and software requirements are.

A couple of cautions when you use this section. First of all, the electronic database field is one of the fastest changing industries

around today. You're almost certain to find that some products listed here no longer exist, new ones have been introduced that aren't listed, and some vendors and producers have either moved or changed their product line. This is a field that's very difficult to stay current with. The best advice I can give you here is to subscribe to a few of the professional journals listed in appendix C, as those magazines regularly report on new online and CD-ROM databases. If you want to stay even more current with new product releases, you might want to consider using an online host that offers a news monitoring service. For example, CompuServe's Executive News Service (as described in chapter 2) allows you to create keywords that the service uses to monitor newswires and cull stories that match your terms. You might also want to monitor the major press release wires (PR Newswire and BusinessWire) to keep up with new product releases.

Also, keep in mind that there is a distinction between a CD-ROM producer and a CD-ROM vendor. It can be a bit confusing, and there's often some overlap between the terms, but generally a *producer* is an organization that was responsible for gathering data and creating the product, while a *vendor* markets and sells it. Most companies listed in the section *CD-ROM producers and online vendors*, near the end of the chapter, provide the vendor contact, since this is the place you're most likely able to easily buy the CD. However, in some cases where it seemed appropriate, I listed the producer instead. In either case, the source should allow you to make contact and place an order.

Finally, while I've tried to make the topic categories as useful as possible, there's also some inevitable overlap. So if there's a related category to the one you're checking, you should look at that one too. For example, while I've created a separate category for astronomy and for meteorology, those topics will also be covered in the *Science and engineering* section. And if you're checking food and diet, you might also want to look at the *Health and medical information* section.

⇨ Address and phone directories

➤ Where can I find the phone number or fax number for a business I need to contact?

➤ Where can I find an address for a business I need to contact?

➤ Where can I find the home phone number or address of someone living in the U.S.?

➤ How can I find out what businesses in the country make a certain product or sell a particular service?

➤ Where can I locate a particular government body or institution?

❋ CD-ROMs

American Business Phone Book
American Business Information
10 million business phone numbers, searchable by partial name, phone number, city, state, or zip code.

North American Facsimile Book
Quanta
150,000 fax numbers for Canadian, U.S., and Mexican companies. Searchable by company name, address, city, state province area, and zip code.

PhoneDisc QuickRef
Phone Disc USA
100,000 listings, including businesses, educational, and government.

ProPhone
ProCD
70 million residential listings and 7 million business listings. Searchable by name, address, and phone number. Boolean searching supported.

PhoneDisc, USA
Digital Directory Assistance, Inc.
80 million residential names, phone numbers, addresses, and zip codes.

❋ Online services

PhoneFile
CompuServe/IQ
The names, addresses, and phone numbers for more than 75 million households.

⇨ Agriculture

➤ Where can I locate comprehensive reports and analyses on agriculture and biology?

➤ What are the latest statistics on U.S. agriculture?

➤ Where can I find the results from the latest agriculture research?

➤ How can I learn about veterinary medicine?

✳ CD-ROMs

1987 U.S. Census of Agriculture
Bureau of the Census
County-level data on agriculture in the United States.

Agri/Stats 1
Hopkins Technology
Information on U.S. agricultural industry, including crops, grains, livestock, and cattle.

Agriculture & Life Sciences
IDD
Over 50,000 pages of information drawn from periodicals, government documents, and various handbooks on the United States agricultural industry.

Compact International Agricultural Research Library
Consultative Group on International Agricultural Research
Agricultural research worldwide.

Food, Agriculture, and Science
Knowledge Access
Documents from 20 international agricultural research centers.

National CD-ROM Sampler: An Extension Reference Library
Virginia Tech
Agricultural information from the U.S.

National Dairy Database
Interactive Design
Fulltext of 700+ documents on dairy farms management.

✳ CD-ROMs in libraries

Agricola
SilverPlatter
Covers agriculture, forestry, soils, ecology, flora and fauna, nutrition, biotechnology, and more.

Biological and Agricultural Index
H.W. Wilson Co.
Indexes 225 key periodicals in the life sciences and agriculture. Major areas covered include: agriculture, agricultural chemicals, animal husbandry, biochemistry, biology, biotechnology, botany, cytology, ecology, entomology, environmental science, fishery sciences, food science, forestry, genetics, horticulture, limnology, microbiology, nutrition, physiology, plant pathology, soil science, veterinary medicine, and zoology.

CAB Abstracts
SilverPlatter
Scans over 14,000 journals, books, reports, and other published literature on all aspects of agriculture, and provides abstracts. Topics include plant protection, forestry engineering, animal and crop husbandry, animal and plant breeding, veterinary medicine, human nutrition, and more.

✳ Online services

Agricola
CompuServe/Knowledge Index
Worldwide information on agriculture.

CAB Abstracts
CompuServe/Knowledge Index
Detailed summaries of worldwide agricultural and biological research. Bibliographic database.

CAB Abstracts
CompuServe/Knowledge Index
Detail summaries of worldwide agricultural and biological research.

⇨ Animals and wildlife

➤ What is the natural habitat of a certain animal?

➤ What are the habits of certain animals? How do they look and act?

> ➤ What are the different types of birds, and what do they look like?

> ➤ Where can I learn about the diseases and health problems of my pet?

✳ CD-ROMs

About Cows
Quanta
Everything you'd ever want to know . . . about cows.

Mammals: A Multimedia Encyclopedia
National Geographic
Encyclopedia information on over 200 mammals, corresponding to the equivalent print book.

Microsoft Dinosaurs
Microsoft Corporation
Over 1,000 full-color illustrations and photos and about 200 articles on dinosaurs. Also includes audio.

Multimedia Audubon's Birds
Creative Multimedia
Complete text of Audubon's *Birds of America*, published in 1840.

Multimedia Audubon's Mammals
Creative Multimedia
Complete text of Audubon's *Quadrupeds of North America*, published in 1840. Includes 150 full-color lithographs.

Multimedia Encyclopedia of Mammalian Biology
McGraw-Hill, Inc.
Text, still images, sound, and full-motion video are used in this CD-ROM encyclopedic version of the five volumes of the respected Grzimek's *Encyclopedia of Mammals*. Over 3,500 full-color images and nearly 500 maps.

The Animals
Software Toolworks
Experts from the renowned San Diego Zoo offers movies, sounds, stories, photographs, and text about exotic animals around the world.

✳ Online services

PetCare Guide
Prodigy
Tips and advice on caring for your pet and helping with any health problems.

⇨ Art and music

> ➤ When was Monet's *Water Lillies* painted?

> ➤ What does an oboe sound like? What do other musical instruments sound like?

> ➤ What is the musical structure of the beginning of Beethoven's 9th Symphony?

> ➤ Where can I find a comprehensive compilation of reports, articles, and studies in the art field?

✳ CD-ROMs

Coates Art Review—Impressionism
Quanta
Comprehensive review of impressionist work and art. Masters included as well as lesser-knowns. You can search for specific paintings, drawings, sculptures, background information, images, etc.

Igor Stravinsky: The Rite of Spring
Voyager
Audio, text, and images of Stravinsky's The Rite of Spring.

Jazz: A Multimedia History
Ebook
Contains selected recordings—as well as photos, interviews, and quotes—from major figures in jazz, such as Duke Ellington, Charlie Parker, Louis Armstrong, Miles Davis, Herbie Hancock, and others.

Ludwig Van Beethoven's Symphony No. 9
Voyager
Audio, text, and images of Beethoven's 9th Symphony.

Microsoft Musical Instruments
Microsoft Corporation
Information on over 200 musical instruments, including photos and sounds.

✳ CD-ROMs in libraries

Art Index
H.W. Wilson Co.
Indexes 213 U.S. and non-U.S. periodicals, yearbooks, and museum bulletins. Major areas include: advertising art, antiques, archaeology, architecture and architectural

history, art history, city planning, computers in archaeology, architecture and art, crafts, folk art, glassware, graphic arts, interior and industrial design, jewelry, landscape architecture, motion pictures, museology, painting, photography, pottery, sculpture, television, textiles, video, and woodwork.

Muse
NISC
Contains the International Repertory of Music Literature's 135,000 abstracts along with 105,000 records from the music catalog of the U.S. Library of Congress. Covers all significant literature on music history, theory, analysis, performance, instruments, voice, and related issues and disciplines.

✳ Online services

Art Bibliographies Modern
CompuServe/Knowledge Index
Comprehensive coverage of all modern art.

Art Literature International (RILA)
CompuServe/Knowledge Index
Worldwide historic coverage of Western art.

➡ Astronomy and space

➢ Where can I find information on the Apollo, Viking, and Voyager space expeditions?

✳ CD-ROMs

Space Science Sampler
University of Colorado
Data and pictures from the Viking and Voyager trips.

Space Series—Apollo
Quanta
Chronology of Apollo space ventures, from Apollo 1 to the Apollo-Soyuz program. Historical information plus hundreds of photographs.

➡ Biographical information

➢ When was a certain person born, where did he or she go to school, and what were the highlights of his or her life?

➤ What were a person's major accomplishments?

➤ How and where can I write to a particular person?

✳ CD-ROMs in libraries

Biography Index
H.W. Wilson Co.
Indexes a broad range of biographical material, including: 2,700 periodicals; English-language books including over 1,800 annual works of individual and collective biographies; autobiographies, memoirs, journals, diaries, letters, interviews, bibliographies, and obituaries; biographical novels, drama, pictorial works and poetry; juvenile literature; and biographical information from otherwise nonbiographical works.

✳ Online services

Marquis Who's Who
CompuServe/Knowledge Index
CompuServe/IQ
Detailed biographies on nearly 75,000 professionals and well-known individuals.

Business and company information

➤ Where can I find out how to start up and manage a new small business?

➤ Where can I find the latest business news and analyses of what's happening in the business world?

➤ Where can I find out about opportunities to sell my product overseas?

➤ What are the latest developments regarding a particular industry?

➤ What are the latest management strategies, and which firms are trying them out?

General business information

✳ CD-ROMs

Microsoft Small Business Consultant
Microsoft Corp.
How to start and manage a small business.

Trade Opportunities
Wayzata
Trade information collected from the U.S. Department of Commerce and other agencies and departments providing statistics and advice on exporting.

✳ CD-ROMs in libraries

ABI/Inform
UMI/ProQuest
Provides 150 word abstracts from articles published in major leading business periodicals.

Business Periodicals Index
H.W. Wilson Co.
Indexes 345 leading business magazines. Major areas include: accounting, acquisitions and mergers, advertising, banking, building and construction, communications, computers, economics, electronics, engineering, finance and investments, government regulations, industrial relations, insurance, international business, management, marketing, occupational health and safety, oil and gas, personnel, publishing, real estate, small business, and taxation.

F&S Index Plus Text
SilverPlatter
Indexes, abstracts, and in some cases provides the fulltext of recent articles from over 1,000 sources on companies and industries.

Wilson Business Abstracts
H.W. Wilson Co.
Indexes and abstracts articles published in 345 major business journals.

✳ Online services

ABI/Inform
CompuServe/Knowledge Index
Business practices, corporate strategies, and trends.

Chemical Business Newsbase
CompuServe/Knowledge Index
International trade and business coverage of the chemical industry.

DowQuest
Genie gateway: Dow Jones
One year of information from approximately 400 national, regional, and industry publications, including exclusive information from Dow Jones News sources.

Harvard Business Review
CompuServe/Knowledge Index
Complete text of the *Harvard Business Review*. Covers the full range of strategic management subjects.

Marketing/Management Research Center
CompuServe/IQ
A gateway to nine different databases on Dialog: ABI/Inform, Findex, FINIS, Industry Data Sources, Infomat International Business, McGraw-Hill Publications Online, PTS MARS, PTS New Product Announcements, and PTS PROMT. Some contain fulltext, others abstracts, and some bibliographic information. Coverage and update frequency varies by database.

Microsoft Small Business Center
America Online
A variety of how-to and advisory files and libraries designed for start-up and small businesses.

Standard & Poor's Register, Biographical
CompuServe/Knowledge Index
Information on approximately 72,000 key business executives.

Trade and Industry Index
CompuServe/Knowledge Index
Indexes of popular general business publications and industry trade journals.

 # Business and company news

> What is the latest news on companies, industries, technologies, management, and other key business issues?

> What are the latest products and services introduced by major U.S. companies?

✳ CD-ROMs in libraries

Business Index
InfoTrak
Abstracts 700 journals, plus the *Wall Street Journal*, *New York Times*, *Asian Wall Street Journal*, and *Financial Times of Canada*.

Business ASAP
InfoTrak
Provides the fulltext of articles found in 350 journals selected from the Business Index.

❋ Online services

Barron's
GEnie gateway: Dow Jones
Exclusive source of Barron's fulltext articles from January 1987.

Business and Financial Report
GEnie gateway: Dow Jones
Continuously updated business and financial news culled from the *Wall Street Journal*, the Dow Jones News Service, and other newswires.

Business Database Plus
CompuServe/Ziff Davis
Provides the fulltext from about 500 regional, national, and international business and trade publications, as well as a selection of industry newsletters.

The Business Library
GEnie gateway: Dow Jones
Text of selected articles from *Forbes, Fortune, Inc., Money, Time, The Economist, Financial World, American Demographics*, and over 200 other publications.

Business Week
GEnie gateway: Dow Jones
Fulltext of all articles from *Business Week* back to January 1985.

BusinessWire
CompuServe/Knowledge Index
Delphi
Unedited text of news released from over 10,000 U.S. organizations and corporations, with an emphasis on U.S. companies.

Company and Industry News
Prodigy
Recent news on major companies and various industries, reported by Dow Jones news.

Dow Jones International News
GEnie gateway: Dow Jones
Up-to-the-minute international business news from Dow Jones' international newswires, the *Wall Street Journal, Wall Street Journal Europe*, and *Asian Wall Street Journal*. News on corporations, currency markets, the world stock market, and more.

Dow Jones News
GEnie gateway: Dow Jones
Stories from the *Wall Street Journal*, *Barron's*, Dow Jones News Service, and the Canadian Dow Jones News Service.

Dow Jones QuickSearch
GEnie gateway: Dow Jones
A complete corporate report including the latest information from *Dow Jones News*, current stock quotes, financial overviews, company vs. industry performance, income statements, and more.

Japan Economic Daily
GEnie gateway: Dow Jones
Same-day coverage of major business, financial market, and political news from the Kyodo News Service in Japan.

PR NewsWire
CompuServe/Knowledge Index
Delphi
Complete text of news releases covering the entire spectrum of news.

Press Release Wires
GEnie gateway: Dow Jones
News releases from corporations, government agencies, industry associations, labor unions, and stock exchanges.

Textline
CompuServe/IQ
A collection of prominent newspapers and newswires in English, originating from countries around the world. Provides comprehensive coverage of world, national, domestic, political, economic, financial, industry, and commercial news.

UPI Business News
Delphi
Up-to-the-minute news, as filed by United Press International reporters.

The Wall Street Journal Full-Text Version
GEnie gateway: Dow Jones
The complete text of the *Wall Street Journal* newspaper.

Wall $treet Week Online
GEnie gateway: Dow Jones
Transcripts of the public broadcasting program "Wall $treet Week."

⇨ U.S. company directories

➤ Where can I find the names, addresses, and phone numbers of manufacturers or providers of a certain product or certain service?

➤ Where can I find basic identifying information for certain companies?

➤ Where can I find sales information for large, well-known companies?

✳ Online services

Business Resource Directory
GEnie
Lists information on very small businesses and contains information mainly on small businesses owned or managed by GEnie's own membership.

Corporate Affiliates Research Center
GEnie gateway: Dialog
Business profiles and corporate linkage for 100,000 companies worldwide.

Corporate Affiliations
CompuServe/IQ
Information on the relationships between parent and subsidiary firms for most large U.S. public companies. A typical record includes the business name, address, phone number, business description, names of executives, and where the company fits in the corporate family hierarchy.

Corporate Ownership Watch
GEnie gateway: Dow Jones
Summaries of 5% ownership and the names of all tender offer filers. Insider trading information on over 8,000 publicly held companies plus data on individuals (officers, directors, and owners with more than 10% ownership).

D&B Business Locator
GEnie gateway: Dialog
Identification information on over 8 million public and private U.S. companies (same as Dun's Electronic Business Directory on CompuServe).

D&B U.S. Company Profiles
GEnie gateway: Dialog
Detailed information for over 7.5 million U.S. business establishments.

Dun's Electronic Business Directory
CompuServe/IQ
Information on over 8 million public and private U.S. companies. Each record
contains the company name, address, phone number, type of business, and SIC
code. Many also provide the number of employees, information on parent company,
and other data.

Dun's Market Identifiers
CompuServe/IQ
Dun's Market Identifiers contains information on over 2 million U.S. public and
private establishments having either more than 5 employees or over $1 million in
sales. Information on a listed company includes its name, address, phone number,
sometimes number of employees, sales figures, corporate family relationships, and
executive names and titles.

Executive Desk Register
Delphi
Basic directory data for 5,000 public companies that trade their stock on the New
York, American, or NASDAQ exchanges.

NYNEX Northeast Access
Delphi
Directory data for companies located in the yellow pages or business-to-business
listings for the states of New York, Connecticut, Maine, Massachusetts, New
Hampshire, Rhode Island, and Vermont.

Standard & Poor's Corporate Descriptions
CompuServe/Knowledge Index
Information and news on over 12,000 publicly held U.S. companies.

Thomas' Register Online
GEnie gateway: Dialog
CompuServe/IQ
Names, addresses, and products produced by 150,000 public and private
companies.

International company directories

> Where can I find the names, addresses, and phone numbers of
> non-U.S. manufacturers or providers of a certain product or
> service?

> Where can I find basic identifying information for certain non-
> U.S. companies?

> ➤ Where can I find sales information for large well known non-U.S. companies?

✳ Online services

CC British Company Directory
CompuServe/Knowledge Index
Listing of *every* limited-liability company in England, Scotland, and Wales.

Corporate Canada Online
GEnie gateway: Dow Jones
News and detailed financial and market information on 2,200 public, private, and government-owned Canadian companies from InfoGlobe, publishers of Canada's national newspaper the *Globe and Mail*.

D&B Duns Australian Duns Market Identifiers
D&B Duns New Zealand Market Identifiers
CompuServe/IQuest
Information on a total of 95,000 Australian and New Zealand businesses.

D&B Duns Canadian Company Profiles
GEnie gateway: Dialog
A directory file containing key information for over 350,000 Canadian companies.

D&B Duns Canadian Market Identifiers
CompuServe/IQuest
Contains data on over 350,000 Canadian companies.

D&B European Company Profiles
GEnie gateway: Dialog
A directory file providing detailed information on over 2 million businesses located in 26 European countries.

D&B International Duns MI
CompuServe/IQuest
Over 200,000 firms in more than 90 countries.

D&B International Company Profiles
GEnie gateway: Dialog
A directory file containing key information for parent companies for over 2.4 million Asian, African, European, Indian and other non-U.S. companies.

European Company Library
CompuServe/IQuest
Directory and financial data on over 2 million European firms.

German Company Library
CompuServe/IQuest
Contains directory, financial, and product information for over 48,000 public and
private German companies.

Company financials

> Where can I locate in-depth financial information on U.S.
> public companies?

> Where can I locate in-depth financial information on non-U.S.
> companies?

> Where can I locate credit and credit rating information on U.S.
> companies?

✳ CD-ROMs in libraries

Compact Disclosure/U.S.
Disclosure Inc.
Financial data on 11,000 U.S. companies, including detailed financial statements,
description of business, President's letter to shareholders, management discussion
from the annual report, and so forth.

Compact Disclosure/World
Disclosure Inc.
In-depth financial data on companies worldwide.

Laser Disclosure
Disclosure Inc.
The fulltext and reproductions of complete images of corporate annual reports,
10Ks, and proxy statement for all companies listed on the New York and American
stock exchanges and the NASDAQ companies. This is not technically a database,
but a "document delivery" system producing full-image printouts.

SEC Online
SilverPlatter
Fulltext database containing 10Ks, 10Qs, annual reports, proxy statements, and
20Fs for all companies listed on the New York and America stock exchanges, as well
as selected NMS/NASDAQ firms. A total of 4,500 firms are included.

✳ Online services

Disclosure
CompuServe

GEnie gateway: Dow Jones
10K extracts, company profiles, and other detailed data on 12,000 publicly held companies from reports filed with the SEC and other sources.

Extel News Cards
CompuServe/IQ
Financial and statistical information on 5,400 companies and 180 industries. Compare company versus industry, company versus company, and industry versus industry.

Media General Financial Services
GEnie gateway: Dow Jones
Financial and statistical information on 5,400 companies and 180 industries.

Standard & Poor's News
CompuServe/Knowledge Index
Financial news on U.S. public companies.

S&P Online
CompuServe/IQ
GEnie gateway: Dow Jones
Information on approximately 5,600 companies, including data such as earning outlooks, historical earnings, dividends, and business summaries.

TRW Business Profiles
CompuServe/IQ
GEnie gateway: Dialog
Data on how over 13 million organizations pay their bills, and their credit histories. Information in a credit report typically contains credit histories, financial information and ratios, UCC filings, tax liens, judgments, bankruptcies, and an executive summary.

Worldscope
GEnie gateway: Dow Jones
Comprehensive information on more than 4,500 corporations in 25 countries.

Zack's Corporate Earnings Estimator
GEnie gateway: Dow Jones
Consensus earnings-per-share estimates and P/E ratio forecasts for 3,500 companies. Industries' earning estimates and five-year growth rates.

⇨ Company and industry analyses

> ➤ Where can I find profiles and background information on smaller, private firms?

281

- Where can I find insider analyses of large U.S. companies, such as strategic direction, competition, sales forecasts, management structures, and so forth?
- How can I find out about the trends and outlook for a particular industry?

✳ CD-ROMs in libraries

Business Dateline
UMI/ProQuest
Provides the fulltext of articles from 350 regional business journals. Coverage extends back to 1985.

✳ Online services

Business Dateline
CompuServe/IQ
GEnie gateway: Dow Jones
The fulltext of articles from more than 115 regional business publications in the U.S. and Canada.

Investext
CompuServe/IQ
GEnie gateway: Dow Jones
The fulltext of company and industry research reports compiled during the most recent two years by analysts in more than 50 Wall Street, regional, and international brokerage houses and research firms. Company reports typically include historical information such as a company profile, revenues, earnings, and other financial operating results such as stock performances. Many also contain the research brokerage's recommendations and forecasts.

College information

- Which colleges have the features and characteristics that might appeal to me?
- Which colleges have scholarship money that I'd qualify for?
- Where can I find an up-to-date description of a certain college?

✳ CD-ROMs

The College Handbook
MacMillan New Media
Derived from the College Board, this CD-ROM contains information on 2,700
colleges and universities.

✳ Online services

CASHE
GEnie
College Aid Sources for Higher Education (CASHE) is designed to help prospective
college students pinpoint which, if any, of 14,000 different resources of financial aid
they might qualify for.

College Board
America Online
Allows you to search an online version of the equivalent 2,000-page print
guidebook to colleges, published by the College Board.

Peterson's College Database
CompuServe
CompuServe/Knowledge Index
Provides descriptions of over 4,700 colleges and universities with two- and four-year
degree programs.

Peterson's College Selection Service
GEnie gateway: Dow Jones
A guide to U.S. and Canadian colleges and universities.

Peterson's Gradline
CompuServe/Knowledge Index
Provides descriptions of over 2,600 accredited institutions in the U.S. and Canada
that offer post-baccalaureate degrees.

⇨ Computers and consumer electronics

➢ What is the latest computer industry news?

➢ What are the newest products introduced by major computer
and consumer electronic vendors?

> ➤ Where can I find information on finding the right software for my computer?

> ➤ How do I know whether a particular piece of software is going to do its job well?

✳ CD-ROMs

NewsBytes, volume 2
Wayzata
Up-to-the-minute news on the computer industry.

✳ CD-ROMs in libraries

ComputerSelect
Ziff-Davis
Fulltext of articles from 65 major computer journals.

✳ Online services

Business Software Database
CompuServe/Knowledge Index
Descriptions of software packages that have business applications for use with micro- and minicomputers.

Computer Database
CompuServe/Knowledge Index
Summaries of computer-related articles and publications.

Computer Database Plus
CompuServe/Ziff Davis
Provides abstracts and fulltext from about 200 computer or computer related magazines, newspapers, and journals, and contains over 250,000 articles back through 1987.

Computer & Electronics News Center
GEnie gateway: Dialog

Computer News Fulltext
CompuServe/Knowledge Index
Complete articles from *ComputerWorld* and *Network World*.

DataNet
Delphi
The latest news from the computer industry.

KnowledgeBase
America Online
Microsoft created this database to help users of their software obtain advice and help. Products covered include Works, Word, and Excel, among others. A total of 32,000 articles are made available.

MacWorld
America Online
The fulltext of recent issues from MacWorld magazine.

Microcomputer Software Guide
CompuServe/Knowledge Index
Complete information on available U.S. software programs.

Micro Software Directory
CompuServe/Knowledge Index
Provides critical reviews of leading software packages.

NewsBytes
America Online
GEnie
The latest news from the leading computer-information newswire.

Online Today
CompuServe
Daily updated computer- and information-industry news.

Software Guide
Prodigy
Descriptions and ratings of popular software products, derived from articles published in *Home Office Computing* magazine.

Wired
America Online
Fulltext of the same magazine, covering the technological and sociological impacts of living in the digital age.

⇨ Consumer advice

➤ Where can I find which company makes the highest-rated product?

➤ Where can I get good advice on how to buy a car?

➤ Where can I get good advice on how to buy a computer?

➤ Where can I find good tips on common consumer problems such as managing money, buying health-related products, buying a home, preparing food, and so on?

✳ CD-ROMs

How Computers Work
Warner New Media
Complete text of articles on how computers work, based on two Time-Life books.

Computer Select
Ziff-Davis
The fulltext of nearly 80,000 articles from 71 computer publications, and abstracts from 100 additional ones.

Consumer Information Disk
Quanta
Publications released from the United States Consumer Information Center.

Consumer Reports
Dialog
The fulltext of current and past issues of *Consumer Reports* magazine, fully keyword searchable (unlike most online versions, which are menu-select only).

✳ CD-ROMs in libraries

Consumer Reference Disc
NISC
Combines the Consumer Health & Nutrition Index with Consumers Index to offer 190,000 abstracts and bibliographic citations to keep consumers informed of product evaluations, warnings, recalls, alerts, and health-related issues.

✳ Online services

Consumer Information/David Horowitz
America Online
This popular consumer advocate's advice and reports can be searched and read online.

Consumer Reports
CompuServe
CompuServe/Knowledge Index
Prodigy
Contains the fulltext of stories published in the past 7 years of *Consumer Reports*.

 # Country and geographic information

➤ Where can I find statistical data on countries around the world?

➤ Where can I find discussions and analyses of customs and problems of countries?

➤ How can I locate a particular street in the United States?

➤ Where can I learn about the characteristics of certain U.S. regions?

➤ What are the geographical features of a certain region in the world?

➤ What is the geography like under the oceans?

✳ CD-ROMs

CIA World Factbook
Quanta
Facts on 249 countries

Countries of the World Encyclopedia
Bureau of Electronic Publishing
60,000 screens detailing the culture, history, and economy of every country in the world. Based on U.S. Army handbooks and foreign embassies.

Deep Sea Drilling Project
U.S. National Environment Satellite Data and Information Service
Marine, geological, and geophysical data.

Delorme Street Atlas USA
Delorme Mapping
All U.S. roads and street addresses on CD. Users can type in a zip code, phone prefix, or city name to call up a map covering that particular area.

Electronic Map Cabinet
Highlighted Data
Geographical data that can be used to generate maps.

KGB World Factbook
Quanta
Information on 253 countries, including maps.

Global Ecosystems Data
National Geophysical Data Center
Selected data on global ecosystems, vegetation, climate, topography, soils, and other data.

Middle East Diary on CD-ROM
Quanta
Information on people, history, and conflicts in the Mideast.

Picture Atlas of the World
National Geographic
Information on physical, economic, cultural, and geographic aspects of the world's regions.

Software Toolworks U.S. Atlas
Software Toolworks
250 U.S. regional and topographical maps.

Software Toolworks World Atlas
Software Toolworks
240 world, country, regional, and topographical maps.

Sure!Maps
Horizon Technologies
Combines colorful and detailed raster maps, where the user can plot data.

Svinga
Media Technology Ltd.
A multimedia journey through Zimbabwe.

U.S. Atlas Version 4
Software Toolworks
Regular maps and topographic maps as well as 28 detailed regional city maps; statistical maps; data import and export features; 110 VGA color reference and relief maps; and over 1,000 statistical maps for states and counties.

Wayzata World Factbook 1991 + Navigator
Wayzata
Information on 250 countries.

World Atlas Version 4
Software Toolworks
Over 240 video clips of cities around the world, over 1,000 photos, new country maps to reflect new political boundaries, and 50 regional city maps for major cities. Contains all new and updated data and a currency converter, allowing you to compare data between regions.

✳ CD-ROMs in libraries

GeoRef
SilverPlatter
Comprehensive index of over 1.5 million citations, many with abstracts. You can scan over 3,000 journals in 40 languages as well as books, maps, and most USGS publications.

Notimex on CD-ROM
NISC
Daily news from Latin America, derived from the Spanish wires of the Mexican News Agency. Covers business, economics, finance, politics, religion, culture, sports, entertainment, and general news written by and from the perspective of Latin Americans.

⇨ Demographics and statistics

➤ Which parts of the country are the wealthiest?

➤ Where do the oldest and youngest people live?

➤ In which regions of the country does a high percentage of residents own their homes?

➤ How can I find just the right demographic market for my new product?

➤ Where can I locate facts on the U.S. population?

➤ Where can I locate facts on U.S. business activity?

➤ What is the U.S. population's opinion on a particular social or political issue?

✳ CD-ROMs

American Housing Survey, 1985: National Care
U.S. Bureau of the Census
Data on housing and housing trends in the United States.

County Business Patterns
U.S. Bureau of the Census
Data on U.S. business establishments, broken down by county.

County and City Data Book
U.S. Bureau of the Census
Demographic, economic, and geographical data on U.S. counties and cities.

County-City Plus
Slater Hall
2,000+ demographic data items on counties, MSAs, and states.

Morbidity and Mortality Weekly Report on CD-ROM
MacMillan New Media
Five years of text and tables from the United States Centers for Disease Control.

StatCan: CANSIM Directory Disc
OPTIM
Canadian economic, financial, and demographic statistics.

Test Disc 2
U.S. Bureau of the Census
Information from U.S. censuses: retail trade, agricultural, and other data.

USA State Factbook
Quanta
Information on the U.S. and its territories. Provides information on state geography, vital statistics, government and politics, economics, lines of communication, transportation, and other information.

World Almanac and Book of Facts 1992
Metatec/Discovery
One million facts, equivalent to the print book.

World Factbook
Wayzata
Complete text of equivalent print book. Covers geographic, government, and other data on 250 countries. Based on the CIA *World Factbook*.

✳ CD-ROMs in libraries

Census of Population and Housing
U.S. Bureau of the Census
Statistical data on the population of the United States and on housing issues such as occupancy and prices.

Popline
NISC
Derived from the Population Information Program of the Johns Hopkins University of Public Health and the National Library of Medicine. Contains nearly 200,000

citations and abstracts on population, family planning, fertility, population laws, sexually transmitted diseases, and more.

Statistical Abstract of the United States
U.S. Bureau of the Census
All types of U.S.-oriented statistics.

USA Counties
U.S. Bureau of the Census
Statistics on U.S. counties.

✳ Online services

Census Data/Demographics/SuperSite
CompuServe/IQ
Demographic reports covering population, income, housing, education, employment, and forecasts for the entire U.S., each state, county, and metropolitan area. Also available are sales potential reports and target marketing profiles on U.S. households, based on demographic, socioeconomic, and housing characteristics of the neighborhood. Data from SuperSite is derived from the well-known CACI data analysis firm.

Public Opinion Online
GEnie gateway: Dialog
CompuServe/Knowledge Index
Contains the fulltext of public-opinion surveys, collected by the Roper Center for Public Opinion Research.

(*see also* Government information)

Drugs and pharmaceuticals

➢ What are the side effects of a particular drug?

➢ What does the latest research say about the effectiveness of a particular drug?

➢ What is the generic equivalent of a certain drug?

➢ Which drugs are prescribed to treat a certain illness?

✳ Online services

Consumer Drug Information Fulltext
CompuServe/Knowledge Index
Complete text of the *Consumer Drug Digest*.

Drug Information Fulltext
CompuServe/Knowledge Index
Complete text of the *American Hospital Formulary Service* and the *Handbook on Injectable Drugs*.

International Pharmaceuticals Abstracts
CompuServe/Knowledge Index
Research and current health-related drug literature.

The Merck Index Online
CompuServe/Knowledge Index
Updated and expanded version of the *Merck Index*, an internationally recognized encyclopedia of chemicals, drugs, and biologicals.

⇨ Economics

➤ How well did the U.S. economy perform last year, last quarter, etc?

➤ What kinds of businesses are doing well recently, and which are doing poorly?

➤ What do the experts forecast for the world economy over the next few years?

➤ What does the latest economic research say about supply-side economics?

➤ Which regions of the country have the best and the worst economy at the moment?

✳ CD-ROMs

Consu/Stats 1
Hopkins Technology
Information on consumer expenditures, derived from government data.

Econ/Stats/1
Hopkins Technology
Statistical data on the U.S. economy.

Economic Census 1987 VOL 1
Bureau of the Census
1987 economic censuses.

✳ CD-ROMs in libraries

EconLit
SilverPlatter
Comprehensive, indexed bibliography with selected abstract of the world's economic literature, compiled from the American Economic Association's *Journal of Economic Literature* and the *Index of Economic Articles*. 1969+.

✳ Online services

Economic Literature Index
CompuServe/Knowledge Index
Comprehensive coverage of economic research.

Education

> ➤ What are the latest teaching techniques to encourage cooperation rather than competition?

> ➤ What are the pros and cons of the Montessori method of teaching?

> ➤ How are computers being used as teaching aids?

> ➤ What are some successful techniques in battling violence in schools?

> ➤ Which school systems are paying their teachers the most?

> ➤ What does the research say about year-round school?

✳ CD-ROMs in libraries

Education Index
H.W. Wilson Co.
Indexes 400 English-language periodicals, yearbooks, and monographic series from around the world. Key subjects include: audiovisual education, classroom computers, comparative education, competency-based education, educational technology, government funding, language and linguistics, literacy standards, multicultural and

multiethnic education, psychology, religious education, science and mathematics, social sciences, special education, student counseling, teacher education, teacher/parent relations, and vocational education.

ERIC
SilverPlatter
The premier education database. Covers 750 major education journals plus educational documents by 20 ERIC clearinghouses.

OCLC Education Library
SilverPlatter
Indexes 500,000+ books, dissertations, etc., in education and related fields, 1600 to the present.

✳ Online services

A-V Online
CompuServe/Knowledge Index
Information on all nonprint media (films, transparencies, videos, slides, etc.) covering all levels of education.

Educator's Center
GEnie gateway: Dialog
All aspects of education, drawn from several educational databases.

ERIC
CompuServe/Knowledge Index
Research reports, articles, and projects significant to education.

⇨ Employment and careers

➤ Which fields are now doing the most hiring?

➤ Which fields are projected to be doing the most hiring in the next few years?

➤ What is the career outlook for working overseas?

➤ Where can I find out about job openings in other states in my field?

➤ Where can I find a job description for a new career I'm considering?

✳ CD-ROMs

Career Opportunities
Quanta
Data on careers, derived from the U.S. Department of Commerce. Includes job descriptions, employment statistics, etc.

Europe in the Round
Vocational Technologies Ltd.
Education, training, and work opportunities in the 12 member states of the EC/Vocational Technologies.

✳ Online services

Employment Agency Database
America Online
A business directory that identifies and provides information on about 2,000 professional placement firms.

Employer Contacts
America Online
This database contains basic identifying information for about 5,000 U.S. employers.

Job Listings
America Online
Composed of three databases. E-Span contains electronic classifieds, placed by firms around the country who are searching for candidates to fill open positions. Help Wanted-USA contains similar postings and is broken down into two separate files. Finally, a feature called the Classifieds Bulletin Board allows users to place their own ads or read ads placed by other America Online members.

Encyclopedias

➢ Where can I find background information on a particular topic?

➢ Where can I get a clear definition and description of a technical or scientific matter?

✳ CD-ROMs

Aircraft Encyclopedia
Quanta
Descriptions and images of aircrafts.

American Heritage Illustrated Encyclopedic Dictionary
Xiphias
80,000-word dictionary, based on the equivalent print version.

Compton's Multimedia Encyclopedia
A complete multimedia encyclopedia, containing 33,000 articles, 10,000 pictures, timelines, animation, video, and special work features such as a "virtual workspace" and advanced article retrieval. $395.

The New Grolier Multimedia Encyclopedia
Grolier Electronic Publishing
Electronic equivalent to the 21-volume *Academic American Encyclopedia*, containing 33,000 articles, 10 million words, and multimedia features such as movies, sound, maps, pictures, narrated animations, timelines, and other features. $395 list price. (When packaged with other CD products, this product's producer is Software Toolworks.)

Information Finder
World Book Publishing
Contains the fulltext from the *World Book Encyclopedia*. Contains over 17,000 articles.

McGraw-Hill Concise Encyclopedia of Science & Technology
McGraw-Hill, Inc.
Electronic version of the 20-volume *McGraw-Hill Encyclopedia of Science & Technology*, offering information on over 75 major areas of theoretical and applied science. Includes 1,700 photographs, line drawings, graphs, tables, and charts.

McGraw-Hill Dictionary of Scientific and Technical Terms
McGraw-Hill, Inc.
Over 117,000 definitions of over 100,000 terms.

Microsoft Encarta Multimedia Encyclopedia
Microsoft Corporation
A multimedia Windows-based electronic version of the 29-volume *Funk & Wagnalls New Encyclopedia*, supplemented with additional articles, color maps and illustrations, animation, and other features, including an 83,000-word dictionary. $395.

Multimedia Space Encyclopedia
Updata
Provides a variety of information on space exploration, such as a timeline, hundreds of images, quicktime movies, biographical profiles of space explorers, and more.

❊ Online services

Compton's Encyclopedia
America Online
Compton's is a fully searchable online encyclopedia, which contains 5,200 articles and 8.7 million words.

Everyman's Encyclopaedia
CompuServe/Knowledge Index
Comprehensive reference work providing detailed and informative articles that cover the full range of human knowledge.

Grolier's Academic American Encyclopedia
CompuServe/Delphi/GEnie/Prodigy
A fulltext encyclopedia consisting of 21 volumes, 33,000 articles, and 10 million words.

⇨ Entertainment

➤ Who won a Grammy award as best new artist in 1992?

➤ Where can I find movie and video reviews?

➤ Where can I find background information on old classic movies?

➤ When did talking motion pictures first begin?

➤ Which television shows are most appropriate for children?

➤ Where can I find a historical account of an art- and entertainment-related event?

❊ CD-ROMs

1992 Grammy Awards on Disc
UniDisc
35-year retrospective on the Grammy awards show. Updated yearly.

Cinemania
Microsoft Corporation
Movie reviewer Leonard Maltin's movie reviews on disc. Also biographies, pictures, photographs, and facts for 19,000 films and 3,000 film stars. Interactive products includes over 1,000 photos, about 100 spoken clips of famous lines, a glossary, and other cinema-related features.

The Compleat Beatles
Comptons New Media
Contains the entire two-hour film of *The Compleat Beatles*, plus the text of the same book, tracing the evolution of the rock group. Supplemented with facts and trivia about the band.

Magill's Survey of Cinema CD-ROM
Salem Press
Summaries of 3,500+ classic and contemporary films.

Roger Ebert's Movie Home Companion
Quanta
1,000 movie and video reviews from film critic Roger Ebert.

Scanrom Horror & Science Film Guide
Scanrom
More than 2,300 horror and science fiction films described. Includes story lines, names of directors and stars, detailed facts, and so on.

Time Table of Arts and Entertainment
Xiphias
Describes over 4,000 events in the history of art, music, literature, and performing arts.

✳ Online services

Home Video Update/Movie Reviews
America Online
Movie Reviews. Reviews of current and older videos and movies, searchable by menu.

Kidsnet
America Online
Allows parents, teachers, and other interested users to locate information on television shows geared specifically for children.

Magill's Movie Guide
Prodigy
Provides 13,000 movie reviews, drawn from the print version of Magill's movie guide. Searchable by several criteria: title, genre, star, director, or year.

Magill's Survey of Cinema
CompuServe/Knowledge Index
Review articles for over 1,800 notable films.

⇨ Environment

➤ What are the long-term health effects of a certain chemical substance?

➤ Which states have the highest levels of air pollution?

➤ How can I learn strategies to live and act in a more environmentally helpful manner?

✳ CD-ROMs

1987 Toxic Release Inventory
Environmental Protection Agency
Annual estimate of 320 toxic chemicals in the environment.

Registry of Toxic Effects of Chemical Substances
Canadian Centre for Occupational Health
Data on the toxic effects of 100,000 chemicals.

View From the Earth
Warner New Media
Information on and pictures of solar eclipses.

✳ CD-ROMs in libraries

Earth Science Library
SilverPlatter
Index to books, journals, dissertations, etc., on all earth sciences and technological topics. Also includes citations to geologic maps of the United States and cataloging records of the U.S. Geological Survey Libraries since 1975.

✳ Online services

Network Earth
America Online
This database covers topics such as population, energy, wastes and toxics, land use and misuse, biodiversity and habitat preservation, air quality and climate, and oceans and aquatic life.

Pollution Abstracts
CompuServe/Knowledge Index
Information on pollution: its sources and its control.

 # Ethnic and minority information

➤ What is the history of Native Americans in the U.S.?

➤ Where can I find information about the Jewish culture and traditions?

➤ Where can I learn of the cultural habits of various immigrant groups in the U.S.?

➤ What are considered the most pressing concerns and issues facing African Americans today in the U.S.?

✳ CD-ROMs

African American Experience
Quanta
Electronic textbook, history of African Americans from the homeland. You can follow their migration to America and learn about their contributions to history. Covers geography, explorers, freedom fighters, biographies, photographs, and more.

First Electronic Jewish Bookshelf
Updata
Contains a selection of reference materials of interest to or pertaining to Jewish themes, such as the fulltext of *The Jewish Book of Why* and *The Jewish Book of Knowledge*, a concise encyclopedia of Judaism, a Jewish comedy catalog, a kosher cookbook, folklore, and more.

North American Indians
Quanta
Information on the history of Native Americans.

✳ CD-ROMs in libraries

Bibliography of Native Americans on Disc
ABC-CLIO
Corresponding to the print version of *Ethnographic Bibliography of North America*, this CD-ROM contains 60,000 citations to books, journal articles, essays, conference papers, dissertations, and U.S. government documents from the 16th century until the early 1990s.

Ethnic NewsWatch
Softline Information

Index and fulltext of newspapers and magazines from the ethnic and minority press in America. Covers African American, Arab/Middle Eastern, Asian American, European/Eastern European, Hispanic/Latino, Jewish, and Native American publications.

(*see also* Social sciences and humanities)

⇨ Food and diet

➤ Where can I find the latest nutritional information?

➤ How much fat is there in a particular food?

➤ Where can I find some low salt recipes?

➤ Where can I get descriptions of top-rated restaurants in cities around the U.S.?

➤ Where can I locate an appropriate wine to serve with a meal?

➤ What is the latest technologies and approaches towards food preservation?

✳ CD-ROMs

Food/Analyst
Hopkins Technology
Provides nutritional information such as calories, carbohydrates, fat, fiber, sugars, etc., for over 4,800 foods.

Food/Analyst Plus
Hopkins Technology
Similar to the previous product, but providing nutritional information for over 20,000 food items.

Sante
Hopkins Technology
An electronic cookbook, diet analysis, weight control, and exercise CD-ROM with information on over 18,000 foods.

✳ Online services

WineBase
America Online
The database contains information and ratings on thousands of different wines.

Zagat Restaurants
Prodigy
Information and ratings on restaurants located in major U.S. cities.

Food Science and Technology Abstracts
CompuServe/Knowledge Index
Provides access to research and new development literature in the areas related to food science and technology.

(*see also* Agriculture)

Gardening and plants

> ➤ Where can I find out what types of plants do best in city apartments?

> ➤ How can I diagnose and treat my sick plant?

> ➤ What is the best way to take care of a certain plant?

> ➤ Which herbs can be used to promote physical healing?

✳ CD-ROMs

The Herbalist
Hopkins Technology
Information on therapeutic herbalism (the use of medicinal plants).

Plant Doctor
Quanta
Multimedia disc to evaluate, diagnose, and treat unhealthy plants in urban environments.

Urban Phytonarian
Quanta
Fulltext of the same print publication for care of urban plants and trees.

(*see also* Agriculture)

General reference and writing aids

> ➤ Who holds the world record for a particular feat?

> ➤ Where can I find a good quote on a certain subject?

➤ Where can I locate a CD-ROM covering a particular topic?

➤ How can I find the origin of a well-known saying?

➤ What's another way of saying the same thing?

➤ When did a particular historical event occur?

➤ What is the proper spelling and definition of a certain word?

➤ Where can I find some relevant anecdotes for a speech I need to give?

➤ What did the popular news media write about a well-known historical event?

➤ Has a book been published on a particular subject? If so, who published it and when, and who is the author?

➤ Has anyone ever written their PHd thesis on a particular topic?

➤ Where can I find a published review for a certain book?

✳ CD-ROMs

CD-ROM Directory on Disc
TFPL
Describes thousands of CD-ROMs in detail. Also includes related information on CD-ROMs.

CD-ROM SourceDisc
The Disc Company
Information on CD-ROMs and the CD-ROM industry.

CD-ROMs in Print
Meckler
Describes 3,600 CD-ROMs.

Electronic Whole Earth Catalog
Broderbund
The complete text of the *Whole Earth Catalog*.

Findit Webster
Innotech
Definitions for 85,000 words, including over 3,500 audio pronunciations.

Guinness Disc of Records
MirrorSoft
Complete text of *The Guinness Book of World Records.* Includes animations, music, and sound effects plus 300 color photographs.

Guinness Multimedia Disc of Records
Grolier Electronic Publishing
Includes every record, picture, and word from the print book. Contains over 3,000 records, over 600 pictures, and dozens of video sequences, many with synchronized audio.

Microsoft Bookshelf
Microsoft Corporation
Award-winning "reference library" that contains a selection of popular research and writing sources, including a dictionary, almanac, quotation book, style manual, thesaurus, zip-code directory, business information sourcebook, and more. Includes over 3,000 images and maps, dozens of animations and spoken quotations, and more than 65,000 audio pronunciations in the dictionary and encyclopedia. $195.

Oxford English Dictionary
Oxford University Press
An electronic version of the 20-volume *Oxford English Dictionary*, containing over 616,000 English-language words. $895.

Proverbs & Quotes for All Occasions
NISC
Electronic version of two print reference sources: the *Encyclopedia of World Proverbs: A Treasury of Wit and Wisdom Through the Ages*, and Camp's *Unfamiliar Quotations from 2,000 B.C. to the Present.*

Speaker's Lifetime Treasury on CD-ROM
Thousands of quotes, epigrams, stories, similes, metaphors, mythological stories, comedy, audience-control techniques, business quotes, topics and themes, and more.

Time Magazine Compact Almanac
Time-Warner, Inc.
Over 15,000 articles from Time's publishing history, with emphasis on the most recent year, but coverage of older articles as well.

Webster's Ninth New Collegiate Dictionary
Highlighted Data
The CD-ROM version of the equivalent print book.

✳ CD-ROMs in libraries

Books in Print
H.W. Wilson Co.
Provides excerpts from and citations to reviews of current adult and juvenile fiction and nonfiction. Covers over 6,400 English-language books each year, selected from 95 American, British, and Canadian periodicals in the humanities, social sciences, and general sciences, as well as library review media.

Cumulative Book Index
H.W. Wilson Co.
A directory that lists information on English-language books published each year around the world.

Dissertation Abstracts
UMI
The fulltext of hundreds of thousands of doctoral dissertations.

✳ Online services

Books in Print
CompuServe/Knowledge Index
CompuServe/IQ
Currently published, forthcoming, and recently out-of-print books.

Dissertation Abstracts Online
CompuServe/Knowledge Index
Abstracts of all U.S. dissertations since 1861 and citations for some Canadian dissertations. Also includes selected Masters theses since 1962.

GEnie Bookshelf
GEnie gateway: Dialog
Information on over 1 million books in print; can be searched by title, author, or subject.

Magill Book Reviews
GEnie gateway: Dow Jones
Reviews of many recent fiction and nonfiction works. New titles added weekly.

Quotations Database
CompuServe/KNOWLEDGE INDEX
Omnibus file of literary, political, and other quotations of note. Ancient times through 1979.

Government information

➤ Where can I find biographical information on members of Congress?

➤ What are the latest U.S. statistics on battling drugs and crime?

➤ Where can I find the names and titles of people holding various administrative offices in the federal government?

➤ Where can I find historical information on certain bills and acts of legislature?

➤ Where can I get a listing, by subject, of what the government publishes?

➤ How can I locate government statistics and analyses on exporting and selling to other countries?

➤ Where can I get access to the latest government research and scientific reports?

➤ Where can I find the latest economic news from the government?

❉ CD-ROMs

BNA Daily News
CompuServe/Knowledge Index
Daily, comprehensive news coverage of national and international government and private-sector activities.

Congress Stack
Highlighted Data
Congressional directory: staff listing, bios, pictures, and district maps.

Information USA
Information USA
Lists and describes over 45,000 different sources of federal government assistance, such as reports, publications, and sources of money. Includes the fulltext of four popular books by Matthew Lesko on locating information from the federal government.

Microsoft STATPACK
Microsoft Corporation
Statistics on U.S. agriculture, wages, business, public lands, etc.

NIJ Drugs and Crime CD-ROM Library
U.S. National Institute of Justice
Provides a variety of information on drugs and crime, gathered from both private and public sources. Includes statistics, research results, full text from scholarly and technical journals, and more.

U.S. Government Manual on CD-ROM
Updata
Listing of department and agency personnel, phone numbers, missions, etc.

✳ CD-ROMs in libraries

Congressional Masterfile 2
Congressional Information Service Inc.
Index to U.S. Congressional activities, 1970+.

Government Publications Index
InfoTrak
An index to the monthly catalog of the government printing office. Includes indexing to public documents generated by legislative and executive branches of the U.S. government.

GPO on SilverPlatter
SilverPlatter
Citations to various reports and publications issued by the U.S. government. Contains over 300,000 records.

Monthly Catalog of U.S. Government Publications
Marcive
Primary database of U.S. government publications. Contains bibliographic citations to documents published by federal government agencies, including books, reports, studies, serials, and maps covering a wide range of topics.

National Trade Data Bank
GPO
NTDB offers a huge amount of information on exporting collected by the U.S. government. Among it are in-depth studies on the market potential of specific products in foreign countries, export/import statistics by commodity, how-to articles, and economic and demographic data on countries around the world.

NTIS
SilverPlatter
Bibliographic descriptions for over half a million U.S. government research and development reports, created by federal, state, and local government agencies.

✳ Online services

Commerce Business Daily
GEnie gateway: Dialog
CompuServe/IQ
The fulltext of U.S. Commerce Department publications, listing all significant federal contracts, requests for proposals, and related data.

Government Publications
CompuServe/IQ
Includes both a catalog of government publications and books with online ordering, as well as online consumer information articles from government publications covering topics such as personal finance, health, automotive, food, parenting, and so on.

NTIS—Government Sponsored Research
CompuServe/IQ
The U.S. National Technical Information Service is the source of government-sponsored research, development, and engineering reports. This database does not provide the actual reports but references key information so users can place an order for what they need.

GPO Publications Reference File
CompuServe/Knowledge Index
Publications for sale by U.S. Superintendent of Documents.

NTIS—Government Sponsored Research
CompuServe/IQ
Indexes U.S. government-produced technical reports. 1964 to present.

⇨ Health and medical information

➤ What are the symptoms of a certain disease? How is it treated?

➤ How can I best treat a particular health problem?

➤ How can I learn about the various methods for treating mental illness, and how effective the approaches are?

➤ What is the latest medical research status on treating a certain form of cancer?

➤ How safe is heart bypass surgery? What makes for the most successful operation?

➢ What is the latest research in preventing common childhood diseases?

➢ Where can I find the professional literature that doctors use?

➢ What does the latest research say about the relationship of diet to cancer?

➢ How can I learn about the latest developments in treatment of AIDS?

➢ What does the popular press say about the role of exercise in preventing heart disease?

➢ Where can I learn about issues facing the nursing field?

➢ What does the latest research say about the effect of second-hand smoke?

✳ CD-ROMs

American Family Physician
Creative Multimedia Corporation
Provides the fulltext of the health journal *American Family Physician*, which covers family medicine, diagnostic and therapeutic techniques, medical developments, and so forth.

British Medical Journal
Macmillan New Media
Five years of articles and text.

Cancer on Disc
Creative Multimedia Corporation
The fulltext of the journal *Cancer*.

Cardiology Medline
Macmillan New Media
200,000 citations and abstracts on articles dealing with cardiology.

The Family Doctor
Creative Multimedia
Home medical guide written for consumers. Hyperlinked Windows version available.

Health and Medical Care Directory on CD-ROM
Innotech
Data on thousands of American health-related businesses, arranged like a yellow-page directory.

Mayo Clinic Family Health Book
Sony Electronic Publishing
From the 9,300-page classic home medical reference. Includes 90 minutes of audio, video footage of 45 animated illustrations, and 500 color illustrations and photographs.

Nursing Indisc
Knowledge Access
220,000 citations to worldwide literature on nursing and nursing research.

Pediatric Infectious Disease Journal, The
Creative Multimedia Corporation
1984–91, articles and supplements from same.

Pediatrics in Review 1985–91
Creative Multimedia Corporation
Online version of print book of the same name, also includes the "redbook" from American Academy of Pediatrics.

Pediatrics on Disc
Creative Multimedia Corporation
Provides the fulltext of the publication *Pediatrics*, published by the American Academy of Pediatrics.

Prescription Drugs: A Pharmacist's Guide
Quanta
Manufacturing, dosage, side effects, and other related information on the most widely used prescription drugs.

Vital Signs: The Good Health Resource
Texas Caviar
A library of health information on hundreds of ailments and related medical information.

Wilm's and Other Renal Tumors of Children
Creative Multimedia
Information on renal tumors in children.

Year Books on Disc
Creative Multimedia
Developments in medical fields of popular interest.

✳ CD-ROMs in libraries

AIDSLINE
U.S. National Library of Medicine
Scans 3,000 journals and covers all aspects of AIDS.

CancerLit
Cambridge Scientific Abstracts
The National Cancer Institute's database of approximately 500,000 citations, most with abstracts, to journal articles, meeting reports, books, government documents, and other publications.

Health Index
InfoTrak
An index to over 160 core publications on health, fitness, nutrition, and medicine. Also includes health-related articles from approximately 3,000 other magazines and newspapers.

Health Reference Center
InfoTrak
Provides the fulltext of 150 titles on health, fitness, nutrition, and medical issues. Includes 100 consumer-oriented magazines and 500 medical educational pamphlets.

MDX Health Digest
SilverPlatter
Contains citations and abstracts to various consumer-oriented, health-related issues derived from periodicals, newspapers, and selected medical journals.

Medline
SilverPlatter/Cambridge/Dialog
A comprehensive professional medical database of 6 million citations from 1966 to the present; divided into four timespans. One of the world's largest medical databases. Medline is derived from the Index Medicus, Index to Dental Literature, and the International Nursing Index.

Physician's Desk Reference
Medical Economics Co.
Provides the fulltext from the well-known *Physicians Desk Reference*, as well as supplementary volumes covering drug descriptions and other topics.

The Physician's Medline (plus the New England Journal of Medicine, Journal of the American Medical Assoc, Annals of Internal Medicine, The Lancet, Brigthish Medical Journal, and American Journal of Public Health)
Macmillan New Media
Massive file of reports, articles, and research results from all major leading medical periodicals, research centers, organizations, etc. 1987 to 1991.

✳ **Online services**

AIDSline(TM)
CompuServe/Knowledge Index
Provides complete access to medical literature related to AIDS.

CAIN
Delphi
CAIN stands for the Computerized Aids Information Network. The database indexes and offers abstracts and fulltext for over 3,000 sources of information on AIDS, including data from the FDA, the National Institutes of Health (NIH), the National Library of Medicine, general-interest and medical journals, and a variety of other government and public data sources.

Cancerlit
CompuServe/Knowledge Index
Wide coverage of cancer research.

Consumer Medicine
GEnie gateway
Consumer Medicine is a gateway into Dialog's Medline database, which indexes biomedical information from 3,700 international journals published in over 70 countries.

Consumer Reports Drug Reference
CompuServe
Provides descriptive information on approximately 700 prescription and over-the-counter drugs. Includes advice on proper usage, side effects, general cautions, and more.

Embase
CompuServe/Knowledge Index
One of the leading sources for searching biomedical literature.

Health Database Plus
CompuServe/Ziff-Davis
Over 100,000 articles, derived from both technical health journals as well as consumer magazines.

HealthNet
CompuServe/Delphi
A fulltext encyclopedia, searchable by menu only.

Health Planning and Administration
CompuServe/Knowledge Index
Nonclinical research on all aspects of health care.

Mental Health Abstracts
CompuServe/Knowledge Index
Worldwide information on mental health from 1,200 journals.

Medical Professionals Center
GEnie gateway: Dialog
Consists of a series of Dialog databases:

> Ageline, produced by the American Association of Retired Persons

> AIDSline, produced by the U.S. National Library of Medicine

> Biosis Previews, produced by BIOSIS

> Cancerlit, produced by the U.S. National Cancer Institute

> Consumer Drug Information Fulltext, produced by the American Society
of Hospital Pharmacists

> Health Devices Alert & Health Devices Sourcebook, produced by ECRI

> Health Planning and Administration, produced by the U.S. National
Library of Medicine

> Medtext, produced by the American Medical Association

Medline (1983 to present)
CompuServe/Knowledge Index
Biomedical literature and research.

Medline (1966 to present)
CompuServe/Knowledge Index
Biomedical literature and research.

Nursing and Allied Health
CompuServe/Knowledge Index
Covers all aspects of nursing and related health fields.

PDQ Cancer-Patient Information File
CompuServe/IQuest
Information on 80 cancer types, treatment alternatives, and related data.

Smoking and Health
CompuServe/Knowledge Index
Information from journal articles, reports, and other literature concerning the effects
of smoking on health.

⇨ History

- ➢ When did a particular historical event occur in U.S. history?

- ➢ What is the background and historical significance of a particular event?

- ➢ Where can I learn about the lives of royal figures in European history?

- ➢ Where can I learn of the lives and significant events of U.S. presidents?

- ➢ Where can I find out about significant events in world history?

✳ CD-ROMs

CD Sourcebook of American History
InfoBases
Contains over 20,000 pages of historical reference works, such as the Declaration of Independence, The Constitution, Federalist Papers, accounts of the revolutionary war, and many other works by historians and other significant figures in American history.

European Monarchs
Quanta
Births, deaths, heritages, successions, etc., for the royal families of Europe.

Presidents: It All Started With George
National Geographic
Encyclopedic information on the first 40 U.S. presidents.

Time Table of History: Business, Politics & Media
Xiphias
6,000 events in the history of business, politics, and media.

Twelve Roads to Gettysburg
Hawks Interactive Systems
An interactive study of the Battle of Gettysburg.

U.S. History on CD-ROM
Bureau of Electronic Publishing
Covers U.S. political, military, and social history by providing the fulltext of over 100 books. Included are over 1,000 photographs, maps, and other illustrative materials.

U.S. Presidents
Quanta
Biographical and statistical information of 41 U.S. presidents.

✳ CD-ROMs in libraries

Historical Abstracts on Disc
ABC-CLIO
Provides abstracts to citations for 2,100 scholarly journals covering world history, except U.S. and Canada, since 1450.

✳ Online services

America: History and Life
CompuServe/Knowledge Index
Wide range of information on U.S. and Canadian history. 1964 to present.

Historical Abstracts
CompuServe/Knowledge Index
Article summaries of the history of the world from 1450 to present. 1973 to present.

⇨ Law and legal information

➤ Where can I find scholarly analyses of current legal issues?

➤ How can I find the history and results of a landmark legal case?

✳ CD-ROMs in libraries

Index to Legal Periodicals
H.W. Wilson Co.
Indexes 620 legal periodicals, including law reviews, bar association journals, yearbooks, institutes, and government publications. Also included is a table of cases, table of statutes, and book reviews.

LegalTrac
InfoTrak
An index to over 800 legal publications. Sources include all major law reviews, seven legal newspapers, law specialty publications, and bar association journals.

✳ Online services

Legal Resource Index
CompuServe/Knowledge Index
Indexing of over 750 law journals and reviews.

⇨ Literature

➢ Where can I read and analyze the works of Shakespeare?

➢ Where can I read and analyze the works of Sherlock Holmes?

➢ Where can I locate key passages and specified phrases in great works of literature?

✳ CD-ROMs

Complete Works of Shakespeare
Creative Multimedia Corporation
All plays, poems, and sonnets.

Complete Works of Sherlock Holmes
Creative Multimedia Corporation
Solves crimes. With linoleum block prints.

Gale Literary Index CD-ROM
Gale Research
Indexes over 110,000 authors' names and corresponding literary works.

Ghost Tracks
Falcon Scan
Complete text of 500 stories on the supernatural by 75 authors.

Great Literature
Bureau of Electronic Publishing
1,896 of the greatest literary works of all time. Pictures and sounds, celebrity narrations, critical commentary, and bibliographies. Fully indexed.

Greatest Books Collection
World Library Inc.
150 great works by Aristotle, Confucious, Plato, Poe, Twain, etc.

Library of the Future
World Library Inc.
450 of the world's most important literary titles.

Masterpiece Library
Pacific Hitech
1,338 classic pieces of literature, including Milton, Poe, Yeates, Dickens, and many more.

Monarch Notes on CD-ROM
Bureau of Electronic Publishing
Complete text of entire Monarch note collection on classic U.S. and world literature.

Magazines and journals (popular)

➤ Where can I find hundreds of thousands of articles published in the popular press on a wide variety of general-interest subjects?

✳ CD-ROMs

ComputerWorld on CD
International Data Group
The fulltext and selected graphics from the past four years of *ComputerWorld*. Designed for use with Sony's Multimedia player. $295.

MacLeans
Optim
Complete text of the same magazine, annually updated.

Nautilus
Nautilus
A multimedia magazine covering computing, entertainment, education, music, and more with downloadable software.

✳ CD-ROMs in libraries

Academic Index
InfoTrak
Indexing of approximately 400 scholarly and general-interest journals, including substantial abstracts for most titles. Also provides six months coverage of the *New York Times*. (The Expanded Academic Index includes approximately 1,500 journals.)

General Periodicals Index
InfoTrak
Indexes and abstracts 1,100 business and general-interest periodicals, as well as the *New York Times*, *Wall Street Journal*, and *Christian Science Monitor*.

Magazine ASAP Plus
InfoTrak
Provides the fulltext of articles found in 100 titles selected from Magazine Index
Plus.

Magazine ASAP Select
InfoTrak
Provides the fulltext of 50 titles selected from Magazine Index Plus.

Magazine Index/Plus
InfoTrak
Contains bibliographic information and some abstracts for articles in over 400
general-interest popular magazines, as well as the *New York Times*.

Periodical Abstracts
UMI/ProQuest
Abstracts hundreds of popular magazine articles. There are three versions of this
database: one abstracts 1,500 journals, extends back to 1986, and also includes the
last six months of the *New York Times* and *Wall Street Journal*; the second
contains abstracts from 950 journals and also extends back to 1986; and the third
abstracts 500 journals back to 1986 and covers six months of the *New York Times*
plus *USA Today*.

Readers' Guide Abstracts
H.W. Wilson Co.
Indexes and abstracts articles from every article in the 240 periodicals covered in the
Readers' Guide.

Readers' Guide Abstracts/Select Edition
H.W. Wilson Co.
Indexes and abstracts articles from a select group of 25,000 articles from the 240
periodicals in the Readers' Guide.

Readers' Guide to Periodical Literature
H.W. Wilson Co.
Indexes 240 popular magazines.

Resource One
UMI/ProQuest
Provides abstracts of articles from 140 periodicals extending back to 1986, *USA
Today* to 1991, and a selection of articles from the *New York Times*.

✳ Online services

Academic Index
CompuServe/Knowledge Index

Provides one-stop access to general-interest, social science, and humanities literature with an emphasis on academic journals.

Canadian Business and Current Affairs
CompuServe/Knowledge Index
Index to articles appearing in 180 Canadian business publications, nearly 300 popular magazines, and 10 newspapers.

GEnie's NewsStand
GEnie gateway: Dialog
Contains the fulltext of articles from hundreds of popular magazines and several well-known national newspapers.

GEnie's Reference Center
GEnie gateway: Dialog
Composed of over 20 different databases covering a wide field of subjects, ranging from computers and education to philosophy, history, and much more.

Magazine Database Plus
CompuServe/Ziff-Davis
Provides the fulltext to magazine articles for over 90 popular periodicals.

Magazine Index
CompuServe/Knowledge Index
Index to articles in over 400 general-interest U.S. magazines.

McGraw-Hill Library
GEnie gateway: Dow Jones
Fulltext articles published in McGraw-Hill's industry-specific publications including *Aviation Week*, *Byte*, *Chemical Engineering*, *Electric Utility Week*, *ENR*, and *Platt's Oilgram Price Report*.

New Republic
America Online
Covers political and social issues from a liberal perspective.

Worth Magazine
America Online
Covers investment information.

Meteorology/Weather

➤ What is the weather going to be like this week?

➤ What are the general weather trends in North America?

✴ CD-ROMs

National Meteorological Center Grid Point Data Set
University of Washington
Atmospheric data on the Northern Hemisphere.

✴ Online services

Dow Jones News/Retrieval Weather Report
GEnie gateway: Dow Jones
Three-day Accu-Weather forecasts for 100 U.S. and foreign cities.

⇨ Military

> ➤ Where can I learn about the details, battles, and historical and political significances of various U.S. wars?

✴ CD-ROMs

Desert Storm: The First Draft of History
Warner New Media
A chronological look at operation Desert Storm.

Officer's Bookcase
Quanta
Military defense terms and acronyms.

USA Wars—Civil War
Quanta
Fulltext and pictures covering chronologies, battles, biographies, campaigns, and other related information.

USA Wars—Desert Storm with Coalition command
Quanta
Fulltext and pictures covering chronologies, battles, biographies, campaigns, and other related information.

USA Wars—Korea
Quanta
Fulltext and pictures covering chronologies, battles, biographies, campaigns, and other related information.

USA Wars—Vietnam
Quanta
Fulltext and pictures covering chronologies, battles, biographies, campaigns, and other related information.

News

> Where can I locate today's news articles from a variety of national newspapers?

> Where can I find older, previously published articles?

> Where can I find news published in the Soviet Union?

> Where can I find the latest news reports, just filed by reporters over the electronic wires?

> Where can I locate news published in smaller, regional U.S. newspapers?

✳ CD-ROMs

Front Page News 1991
Wayzata
Fulltext of 200K news articles from 10 news sources.

Pravda 87
Alde
Complete text of the English-language translation of Pravda during the year 1987.

USA Today: The '90s, vol. 1
Compton's New Media
100,000 stories published in *USA Today* from January 1990 to August 1992.

Washington Times and Insight on the News
Wayzata
Complete text of the *Washington Times* (1990 to 1992) as well as *Insight*, a weekly news magazine.

✳ CD-ROMs in libraries

Federal News CD-ROM
NISC
Fulltext of approximately 500 federal-level political and business news events per month, broadcast by satellite transmissions and covered as they occur. Includes

official briefings, presidential campaigns, press conferences, diplomatic meetings, congressional hearings, and so on.

National Newspaper Index
InfoTrak
Indexing of five national newspapers combined in one source. Covers indexing of the *New York Times*, *Wall Street Journal*, *Christian Science Monitor*, *Washington Post*, and *Los Angeles Times*.

NewsBank Electronic Index
NewsBank Inc.
Indexes approximately 1 million articles from 500 U.S. newspapers. 1981 to date.

Newspaper Abstracts
UMI/ProQuest
Provides indexing (and brief abstracts) for eight major national newspapers: the *New York Times*, *Atlanta Constitution*, *Boston Globe*, *Chicago Tribune*, *Christian Science Monitor*, *Los Angeles Times*, *Wall Street Journal*, and *Washington Post*. Coverage extends back to 1985.

Newspapers Fulltext
UMI/ProQuest
Provides the fulltext of *American Banker*, *Atlanta Constitution* and *Atlanta Journal*, *Christian Science Monitor*, *New York Times*, *San Francisco Chronicle*, *USA Today*, *Wall Street Journal*, and *Washington Post*. Coverage extends back two years.

New York Times Ondisc
UMI/ProQuest
Provides the fulltext of articles printed in the *New York Times*. Updated monthly.

✳ Online services

AP Online
CompuServe
The latest headlines and news from the Associated Press.

Chicago Online
America Online
Unusual online service that offers regional news and features from the Chicago area of potential interest to people living outside of region as well.

Current Digest of the Soviet Press
CompuServe/Knowledge Index
Translations and abstracts from major Soviet newspapers and magazines.

DataTimes
GEnie gateway: Dow Jones
Fulltext of articles from 34 regional newspapers, two AP newswires, the
Congressional Quarterly, Gannett News Service, and *USA Today*.

Dow Jones News/Retrieval World Report
GEnie gateway: Dow Jones
Continuously updated national and international news from the Associated Press,
the Dow Jones News Service, and broadcast media.

Executive News Service
CompuServe/IQ
An electronic news-clipping service that monitors AP newswires, the *Washington
Post*, UPI, and Reuters newswires for stories that contain user-specified words and
phrases. Stories are "clipped" for you as they come across the wires and held in
electronic folders for you to review at your convenience.

National Newspaper Index
CompuServe/Knowledge Index
Indexes the *Wall Street Journal*, *New York Times*, *Christian Science Monitor*,
Los Angeles Times, and *Washington Post*. Other newspapers are also covered
selectively.

NewsGrid
CompuServe
A newswire covering U.S. and world news.

Newspaper Library
CompuServe/IQ
The fulltext (except for advertisements) for 48 daily newspapers from cities around
the country. The file is updated daily, but there is a two-day time lag between the
time a newspaper is updated and when it's available online.

Newspapers (individual daily newspapers)
All available through CompuServe's Knowledge Index:

➤ Akron Beacon Journal

➤ Arizona Republic/Phoenix Gazette

➤ Atlanta Journal/Atlanta Constitution

➤ Baltimore Sun

➤ Boston Globe

➤ Charlotte Observer

➤ Chicago Tribune

➤ Christian Science Monitor

➤ Columbus Dispatch

➤ Daily News of Los Angeles

➤ Detroit Free Press

➤ Houston Post

➤ Los Angeles Times

➤ Miami Herald

- ➤ Newsday and New York Newsday
- ➤ Oregonian (Portland)
- ➤ Orlando Sentinel
- ➤ Palm Beach Post
- ➤ Philadelphia Inquirer
- ➤ Pittsburgh Press
- ➤ Richmond News Leader/ Richmond Times Dispatch
- ➤ Rocky Mountain News
- ➤ Sacramento Bee
- ➤ San Francisco Chronicle
- ➤ San Jose Mercury News
- ➤ Seattle Times
- ➤ St. Louis Post-Dispatch
- ➤ St. Paul Pioneer Press
- ➤ Sun-Sentinel (Fort Lauderdale)
- ➤ Times-Picayune (New Orleans)
- ➤ USA Today
- ➤ Washington Post Online
- ➤ Washington Times

NewsSearch
America Online
A continuously updated newswire delivered by a third-party electronic news-gathering organization called Comtex.

Reuters Newswires
Delphi, GEnie
News headlines and stories from the London-based wire service Reuters.

UK News Clips
CompuServe
Up-to-the-minute political, economic, and financial news from the U.K.

UPI
CompuServe/Knowledge Index
Delphi
Up-to-the-minute news headlines and stories from the UPI newswire service.

The Washington Post, Fulltext Version
GEnie gateway: Dow Jones
The fulltext of the *Washington Post* newspaper.

⇨ Parenting

- ➤ How should I handle a discipline problem with my child?
- ➤ Where can I learn about a health or safety issue relating to children?

> Where can I find some valuable educational magazines for my child?

> How can I get some tips on better relating and talking to my child?

✳ Online services

Educational Magazines
America Online
Bibliographic information on over 300 different educational magazines, journals, newsletters, annual reports and guides, and periodicals ranging from *Highlights* to *American Educator* to *Nature* to *National Geographic*.

ParentNet
Delphi
Encyclopedia-type database containing articles on various aspects of parenting. It's produced by a third-party nonprofit organization that gathers a wide variety of material from numerous social-service agencies.

Parents Information Network
America Online
Offers parents interactive forums on issues of importance to them, bibliographic citations to articles from major educational periodicals, databases, real-time conferencing, guides to other parts of the America Online service, and more.

Parenting Guide
Prodigy
Contains 600 articles covering a number of basic issues that concern parents.

⇨ Patents and trademarks

> Has anyone filed a patent application on a certain invention?

> How can I find the background and history of a certain invention?

> Where can I learn which companies use which trademarks?

> Who received a patent for a particular device? When was it issued?

✳ CD-ROMs

Assist
U.S. Patent and Trademark Office
Provides identifying information on U.S. patents, such as patent number and
assignee name, for all patents issued from 1977. Also provides contact information
for attorneys licensed to practice before the Patent and Trademark Office.

Canadian Patent Index
University of British Columbia Library
200,000 citations to Canadian patents.

Who Invented What 1992
MicroPatent
Answers questions on which companies patented what products, and contains the
fulltext abstracts of every patent issued in the U.S. during 1992.

✳ CD-ROMs in libraries

CASSIS/Patent Data Library Program
U.S. Patent and Trademark Office
U.S. Patent Office data on more than 5 million U.S. and non-U.S. patents.

✳ Online services

Patent Research Center
CompuServe/IQ
Contains summaries of U.S. patents granted in chemical, mechanical, electrical, and
design areas, as well as international patent summaries from the middle of the
1970s.

TradeMark Center
GEnie gateway: Dialog
Contains 1.2 million registered trademarks from the U.S. Patent and Trademark
Office, as well as information on trademarks and service marks registered with the
Secretaries of State of all 50 U.S. states and Puerto Rico.

Tradenames
GEnie gateway: Dialog
A worldwide directory of 304,000 consumer brandnames and their owners.

Worldwide Patents Center
GEnie gateway: Dialog
Contains data on millions of patents registered at the U.S. Patent Office and at
other patent offices around the world.

⇨ Political news and reports

➢ Where can I find transcripts of events and speeches from the White House?

➢ Where can I locate the fulltext of the Supreme Court's decisions on key cases?

➢ How can I learn about terrorist political groups?

➢ Where can I learn how candidates try to win political office?

✳ CD-ROMs

Supreme Court on Disc
HyperLaw
Fulltext of 116 opinions of the 1990 to 1991 court. Updated annually.

Terrorist Group Profiles
Quanta
Profiles terrorist groups worldwide.

U.S. Civics/Citizenship Disc
Quanta
Complete text of publications by the federal government to those who want to be citizens.

Winning Elections
Wayzata
Corresponds to seven print reference on how to seek political office.

✳ Online services

White House Press Releases
America Online
Transcripts of official press releases from the U.S. White House.

⇨ Religion

➢ Where can I find where a certain phrase or passage in the Bible can be found?

> How can I research the history, background, and beliefs of certain religions?

> Where can I find comprehensive analyses of key issues of concern to religious leaders and the religious population?

✳ CD-ROMs

The Bible Library
Ellis Enterprises
The fulltext of 9 Bibles and 20 reference books relating to religion.

Master Search Bible: Concise Edition
Tri-Star Publishing
The fulltext of 4 Bibles and 10 religious works.

Master Search Bible
Tri-Star Publishing
The fulltext of 4 Bibles and 10 reference books relating to religion.

Multi-Bible Volume
Innotech
Complete text of 5 Bibles and a religious reference work.

The New Bible Library
Ellis Enterprises Inc. (EEI)
Contains more than 80 volumes and features 16 bibles and 25 reference works. Also includes transliterations of Hebrew and Greek versions of the Bible and dictionaries, and full color maps of the Holy Land. Advanced search and electronic manipulation features.

✳ CD-ROMs in libraries

Religion Index
H.W. Wilson Co.
CD-ROM version of the major printed religious periodical indexes, containing over 600,000 citations to articles, reports, theses, and other projects relating to religion.

✳ Online services

The Bible
America Online
The King James version. You can enter keywords and phrases to locate relevant passages and text.

Religion Index
CompuServe/Knowledge Index
Index to articles covering church history, the Bible, literature, theology, the history of religions, the sociology and psychology of religion, and related areas.

⇨ Science and engineering

- ➢ Where can I search for certain passages of Charles Darwin's writings?

- ➢ Where can I find technical literature covering all major scientific areas?

- ➢ Where can I find technical literature covering all major engineering areas?

- ➢ Where can I find in-depth articles covering issues in biology?

- ➢ Which technical publications provide news and analyses of mathematics and statistics?

- ➢ Where can I research chemicals and chemical engineering?

✳ CD-ROMs

Darwin
LightBinders
The collected works of the writings of Charles Darwin, including illustrations.

Time Table of Science and Innovation
Xiphias
6,200 events in the history of science and innovation.

✳ CD-ROMs in libraries

Applied Science and Technology Index
H.W. Wilson Co.
Indexes 391 key science, trade, and technology periodicals. Subjects include: aeronautics and space science, artificial intelligence and machine learning, chemistry, computer technology, construction, engineering (civil, electrical, and mechanical), engineering materials, environmental engineering and waste management, food, geology, marine technology and oceanography, mathematics, metallurgy, meteorology, mineralogy, neural networks and optical computing, petroleum and gas, physics, plastics, robotics, solid-state technology, telecommunications, textiles, and transportation.

Biological Abstracts
SilverPlatter
Contains bibliographies and abstracts to literature contained in over 7,600 leading periodicals covering biology and related fields.

CSA Life Sciences Collection
Cambridge Scientific Abstracts
Indexes and abstracts worldwide life-science literature. Topics include: animal behavior, biochemistry, amino acids, biological membranes, nucleic acids, biotechnology research, genetics, immunology, microbiology, toxicology, virology, and more. AIDS is covered in detail.

Compendex Plus
Dialog
Primary database for engineering and technology literature worldwide. 1986+.

General Science Index
H.W. Wilson Co.
Designed specifically for students and nonspecialists, this product indexes information from 139 English-language science periodicals. Major areas include: astronomy, atmospheric sciences, biology, botany, chemistry, science, environment and conservation, food and nutrition, genetics, mathematics, medicine and health, microbiology, oceanography, physics, physiology, and zoology.

Inspec
UMI/ProQuest
Abstracts from journals covering IEE journals of electrical engineering, physics, and computing.

MathSci
SilverPlatter
Primary database for mathematics, statistics, and mathematical applications in other disciplines. Contains information from mathematical reviews and current mathematical publications.

Science Citation Index
Institute for Scientific Information
Primary database for citations to articles in 3,300 science journals.

❇ Online services

The Agrochemicals Handbook
CompuServe/Knowledge Index
Detailed scientific data on agrochemicals.

Analytical Abstracts
CompuServe/Knowledge Index
Comprehensive coverage of analytical chemistry.

Chapman and Hall Chemical Database
CompuServe/Knowledge Index
Physical property data on over 175,000 substances.

Chemical Engineering and Biotechnology Abstracts
CompuServe/Knowledge Index
Information on industrial practice and theoretical chemical engineering.

Compendex*plus
CompuServe/Knowledge Index
Comprehensive coverage of 3,000 engineering journals.

Current Biotechnology Abstracts
CompuServe/Knowledge Index
Covers all aspects of biotechnology, including genetic manipulation, monoclonal antibodies, and fermentation technology.

Inspec
CompuServe/Knowledge Index
Physics, electrical engineering, electronics, computers, and control engineering.

Kirk-Othmer Online
CompuServe/Knowledge Index
Online encyclopedia of applied chemical science and industrial technology. Third edition of the *Kirk Othmer Encyclopedia of Chemical Technology*.

Life Sciences Collection
CompuServe/Knowledge Index
Worldwide coverage of research in biology, medicine, biochemistry, ecology, and microbiology.

MathSci
CompuServe/Knowledge Index
Research on pure and applied mathematics.

⇨ Social sciences and humanities

➤ Where can I find broad-based reports and articles on social-science subjects?

➤ How can I learn about linguistics and literature?

➢ What are the latest studies and research on issues relating to aging?

➢ What issues are confronting libraries and information retrieval today?

➢ How can I learn about language and literature?

➢ Where can I find information on how public policy is made?

➢ What are the key issues professional philosophers are debating?

➢ What does the psychological research show regarding a particular disorder?

➢ What are the experts saying about confronting and solving key social problems?

➢ What are the biggest problems confronting the aged, and what are some solutions?

✳ CD-ROMs in libraries

Humanities Index
H.W. Wilson Co.
Indexes 345 English-language periodicals. Subjects include: art, archaeology, classical studies, area studies, dance, drama, film, folklore, history, journalism and communications, language and literature, music, performing arts, philosophy, and religion and theology.

Library Literature
H.W. Wilson Co.
Indexes 219 journals and over 600 monographs per year, plus conference proceedings and collected works.

MLA International Bibliography
H.W. Wilson Co.
The Modern Language Association International Bibliography indexes over 3,000 periodicals and serials, monographs, book collections, dissertation abstracts, and various other sources that cover languages, literature, folklore, linguistics, literary themes and genres, and other related humanity topics.

PAIS
Public Affairs Information Service
Primary database for public-policy questions, providing over 350,000 citations on all issues relating to public-policy making.

Philosopher's Index
Dialog
Indexes and abstracts from over 150,000 citations from books and over 300
journals of philosophy and related interdisciplinary fields. 1940+.

PsychLit
SilverPlatter
Primary database for psychology and behavioral sciences. Includes articles on all
aspects of psychology. Detailed and professionally oriented articles, many research-
based with statistical backing.

Social Sciences Citation Index
Institute for Scientific Information
Comprehensive social-science database covering recent articles in 4,700 journals.

Social Sciences Index
H.W. Wilson Co.
Indexes 342 English-language periodicals. Covers areas such as: anthropology, area
studies, community health and medical care, economics, ethnic studies, geography,
gerontology, international relations, law and criminology, minority studies, planning
and public administration, police science and corrections, policy science, political
science, psychology and psychiatry, social work and public welfare, sociology, and
urban studies.

Social Work Abstracts Plus
SilverPlatter
Contains 25,000 citations from journal articles and doctoral dissertations covering
the social work profession, theory and practice, areas of service, and social issues
and problems. A separate file provides directory and contact information for clinical
social workers in the United States.

Sociofile
SilverPlatter
Primary database for sociology, social policy, and social planning.

✳ Online services

Ageline
CompuServe/Knowledge Index
Indexes journals covering social gerontology: the study of aging in social,
psychological, health-related, and economic contexts.

Linguistics and Language Behavior Abstracts
CompuServe/Knowledge Index
Abstracts of the world's literature on linguistics and language behavior.

PAIS International
CompuServe/Knowledge Index
Broad-based source for all areas of public and current policy.

Philosopher's Index
CompuServe/Knowledge Index
Index to journal articles and books on the subject of philosophy and related fields.

PsychINFO
CompuServe/Knowledge Index
Leading source of published research in psychology and behavioral sciences.

Sociological Abstracts
CompuServe/Knowledge Index
Worldwide coverage of sociological research. 1963 to present.

Sports

➢ Where can I find historical baseball statistics?

➢ Where can I learn the background and statistics of top baseball players?

➢ Where can I search for and find articles previously published in *Sports Illustrated* magazine on a wide variety of sporting news and features?

➢ What are the latest approaches and techniques being used in sports medicine?

➢ What are the results of today's or yesterday's game in baseball, football, hockey, tennis, and other sports?

➢ What are the current standings in baseball, football, and other sports?

✳ CD-ROMs

Baseball's Greatest Hits
Voyager
Statistics on well-known baseball players and quicktime images on 65 memorable moments in baseball. Includes six hours of audio.

Compton's Multimedia Golf Guide
Compton's New Media

A complete reference guide with graphics and photographs to the layout and characteristics of over 750 golf courses in California and Hawaii.

Scouting Report: 1992
Quanta
Statistics and information on major-league baseball and players.

Sporting News
Quanta
Provides the fulltext of *The Sporting News Baseball Guide*.

Sports Adventure
Knowledge Adventure

Sports Illustrated CD-ROM Sports Almanac
Warner New Media
Statistics and information for over 30 professional and amateur sports.

Total Baseball 1993
Creative Multimedia
Baseball statistics and standings for 1891 to 1993, and audio clips of games through the World Series of 1992.

✳ CD-ROMs in libraries

Sport Discus
SilverPlatter
Sports psychology, exercise, coaching, training.

✳ Online services

Dow Jones News/Retrieval Sports Report
GEnie gateway: Dow Jones
Continuously updated scores, standings, stats, schedules, and stories for most major sports.

The Sports Network
GEnie
An independent news-gathering organization whose writers file late-breaking sports stories and report the latest scores, standings, and news.

UK Sports Clips
CompuServe
Contains only the latest headlines and fulltext stories covering a variety of sports and competitions held around the world.

335

Sport
CompuServe/Knowledge Index
Coverage of sports medicine research and fitness. 1949 to present theses and
monographs.

 # Travel

> ➤ How can I find out about what to do, what to see, where to
>   stay, where to eat, and other practical travel information for
>   regions around the U.S.?

> ➤ Where can I learn about traveling to Japan (how to do it, what I
>   should know about Japanese customs, etc.)?

> ➤ How can I find a certain type of bed and breakfast in a certain
>   city I'd like to visit?

> ➤ Where can I get facts and statistics on major U.S. cities?

✳ CD-ROMs

Electronic Traveler: California, San Francisco and Northern California, U.S. and
Worldwide, Western U.S.
EBook
Travel articles on California, San Francisco and Northern California, the United
States, and regions of the world.

Exotic Japan
Voyager
Information on Japan, such as its culture, people, geography, and so on.

Software Toolworks Travel Companion
Software Toolworks
Travel planning information, derived from Frommer's USA Travel Guide. Includes
data on hotels, restaurants, sights, etc.

✳ Online services

B&B Guide
America Online
Lists data for about 9,000 bed and breakfast accommodations.

City Guides
Prodigy

Created and derived from Prodigy's own members' comments on what to do and see in major cities around the U.S.

Mobil Travel Guide
Prodigy
Guide to food and lodging in 3,300 cities around the country.

Trav-Alerts
Delphi
Advisories from the U.S. State department and other organizations regarding travel to various countries around the world.

Worldline Country Search
Delphi
Travel information on over 200 countries.

⇨ CD-ROM producers

Alde Publishing
6520 Edenvale Blvd., Suite 118
Eden Prairie, MN 55346
(612) 934-4239

American Business Information
P.O. Box 27347
Omaha, NE 68127
(402) 593-4595

Broderbund Software Inc.
500 Redwood Blvd.
Novato, CA 94948
(800) 521-6263

Bureau of Electronic Publishing, Inc.
141 New Rd.
Parsippany, NJ 07054
(201) 808-2700

Canadian Centre for Occupational
Health and Safety
250 Main St. E.
Hamilton, ON L8N 1H6
Canada
(416) 572-2981

Compton's New Media
2320 Camino Vida Roble
Carlsbad, CA 92009-1504
800-216-6116

Creative Multimedia Corporation
514 NW 11th Ave., Suite 203
Portland, OR 97209
(800) 262-7668

Delorme Mapping
P.O. Box 298, Lower Main St.
Freeport, Maine 04032
(800) 452-5931

The Disc Company
6609 Rosecroft Place
Falls Church, VA 22043
(703) 237-0682

Ebook Inc.
39315 Zacate Ave.
Fremont, CA 94538
(510) 794-4816

Ellis Enterprises Inc. (EEI)
4205 McAuley Blvd., Suite 385
Oklahoma City, OK 73120
(800) 729-9500

Dialog Information Services
3460 Hillview Ave.
Palo Alto, CA 94304
(800) 334-2564

Digital Directory Assistance, Inc.
P.O. Box 648, 70 Atlantic Ave.
Marblehead, MA 01945
(617) 639-2900

Falcon Scan
263 Laurier Ave. W., Suite B2
Ottawa, ON K1P 5J9
Canada
(613) 236-6655

Gale Research, Inc.
835 Penobscott Building
Detroit, MI 48226
(800) 347-4253

Grolier Electronic Publishing, Inc.
Sherman Turnpike
Danbury, CT 06816
(800) 356-5590

Hawks Interactive Systems
6475 28th St. SE, Suite 132
Grand Rapids, MI 49546

Highlighted Data
4350 N. Fairfax Dr., Suite 450
Arlington, VA 22203
(703) 516-9211

Hopkins Technology
421 Hazel Lane
Hopkins, MN 55343
(612) 931-9376

Horizon Technology, Inc.
P.O. Box 80246
San Diego, CA 92138
(800) 828-3808

Hyperlaw Inc.
P.O. Box 1176, Ansonia Station
New York, NY 10023
(212) 787-2812

IDD
206 Colony Park, 2001 S. Main St.
Blacksburg, VA 24060
(800) 433-9836

Infobases, Infobases International Inc.
1875 South State St., Suite 3100
Orem, UT 84058-8087
(801) 224-2223

Information Access Company
362 Lakeside Dr.
Foster City, CA 94404
(800) 321-6388

Innotech Inc.
110 Silver Star Blvd., Unit 107
Scarborough, ON M1V 5A2
Canada
(416) 321-3838

International Data Group
IDG Communications
P.O. Box 9171, 375 Cochituate Rd.
Framingham, MA 01701
(508) 879-0700

Knowledge Access
2685 Marine Way, Suite 1305
Mountain View, CA 94043
(800) 252-9273

Knowledge Adventure Inc.
4502 Dyer St.
La Crescenta, CA 91214
(800) 542-4240

Lightbinders
2325 3rd St., Suite 320
San Francisco, CA 94107
(415) 621-5746

Macmillan New Media
124 Mount Auburn St.
Cambridge, MA 02138
(617) 661-2955

McGraw-Hill, Inc.
11 W. 19th St.
New York, NY 10011
(800) 262-4729

Meckler Corporation
11 Ferry Lane W.
Westport, CT 06880
(203) 226-6967

Media Technology Ltd.
c/o Bethesda Softworks
(800) 677-0700

Metatec
7001 Discovery Blvd.
Dublin, OH 43017
(614) 761-2000

MicroPatent
25 Science Park
New Haven, CT 06511
(203) 786-5500

Microsoft Corporation
One Microsoft Way
Redmond, WA 98052
(800) 426-9400

MirrorSoft Ltd.
Irsin House, 118 Southwark St.
London SE1 OSW
UK
(011-44) 71-928-1454

National Geographic Society
Educational Services
Washington, DC 20036
(800) 368-2728

National Geophysical Data Center, NOAA
Code E/GC4, Dept. ORD
325 Broadway
Boulder, CO 80303-3328

Nautilus
7001 Discovery Blvd.
Dublin, OH 43017
(800) 637-3472

NISC
Suite 6, Wyman Towers
3100 St. Paul St.
Baltimore, MD 21218
(410) 243-0797

Optim
338 Somerset St. W.
Ottawa, ON K2P OJN
Canada
(613) 232-3766

OrangeCherry New Media
Box 390 Westchester Ave.
Pound Ridge, NY 10576
(914) 764-4104

Oxford University Press
Oxford Electronic Publishing
200 Madison Ave.
New York, NY 10016
(800) 872-2828

Pacific HiTech, Inc.
4530 Fortuna Way
Salt Lake City, UT 84124
(800) 765-8369

PhoneDisc USA
Digital Directory Assistance, Inc.
5161 River Rd., Building 6
Bethesda, MD 20816
(800) 639-2900

PROCD Inc.
8 Doaks Lane
Marblehead, MA 01945
(617) 631-9299

Quanta
1313 5th St. SE, Suite 223A
Minneapolis, MN 55414
(612) 379-3956

Salem Press, Inc.
150 S. Los Robles Ave., Suite 720
Pasadena, CA 91101
(818) 854-0106

Scanrom Publications
POB 72
Cedarhurst, NY 11516
(516) 295-2237

Slater Hall
1301 Pennsylvania Ave. NW, Suite 507
Washington, DC 20004
(202) 393-2666

Software Toolworks
60 Leveroni Court
Novato, CA 94949
(800) 234-3088

TFPL Ltd.
22 Peter's Lane
London EC1M 6DS
UK
(011-44) 71-251-8318

Texas Caviar
3933 Steck Ave., Suite B-115
Austin, TX 78759
(512) 346-7887

Time-Warner, Inc.
Time-Life Building
New York, NY 10020
(212) 522-1212

Trace Center
1500 Highland Ave., Room S-151
Madison, WI 53705
(608) 262-6966

Tri-Star Publishing
275 Gibralter Rd.
Horsham, PA 19044
(800) 292-4253

UniDisc
(order via Compton's New Media)

Updata Publications Inc.
1736 Westwood Blvd.
Los Angeles, CA 90024
(213) 474-5900

U.S. Bureau of the Census
Data User Services Division
Washington, DC 20233
(301) 763-2074

U.S. Department of Commerce
14th St. at Constitution Ave.
Washington, DC 20230
(202) 377-2000

U.S. Environmental Protection Agency
Office of Health and Environment
Review Division
Office of Pollution, Prevention, and
Toxins
401 M. St. SW, MS-TS796
Washington, DC 20460
(202) 260-1513

U.S. National Environmental Satellite,
Data, and Information Service
National Geophysical Data Center
325 Broadway
Boulder, CO 80303
(303) 497-6215

U.S. National Institute of Justice
P.O. Box 6000
Rockville, MD 20850
(800) 851-3420

U.S. Patent and Trademark Office
Office of Electronic Information
Products and Services
Crystal Plaza 2, 9D30
Washington, DC 20231
(703) 308-0322

University of British Columbia Library
1956 Main Hall
Vancouver, BC V6T 1Z1
Canada
(604) 822-5404

University of Colorado
Laboratory for Atmospheric and Space Physics
Campus Box 392
Boulder, CO 80309
(303) 492-7666

University of Washington
Department of Atmospheric Sciences
Mail Stop AK-40
Seattle, WA 98195
(206) 685-0910

Vocational Technologies Ltd.
32 Castle St.
Guildford, Surrey GU1 3UW
UK
(011-44) 83-579472

Voyager
1351 Pacific Coast Hwy.
Santa Monica, CA 90401
(800) 446-2001

Warner New Media
3500 Olive Ave.
Burbank, CA 91505
(818) 955-9999

Wayzata Technology
P.O. Box 807
Grand Rapids, MI 55744
(800) 735-7321

World Book Publishing
525 Monroe St., 20th Fl.
Chicago, IL 60606
(800) 433-6580

World Library, Inc.
12914 Haster St.
Garden Grove, CA 92640
(800) 443-0238

Xiphias
Helms Hall
8758 Venice Blvd.
Los Angeles, CA 90034
(213) 841-2790

⇨ CD-ROM distributors

These firms don't normally create or produce CD-ROMs, but distribute products produced by other original data providers:

Educorp (Macintosh)
7434 Trade St.
San Diego, CA 92121-2410
(800) 843-9497

EEI
Box 40
Lenapah, OK 74042
(800) 729-9500

MAC/PC Connection
(800) 800-3333

Multiple Zones
(800) 248-0800

SilverPlatter Information, Inc.
100 River Ridge Dr.
Norwood, MA 02062
(800) 343-0064

Tiger Software
800 Douglas Entrance, Executive Tower, 7th Fl.
Coral Gables, FL 33134
(800) 666-2562

Updata
1736 Westwood Blvd.
Los Angeles, CA 90024
(800) 882-2844

Walnut Creek CDROM
1547 Palos Verdes, Suite 260
Walnut Creek, CA 94596
(800) 786-9907

⇨ Retail outlets

You can often find consumer-oriented CD-ROMs sold at computer stores and electronic retail outlets. Popular vendors include stores such as Babbages, Best Buy, CompUSA, ComputerCity, Egghead, Software Etc., Waldensoft, and others.

Major online database vendors

 ## Consumer-oriented systems

America Online
8619 Westwood Center Dr.
Vienna, VA 22182
(703) 448-8700

GEnie
P.O. Box 6403
Rockville, MD 20850
(800) 638-9636

CompuServe
P.O. Box 20212
Columbus, OH 43220
(800) 848-8990

Prodigy
P.O. Box 791
White Plains, NY 10601
(914) 993-8000

Delphi
1030 Masachusetts Ave.
Cambridge, MA 02138
(617) 491-3393

 ## Professionally oriented systems

These are generally—though not exclusively—geared to professional
and experienced researchers in business, law, or other professions.
They're normally more expensive than consumer systems, but
provide in-depth powerful information systems:

BRS
8000 Westpark Dr.
McLean, VA 22102
(800) 289-3166

Dialog
Dialog Information Services
3460 Hillview Avenue
Palo Alto, CA 94304
(800) 334-2564

Data-Star
D-S Marketing Inc.
Suite 1110
485 Devon Park Dr.
Wayne, PA 19087
(800) 221-7754

Dow-Jones
Dow Jones Information Services
P.O. Box 300
Princeton, NJ 08543-0300
(800) 522-3567

Lexis/Nexis
Mead Data Central
P.O. Box 933, 9443 Springboro Pike
Dayton, OH 45401

NewsNet
NewsNet
945 Haverford Rd.
Bryn Mawr, PA 19010

A

Price-comparison chart

The following chart is designed to provide you with a good idea of how the various online providers compare in cost. I've set it up so you can first roughly estimate how many hours per month you think you'll use an online service and then run down the chart to find out how much you'll end up paying, depending on the particular service.

To keep this chart manageable and useful, I've had to make some assumptions. It's based on using a 2,400-bps modem; if you use a 9,600-bps one you'll need to inquire about any surcharges from the vendor. Not included is the cost of any one-time membership kits. These usually consist of introductory brochures and some software, and sometimes come bundled free.

Service	Monthly fee/ # of hours	Each addl. hour	3 hrs. /mo.	6 hrs. /mo.	10 hrs. /mo.	20 hrs. /mo.
America Online*	$9.95/5	$3.50	$9.95	$13.45	$27.45	$62.45
CompuServe standard (1st mo. free)	$8.95/unlimited	0 (basic services only)	$8.95	$8.95	$8.95	$8.95
Compuserve alternate (first 2 mo. free)	$2.50	$12.80 (surcharged services extra)	$40.90	$79.30	$130.50	$258.50
Compuserve Knowledge Index only	$2.50 (for alternate plan)	$24	$72	$144	$240	$480
Delphi 10-4 plan**	$10/4	$4	$10	$18	$34	$74
Delphi 20-20 plan**	$20/20	$1.80	$20	$20	$20	$20
GEnie[†] Basic & Value	$8.95/4 hours	$3	$8.95	$14.95	$29.95	$56.95
GEnie Profl. Svcs	$8.95/4 hours	varies	varies	varies	varies	varies
Prodigy Value Plan	$14.95/unlimited core svcs. + 2 hrs plus features	$4[‡]	$18.95	$20.95	$46.95	$86.95
Prodigy Alternate 1	$7.95/2 hours	$4[‡]	$11.95	$13.95	$39.95	$79.95
Prodigy Alternate 2	$19.95/8 hours	$4[‡]	$19.95	$19.95	$27.95	$67.95

* Not including first month, which includes free usage up to 10 hours.

** Weekend and evening searching only! Delphi charges a $9 per hour surcharge for weekday searching, and a $3-per-month premium for accessing the Internet.

[†] Non-prime-time searching only. Prime-time searching (8AM to 6PM weekdays, local time) costs $12.50 an hour. Also, 9,600-bps searchers pay a $6-per-hour surcharge at all times.

[‡] Actual cost is $3.60 to $4.80, depending on the number of additional hours.

What can you make out of this chart? Well, some obvious difference in pricing plans among the vendors emerges, as does the expenses of searching. It's clear, for example, that as of this writing the cheapest services are the Delphi and CompuServe basic plans. Unfortunately, with a couple notable exceptions, there are few in-depth databases

available on Delphi or CompuServe's basic services alone. But if you're mainly interested in getting onto the Internet, you might find Delphi quite a good choice.

You can also see from the chart just how quickly your bill can run into hundreds of dollars per month if you don't watch your searching time carefully. For instance, while $24 per hour to search Knowledge Index is a bargain in the world of online databases, it still translates into 240 bucks if you've used it for 10 hours during the month. At the same time, remember that most searches take just 10 to 15 minutes or so, so 10 hours worth of searching would typically translate into about 50 searches—which that's a lot of searches, but not impossible to imagine if you're working on a major research project.

Caution: When comparing these prices, keep in mind that online service vendors change their pricing plans frequently to remain competitive. You should double check with the vendors to check for any changes in their pricing plans. If so, you can just recalculate these figures yourself with the new data.

B
Boolean searching

Any researcher worth his or her salt must know the basics of properly conducting an online database search. Luckily, though, while database searching is both a science and an art that requires lots and lots of practice, anyone can learn how to get going with just a little initial instruction.

First, let's review a few basic concepts. Remember that what I'm discussing here are searchable databases. A database, if you'll recall, is a collection of related information you can access with your computer. A searchable database is one that's been programmed and configured so you can electronically browse through the individual items (called records) that make up the database to locate just what you need.

There are a number of ways that database producers and online hosts set up their database for searching. The most important and most useful method is the Boolean search, a sophisticated method for using basic keyword searching.

A Boolean search sounds very mathematical and vaguely confusing, but while it is, indeed, mathematical, it doesn't have to be confusing. In fact, it's pretty darn simple—and I think that by the end of this appendix you'll understand its basic operations pretty well.

Before I start defining a Boolean search, I need to first take one step backwards and talk about keyword database searching. To perform a keyword database search, you must determine what subject you need information on and then think up a specific word or words that best describe that subject—these are called keywords. The online database finds relevant items by searching for records that are linked to that word. For example, if you wanted to find information on arthritis, your keyword would be *arthritis* and that's what you would key in to the database. If you had to dig up information on supercomputers, your keyword would be *supercomputers*.

When your subject can't be easily summed up in a single word is when you enter the wonderful, magical world of Boolean searches. A Boolean search allows you to combine multiple keywords by using three of the simplest words in the English language (or, in Boolean-speak, *operators*): AND, OR, and NOT.

Say you needed to search for information on the topic of arthritis in children. First you would choose an appropriate database, for example, one that contained published articles from medical and health-related journals. Your Boolean keyword search that you would enter into the computer might then be:

```
arthritis AND children
```

By using the AND operator, you've narrowed the previously mentioned search on the keyword *arthritis*. Now, in this more restrictive search, an acceptable article must contain both (that's the AND part) the word *arthritis* and the word *children*. If, in another search, you were looking for data on Wyoming or Montana, your Boolean keyword search would be:

```
Wyoming OR Montana
```

In this case, by using the OR operator, you've broadened and expanded your search. Now an acceptable article must contain either (that's the OR part) the words *Wyoming* or *Montana*. You've cast a wider net. And if you wanted information on supercomputers but don't want to retrieve any items that mention IBM, your keyword search would be:

```
supercomputers NOT IBM
```

(Although the NOT operator can be quite useful in certain instances, to try to simplify things I'm not going to spend much time using it in these examples. It isn't likely that you'll use it nearly as often as AND, OR, and some other related functions.)

You can see how using these connecting words allows you to create much more useful and precise searches than just a single keyword or phrase. You can further exploit the power of these searches by connecting a string of Boolean operators together. So let's say that your research project is now to find information on the occurrences of arthritis or diabetes in children living in England. Your Boolean string might initially be configured like this:

```
arthritis OR diabetes AND children AND England
```

Let's look at this statement very carefully. You have (hopefully) just instructed the computer to locate published articles that mention the words *arthritis* or *diabetes*—as well as *children* and *England*.

Here's where things get just a little bit—but only a little bit—tricky. You see, the computer could read that statement in more than one way. And that's not good! For example, the computer might think that you are requiring it to find all articles that mention:

```
arthritis OR
diabetes AND children AND England
```

And if the computer views your search statement like this, it's instructing itself that an acceptable article—one that meets your criteria—is one that mentions arthritis . . . OR diabetes, children, and England. But that's not what you want. You don't want just any article that mentions arthritis—that's much too broad. However, if the computer views that same search statement differently, it will look for a different set of articles:

```
arthritis OR diabetes
AND children
AND England
```

How do you know which way the system will read your search command? Unfortunately, you don't—databases vary in the manner and order they read Boolean searches. All systems have an automatic or *default* order that determines which Boolean operators it will process first, and this default varies from system to system.

351

Fortunately, though, there's a simple way to make sure that the computer reads your statement exactly the way you want it to be read. Just use parentheses, like this:

`(arthritis OR diabetes) AND children AND England`

Parentheses group terms together and instruct the computer to act on the elements enclosed in the parentheses first. So it's always smart to use parentheses whenever you have multiple operators and there's a chance for confusion.

Boolean search tips

Now that you know what a Boolean search is and how to create one, you now need to know how to create *good* Boolean searches, because—as I mentioned earlier—there's an art to searching, and it requires a bit of skill . . . plus a *lot* of practice. Some of the skill part, however, I can impart here with a few tips.

Know what you're searching

This is a major point that sometimes even professional searchers forget. Depending on the particular database that you've chosen, when you enter your search term the computer might search either the various records' titles, their subject headings or descriptors, an abstract, or words contained in the fulltext. Let's look at each of these areas, and examine their ramifications:

✳ Title searching

Many records—especially newspaper and journal articles—have a title or headline. This title is usually written by a staffer from the original source, though sometimes it's written by the database's own indexers. Titles are generally one line, and are typically a very short summary of the whole item.

❋ **Subject headings and descriptors**

Subject headings or descriptors are terms created by the indexers to describe the topics and issues covered in each particular record. These terms are created as a way to provide some consistency for searchers.

❋ **Abstracts**

Usually, these are one or two paragraphs that summarize the main points of the original article or piece.

❋ **Fulltext**

When you search a fulltext database—i.e., a database that contains the complete text of the original articles, reports, or data—you're often searching all the words contained in the original piece. This can be extremely useful for finding citations of more obscure and hard-to-find subjects, but can also be a treacherous area for novice searches.

Unfortunately, for many of the databases found on consumer online services you aren't given a choice as to which of these areas your search statement is applied to. Often, you automatically search the fulltext of the database records.

 # Plan your search statement

This is crucial. You can't expect to sit down in front of your computer, call up a database, and then just wing it. Well, maybe you can for the simplest single-keyword searches, but it's still not advisable. For any kind of complex or involved searching, you need to take just a couple of minutes out to write down a search strategy before going online. In addition to ensuring superior results, this is important because many databases charge you for every minute you spend online. For this reason, pondering over your search phrases is

an easy—and unnecessary—way to run up the meter. Here's how to create your search statement:

✳ Determine the keywords

How do you plan a search? Well, the core of any database search statement is coming up with the keywords. This is an absolutely vital component of the process; along with your choice of database, this step will most directly determine what you get back from your search.

Sometimes coming up with keywords is simple, and requires no great thought. If you're searching for articles in a music database that mentions, say, the singer Enya, you can probably just key in her name. But most of the time it's not going to be that simple.

Here's an example of how to create a search strategy for a somewhat complex research problem. Say you're looking for information on how to check for radon when buying a home. You might think, at first glance, that your Boolean search would be pretty straightforward, such as:

```
checking AND radon AND buying AND home
```

Sorry. It's not that simple. You see, although these keywords are perfectly fine, there are other words that are just as good. And the database might contain those other words instead of yours! If so, the system would skip over all the database records that contained the other words, even though they would be relevant for you. So you need to think a bit—are there common synonyms for the words you've chosen?

✳ Think of appropriate synonyms

Let's start just with that first word: *checking*. Aren't there other words you could use to describe the process of testing a house for radon? Well, how about *testing*, for one? And what about *analyzing* and *examining*? Hmm . . . it seems we'd better broaden that first keyword, and substitute it with:

```
checking OR analyzing OR examining OR testing
```

Are there other words that come to mind? Well, maybe not immediately, but if you think hard enough you're bound to come up with additional ones. Here's where the "art" of searching comes in, and it's a bit difficult to describe. When you have to think too hard to come up with additional keywords, it's less likely that these words will be ones that will occur with any frequency in the database. That's why using a thesaurus to look up synonyms can be a bit dangerous. You don't want to enter every obscure and possible synonym. There's a point of diminishing returns.

But again, remember there rarely is a "perfect" search statement. In fact, it would be just about impossible for one to exist, because it's impossible to know all the words that will be used in any single database. You've got to make a reasonable stab, though, at coming up with the most common words used in the appropriate context. The point here is that if there are commonly synonyms, use the OR operator to add those words. Note that this procedure of thinking of synonyms is not normally necessary if you're using a database using subject descriptors.

Let's continue this search and go to our next term: *radon*. Are there any synonyms that readily come to mind? No, there aren't. What's next? The word *buy*. Well, what about *purchase*? That seems like just as good a word as *buy*. Okay, so now the search statement is as follows:

```
(checking OR analyzing OR examining OR testing)
AND radon OR (buying or purchasing)
```

Last on the list is the word *home*. Hmm . . . it seems that *house* would be at least as good, if not better. Now the search statement, looking a bit unwieldy, reads like this:

```
(checking OR analyzing OR examining OR testing)
AND radon AND (buying OR purchasing) AND home OR house
```

Are we done yet? Can we run the search? Well, if you're a sharp reader, you'll realize that there are still a few flaws in this little search strategy. One of the biggest is in the choice of the words *checking*, *analyzing*, *examining*, and *testing*. Why should we assume that the gerund form of the word is the one that will be linked in the database? Might some records have, for example, a headline that

reads "How to Check Your House for Radon" or even "Have You Checked Your House for Radon?" Computers have an annoying tendency to take everything you tell them literally, and they're not going to cut you any slack. Does this mean you have to think of and key in all possible variations of every keyword? Luckily, no.

✳ Truncate where appropriate

Riding to the rescue is truncation. When you truncate a word, you use a special symbol, usually inserted at the end, to instruct the computer to automatically search for that root word plus all other words off that stem. On most systems, you truncate a word by ending it with a question mark or an asterisk. You can truncate the word *check*, then, by using *check?*, which would instruct the computer to automatically search for:

```
check
checks
checked
checking
checkings
checker
checkers
```

. . . and any other word it finds that begins with *check*—that includes checkmate too! That's one unavoidable drawback to using truncation—you can get variations of a word that have no relevance to what you're looking for.

You could perform the same exercise with the words *analyzing*, *examining*, and *testing*. Those words, truncated, would become *analyz?*, *examin?*, and *test?* so you're saved the hassle of having to think of and then enter into the computer all possible variations. (On many systems you can also enter a similar "wildcard" symbol in the middle of a word. So, for example, if you entered the word *ch?ck*, the system would turn up words like *check*, *chock*, and *chuck*.)

Are there other keywords in the search statement that should be truncated? Radon seems pretty safe as is. But *buy* and *purchase* could and should be truncated to pick up commonly used variations like *buying*, *buyer*, *buys*, *purchases*, *purchased*, and *purchasing*. And *home* and *house* should certainly be truncated in order to find

occurrences of *homes* and *houses*. So now the latest version reads like this:

```
(check? OR analyz? OR examin? OR test?)
AND radon AND (buy OR purchas?) AND (home OR house)
```

✳ Use proximity operators as needed

You need to know about one last Boolean step: *proximity operators*. You use proximity operators whenever you need to specify exactly how many words apart you want one keyword to be located from another. You can specify that certain words be right next to each other or up to 2, 3, 4, 5, or more words apart. Most of the time, you'll use this function to avoid retrieving records that just coincidentally contain two keywords somewhere in the text, but far apart and with no relationship to each other. This can easily happen in certain databases, especially long fulltext records that run thousands of words long and might contain your keywords, but not with the close relationship you require.

So, again, using the previous example, you could be especially precise by saying that you wanted your first key concept (check? OR analyz? OR examin? OR test?) to be within, say, four words of the next keyword (radon). This would ensure that the first term is directly related to the second. The four-word spread would allow the database to retrieve phrases such as "checking for radon," "radon should be checked," and "why you should check your home for radon." But it would prevent the retrieval of a record that contains, say, the first keyword in the phrase "writing a check" in line 7 and then "radon removal firms" in line 63. On the Dialog online service, you designate proximity operators by replacing the broader AND statement with a number that represents the specified maximum word spread, followed by the letter *n*. So now the final version of the original search statement would be as follows:

```
(check? OR analyz? OR examin? OR test?)
4n radon AND (buy? OR purchas?) AND (home? OR house?)
```

How do you know when you should use proximity operators and, when you *do* use them, how do you know how large a word separation to specify? You should use proximity operators whenever you want to make sure that there is a very close and direct relationship between two

keywords, especially if they're common words that might be sprinkled throughout long articles. As for how large to make the word spread, it really depends on the particular search, though you'd rarely specify over a 7- to 8-word spread. The best way to get a feel for all of this is to practice, practice, practice . . . and then practice some more.

 # Troubleshooting

Let's say you've spent time carefully constructing a search and have still ended up with poor results. Well, it normally means one of three things:

➤ Not enough items ("hits") retrieved—or none at all!

➤ Too many hits

➤ Irrelevant hits

Let's start with the first problem: too few or no hits. What might be the problem? There are a number of possible causes:

You made a typo when entering your search If you asked the database to search for records that contained the word *Dusneyland*, you're not going to find too much! Remember, your computer won't engage in creative brainstorming to solve your problems! Key in your searches carefully, and read them over for any possible typos.

You're searching in the wrong database While not as embarrassing as being in the wrong restroom, discovering that you're using the wrong database can cause problems. Today there are many databases that cover similar-sounding subjects, but actually differ quite a bit. Before searching a database, carefully consider which one is most likely to contain sources of data that cover your subject of interest and take a perspective of most use to you (e.g., a business, scientific, or journalism perspective).

The only way to find this out is to become familiar with many databases so you can make appropriate choices. You don't need to— and cannot—be familiar with *every* database since there are thousands. But you *can* become familiar with several of the leading

databases or more niche ones that are of special interest to you. The best way to become familiar with a database is by reading a description of what it contains and practicing using it. An easy way to find out what many leading databases cover is to obtain a catalog from a major online vendor, such as Dialog.

The following are potential causes of obtaining any of the cited problems: too few hits, too many hits, or irrelevant ones.

You aren't using the best keywords This is a tricky one. It's pretty darn hard to always come up with which few words in the English language are the ones most likely to retrieve what you want. But arriving at the right keywords is crucial to the success of your search.

Usually, the problem with a keyword that isn't working is that it's too broad or too narrow. A word that's too broad, for example a common word very frequently encountered, will result in too many hits. Obvious examples of words that are too broad for, say, a business-related database are ones like *management*, *company*, and *sales*. In a news database, you'd have the same problem with words like *president*, *United States*, *economy*, *healthcare*, and so on. This doesn't mean that it's never appropriate to use one of these terms, but you might need to prepare yourself to narrow down an unmanageable number of hits.

In contrast, using a word that's too narrow, e.g., an obscure or rarely encountered word, might result in retrieving few or no records. This isn't always bad—sometimes you're hoping for only one or two items. Other times you might be wondering if there are any items in the database covering your subject, and your discovery that there isn't is actually an answer to your question. Most of the time, though, when you get too many or too few hits you need to look at your keywords to see if they can be broadened or narrowed.

Other times the problem with keywords that aren't retrieving the kind of results you want isn't that they're too broad or too narrow, but that there's some industry jargon that you need to use and aren't aware of. Sometimes the jargon is written by writers, editors, or expert analysts who write the documents contained in a database. For

example, would you know that, if you were searching for information on company research, you might need to look for the term *competitive intelligence*? If you don't know an industry's own jargon, your search might not turn up relevant material.

How can you learn the jargon and buzzwords? Well, if your search has uncovered even just one or two relevant items, read through them carefully to detect any terms you weren't previously aware of and then try using them in the next search. If your search didn't turn up anything at all, you might want to educate yourself a bit by just hopping down to the library and doing some good old-fashioned paper-browsing in some relevant trade journals and newspapers to spot those words. Or call a professional association (to find one, check a library copy of Gale Research Company's *Encyclopedia of Associations*) and have them send you some of their literature.

Sometimes, though, you'll encounter a different type of jargon—not from the writers and industry experts who wrote the original documents, but by the database's own indexers and abstractors. These people, as part of their job, must consistently employ standardized indexing terms that describe the various topics and events described in each database record. These words are known by one or more of the following terms:

➤ Index terms

➤ Descriptors

➤ Subject headings

➤ Controlled vocabulary

These names are interchangeable for the most part, and are simply used to describe broad subject categories that database indexers assign to each article, report, or data item in the database. Subject descriptors in a business news database, for example, might be: management, strategic planning, financial reports, new products, marketing, and sales. If a particular database record contained these terms, it would mean that ABI/Inform's abstractors determined that those words would best describe the subject matter of that article.

When you're using a database that employs these types of index terms, it's very important for you to know what they are. The reason is that, by knowing these terms, your searches can be made much more precise and the odds are much better that your search will be successful if you can "speak the same language" as the database provider and use those exact words when you construct your search.

Many databases, in fact, are configured to allow you to search just specific sections of the records. These sections are called *fields*, in database lingo. When you do a *descriptor field* search, you're instructing the computer to check if the keywords you've entered match any of the ones the database producer created as descriptors.

What this means is that, if you know a database's descriptor terms, you have a big leg up in your search. Instead of guessing words that might be used in the database, you know ahead of time what the database producer has already determined will be the standard terms employed. So, for example, if you discover that a database has created the descriptor term *cellular telephone industry*, you don't need to come up with synonyms or other concepts. Instead, you know that if you tell the system to search its descriptor fields for the phrase *cellular telephone industry*, it will automatically zero in on precisely those records and pull them out for you. A database indexer has already done the work of grouping all related articles, using various synonyms and similar terms under this single heading.

How do you get a listing of a database's descriptors? There are usually a couple of ways. Many database producers will send you (or tell you how to find online) a listing of its descriptors. A simpler ad-hoc way is to first do a general search, using keywords you think best describe your subject of interest. Then review a handful of actual records you've retrieved and note which, if any, were either right on the mark or close to it. Read the descriptor terms assigned to those records. Then go online again and do a descriptor search using that term or terms.

In summary, here are the basic steps involved in conducting a Boolean search:

❶ Plan your search beforehand.
- Select the most appropriate database.
- Take a few minutes to study the make-up of the database.
- Note if there are descriptor fields available for searching.
- Think of keywords and appropriate synonyms. Use industry terms if possible.
- Truncate where necessary.
- Use proximity operators if needed.

❷ Enter your search statement.

❸ Review your results.
- Too many hits? Narrow your search with less inclusive words or add additional AND statements.
- Too few or no hits or irrelevant hits? Check for typos, check that you're in the right database, broaden the search with more inclusive words or additional OR statements, or check descriptor terms, if available, for more precise terms.

C

Recommended resources

This chapter lists recommended resources covering the electronic information industry and online database searching.

⇨ Books on database searching

Banks, Michael A. *Delphi: The Official Guide*, 2nd edition (General Videotex, 1990).

Basch, Reva. *Secrets of the Super Searchers*, (Eight Bit Books, 1993).

Bowen, Charles. *How to Get the Most Out of CompuServe* (Bantam, 1993).

Crowe, Elizabeth. *The Electronic Traveller* (Windcrest/McGraw-Hill, 1993).

Glossbrenner, Alfred. *The Complete Handbook of Personal Computer Communications, 3rd edition* (St. Martins Press, 1989).

Glossbrenner, Alfred. *How to Look it Up Online* (St. Martins Press).

Glossbrenner, Alfred. *The Master Guide to CompuServe* (Sybex, 1991).

Glossbrenner, Alfred. *The Master Guide to GEnie*.

Jacso, Peter. *CD-ROM Software, DataWare, and Hardware: Evaluation, Selection, and Installation* (Libraries Unlimited, 1992).

Kane, Pamela. *Prodigy Made Easy* (Osborne/McGraw-Hill, 1992).

Lichty, Tom. *The Official America Online Tour Guide* (Ventana Press, 1993).

Rugge, Sue and Glossbrenner, Alfred. *The Information Broker's Handbook* (Windcrest/MGraw-Hill, 1993).

⇨ Books on the Internet

Books on this topic have exploded over the past year. To choose a good one, look for reviews in computer and library publications. Here are the names of a few new ones that might be particularly helpful:

Estrada, Susan. *Connecting to the Internet: an O'Reilly Buyer's Guide* (O'Reilly & Associates, 1993).

Hardie, Edward T. *Internet Mailing Lists* (Prentice Hall, 1993).

Krol, Ed. *The Whole Internet Users Guide & Catalog, 3rd Edition* (Prentice Hall, 1993).

LaQuey, Tracy and Ryer, Jeanne C. *The Internet Companion, plus a beginner's start-up kit for global networking* (Addison-Wesley, 1993).

Newby, Gregory B. *Directory of Directories on the Internet* (Meckler Corp., 1993).

⇨ Books on general research sources and strategies

Berkman, Robert I. *Find it Fast: How to Uncover Expert Information on Any Subject* (HarperCollins, 1994).

Barzun, Jacques and Graff, Henry. *The Modern Researcher* (Harcourt Brace Jovanovich, 1993).

Garvin, Andrew. *The Art of Being Well Informed* (Avery Press, 1993).

⇨ Magazines

Magazines that cover the online and CD-ROM markets run the gamut from very basic to technical and scholarly. I've marked the ones geared to novice searchers with an asterisk.

Canadian CD-ROM News
c/o Paul Nicholls
School of Library and Information Science
London, ON N6G 1H1
Canada
(519) 679-2111

CD ROM Librarian
Meckler Corp.
11 Ferry Lane West
Westport, CT 06880
(203) 226-6967

CD-ROM Professional
Pemberton Press
462 Danbury Road
Wilton, CT 06883
(203) 761-1466

CD-ROM World *
Pemberton Press
462 Danbury Road
Wilton, CT 06883
(203) 761-1466

CompuServe *
CompuServe Information Service
P.O. Box 20212
Columbus, OH 43220
(800) 848-8990

Database
Online Inc.
11 Tannery Lane
Weston, CT 06883
(203) 227-8466

Information Advisor
FIND/SVP
625 Avenue of the Americas
New York, NY 10011
(212) 645-4500

Information Today
Learned Information Inc.
143 Old Marlton Pike
Medford, NJ 08055
(609) 654-6266

Information World Review
Learned Information (Europe)
Woodside, Hinksey Hill
Oxford OX1 5AU
UK
(011-44) 86-573-0275

Internet World *
Meckler Corporation
11 Ferry Lane W.
Westport, CT 06880
(203) 226-6967

Link-Up *
Learned Information Inc.
143 Old Marlton Pike
Medford, NJ 08055
(609) 654-6266

Online
Online Inc.
11 Tannery Lane
Weston, CT 06883
(203) 227-8466

Online Access *
920 North Franklin St., Suite 203
Chicago, IL 60610
(312) 573-1700

Searcher
Learned Information Inc.
143 Old Marlton Pike
Medford, NJ 08055
(609) 654-6266

Wired
544 2nd St, 3rd Fl.
San Francisco, CA 94107
(415) 904-0660

Also keep in mind general-interest computer magazines, which often report on developments in online searching. Periodicals you can commonly find in your local library include: ComputerWorld, Home Office Computing, PC Magazine, PC Week, Byte, InfoWorld, MacWorld, and MacUser.

Database directories

You can find these comprehensive directories at the general-reference department of your library. Because the electronic information industry changes so quickly, you should be sure they're the most recent version or at least no older than a year.

The CD-ROM Finder, 5th edition
1993, Learned Information

The CD-ROM Directory
Task Force Pro Libra Ltd.

CD-ROMs in Print
Meckler Corporation

CD-ROM Sourcebook
Helgerson Associates Inc.

Gale Directory of Databases
Gale Research Inc.

Associations

Professional associations can be a wealth of useful information and advice. In addition, they usually offer training classes, hold conferences, and publish reports and periodicals.

American Society of Information Science
8720 Georgia Avenue, Suite 501
Silver Spring, MD 20910
(301) 495-0900

Association of Independent Information Professionals
c/o Burwell Enterprises
3724 FM 1960 West, Suite 214
Houston, TX 77068
Attention Sue Feldman, DataSearch 607-257-0937
or Susan Detweiler 219-269-5254

The Internet Society
Suite 100
1895 Preston White Dr.
Reston, VA 22091
(703) 648-9888

Special Libraries Association
1700 18th St. NW
Washington, DC 20009
(202) 234-4700

Conferences and seminars

Two of the largest U.S. online database conferences are Online and National Online. Both are held annually and are geared to a fairly sophisticated audience of professional searchers. Online is sponsored by Online Inc. (Wilton, CT) and is held every November in varying locations. National Online is sponsored by Learned Information (Medford, NJ) and is held every May in New York City.

These conferences usually offer database search workshops, sponsored both by online vendors as well as experts such as Sue

Rugge of the Berkeley-based Information Professional Institute. Many of these workshops are oriented towards the beginning searcher.

⇨ Other useful resources

FISCAL Directory of Fee-based Research and Information Services
FYI County of Los Angeles Public Library
12350 Imperial Highway
Norwalk, CA 90650
(213) 868-0775
(Identifies and describes organizations specializing in document delivery.)

Burwell Directory of Information Brokers
109 Randolph Road
Ithaca, NY 14850
(607) 257-0937
Attention: Susan Feldman
(Over 1,000 international brokers, freelance librarians, etc., who will conduct research for a fee.)

Bibliodata Fulltext Sources Online
Bibliodata
P.O. Box 61
Needham Heights, MA 02194
(617) 444-1154
(Over 2,500 periodicals, newspapers, etc., available online.)

Index

CompuServe.

The difference between your PC collecting dust and burning rubber.

No matter what kind of PC you have, CompuServe will help you get the most out of it. As the world's most comprehensive network of people with personal computers, we're the place experts and novices alike go to find what's hot in hardware, discuss upcoming advances with other members, and download the latest software. Plus, for a low flat-rate, you'll have access to our basic services as often as you like: news, sports, weather, shopping, a complete encyclopedia, and up to 60 e-mail messages a month. And it's easy to begin. All you need is your home computer, your regular phone line, a modem, and a CompuServe membership.

To get your free introductory membership, just complete and mail the form on the back of this page. Or call 1-800-524-3388 and ask for Representative 449. Plus, if you act now, you'll receive one month free unlimited access to basic services and a $15 usage credit for our extended and premium services.

So put the power of CompuServe in your PC — and leave everyone else in the dust.

SM **CompuServe**® The information service you won't outgrow.™

Put the power
of CompuServe
at your fingertips.

Join the world's largest international network of people
with personal computers. Whether it's computer support,
communication, entertainment, or continually updated
information, you'll find services that meet your every need.

Your introductory membership will include one free month
of our basic services, plus a $15 usage credit for extended and
premium CompuServe services.

To get connected, complete and mail the card below. Or call
1-800-524-3388 and ask for Representative 449.

Yes! I want to get the most out of my PC. Send me my FREE
CompuServe Introductory Membership, including a $15 usage credit and
one free month of CompuServe basic services.

Name: _____

Address: _____

City: _____ State: _____ Zip:_____

Phone: _____

Clip and mail this form to: CompuServe
                                P.O. Box 20212
                                Dept. 449
                                Columbus, OH 43220